Personal transformations
in small groups

The International Library of Group Psychotherapy
and Group Process

General Editor

Dr Malcolm Pines
Institute of Group Analysis, London, and formerly of the Tavistock
Clinic, London.

The International Library of Group Psychotherapy and Group Process is
published in association with the Institute of Group Analysis (London)
and is devoted to the systematic study and exploration of group
psychotherapy.

Personal transformations in small groups

A Jungian perspective

Robert D. Boyd

with contributions from

John M. Dirkx, Mary Ellen Kondrat,
J. Gordon Myers, Jean Rannells Saul

London and New York

First published in 1991
by Routledge
11 New Fetter Lane, London EC4P 4EE

Simultaneously published in the USA and Canada
by Routledge
29 West 35th Street, New York, NY 10001

First published in paperback 1994

A Tavistock/Routledge publication

Typeset in Times by LaserScript Limited, Mitcham, Surrey
Printed and bound in Great Britain by
Biddles Ltd, Guildford and King's Lynn

British Library Cataloguing in Publication Data
A catalogue record for this book is available from the British Library

Library of Congress Cataloging in Publication Data
A catalog record for this book has been requested
ISBN 0–415–04363–8

Contents

Figures and tables

Contributors

Robert D. Boyd received his Ph.D. in educational psychology at the University of Chicago. He is a former director of the Group Dynamics Laboratory and is now a professor of education at the University of Wisconsin-Madison. Author of books, articles and research reports on small groups, human development and adult education, he has also served as President of the Commission of Professors of Adult Education for North America. He is a former editor of *Adult Education Quarterly*.

John M. Dirkx received his Ph.D. at the University of Wisconsin-Madison. He is an assistant professor and section head of Adult and Continuing Education at Teachers College, University of Nebraska where he teaches courses in group dynamics and the psychology of the adult learner. His publications and research interests are focused on the dynamics of interactions in adult learning groups and the transformative effects of participating in these groups.

Mary Ellen Kondrat received her Ph.D. in education from the University of Wisconsin-Madison. Her interest in small groups stems from her extensive experiences as a clinical psychiatric social worker. She has been a lecturer and consultant to various professional, service and religious organizations in the areas of communication and group dynamics. She is currently an assistant professor in the School of Social Work at Michigan State University.

J. Gordon Myers senior member of Riggs Associates, has had an extensive career as a consultant to various organizations on management issues and group dynamics. He received his Ph.D. from the University of Wisconsin-Madison. He has been a lecturer at Loyola University in Chicago where he has offered courses on small groups, interpersonal relations, and transitional problems in organizations.

Jean Rannells Saul is an associate professor in the Department of Educational Leadership at Texas Woman's University. She received her Ph.D. from the University of Wisconsin-Madison. She has worked on women's oral history projects and has leadership roles with women in administrative, religious, and learning contexts. Her studies of the individuation processes have been presented at various women's conferences and meetings.

Introduction

All research is conducted within some given context and arises from some historical base. Having a knowledge of these matters gives the basis for understanding why the research pursued a given direction and how the means it adopted were consistent with the realization of its goals. It is from this perspective that the introduction was undertaken. What follows is my attempt to provide a brief account, if you will, a history of the direction our research has been taking and an explanation, brief as it will be, of the means we have adopted in conducting our research.

Our initial studies were conceptually grounded in psychoanalytic thought. That would be expected in view of the fact that my psychological training at the University of Chicago was a study of Freud and the neo-Freudians. I brought to my students what my teachers had brought to me. In the early days of the Laboratory we investigated Bion's (1959) theory of Basic Assumption Cultures, mechanisms of defense (A. Freud, 1937; Murphy, 1960), the conflict-free sphere of the ego (Hartmann, 1958), and Erikson's (1950) epigenetic theory. The application of these theories extended our knowledge of the dynamics within the small group. Our contributions were made mainly in the areas of furthering the methodologies and the development of research instrumentations in the study of small groups based upon these theories. The studies and my experiences in working with small groups in a variety of settings were the bases upon which I developed the Three Channel model (Boyd, 1966) of the small group. The Three Channel model interrelates three forms of content that is communicated in the interactions within a small group.

This model proved to be a useful conceptualization in both conducting and investigating the dynamics of small groups (Boyd and Wilson, 1974). The motivation channel, defined by Erikson's epigenetic theory, identified the basic concerns being expressed in the group. The various ways the group used to approach and avoid relationships were defined by Bion's Basic Assumption Cultures. The members' behaviors

1

were specified in terms of valencies (Stock and Thelen, 1958). The third form of content was the work that the group was engaged in and here different conceptual systems were employed. This model was the conceptual framework for several dissertations. As is always the case, when one has scaled a mountain there is the unexplored land that lies beyond. There was something taking place in the group which could not be accounted for by the psychoanalytic theories we had been using in our studies of the small group. At first I could not clearly identify it and I certainly could not name it. In my searching to find what I was intuiting I reread Slater (1966) and came upon a brief reference to Neumann's (1954) work in Slater's book. I began reading Neumann's writings which then lead me further into a study of Jung's works. My initial sense in reading Neumann was that I had found what I had been observing but had not been able to clearly identify. There were archetypal elements at play in the dynamics of the small group and if we were to get a better and deeper understanding of what was taking place in the group and with the members, we had to take account of these archetypal dynamics. This launched a whole new area of study. From these studies I proposed the Matrix Model (1975), which was later published (Boyd, 1983, 1984) in a more expanded version.

Conceptualizing is one part of a two part task, the other being testing the explanations which are set out based upon the conceptual framework. It is this task to which I plan to spend the remaining pages of the Introduction. Thus the Matrix Model, which is described in detail in Chapter One, will be set aside at this time as our focus is now on a discussion dealing with the issues involved in the testing of empirical explanations. The discussion is framed within two traditions: empirical literature in analytical psychology; the dialogs of naive falsification and experiential logic of the soul.

The literature in analytical psychology is rich in case material. The carefully documented accounts of individuals' encounters and struggles with psychic elements of the unconscious have added to a more thorough understanding of the psyche and have made significant contributions to the concretization of theory. Our work has been along similar lines; however, there are differences which set it apart from the mainstream literature in analytical psychology. The similarities can be readily identified. Case material is also the data base of our studies. In the parlance of academic psychology, our work is described as qualitative research studies. Experimental design studies have not been used as they introduce extraneous variables and set up a different context than that which is the focus of our investigations. Individuals come into groups with specific purposes and goals and to alter these in any way for the objective of a scientific investigation alters the nature of the setting. The case material reported in the chapters which follow has been drawn from self-analytic groups which were specifically set up for that purpose. They were videotaped and to that extent we accept the observation that we may have altered the setting; however, the videotapes were made as an instructive device for the members and which they used to review and analyze the dynamics of their group.

Our case material deals with the transactions within small groups and not between a therapist and a client. On an initial consideration, these two contexts may be viewed as being fundamentally different. The small group does present a much more complex system of transactions than is the situation of the therapist/client dyad. The complexity is certainly there but the presence of psychic content in various forms is also there. The leader is the other concern; however, the interventions which are made by the leader are structured within the framework of analytical psychology, as they are for the therapist. There are differences between the two settings but the differences rather than discounting the possible presence of archetypal content and transformation processes, point to their presence in various dynamics within the transactions among the members, the manifestations of the social and cultural systems as well as between the members and the leader.

There is a fundamental difference between most of the studies reported in the literature on analytical psychology and the approach we have taken in our work. It was pointed out above that the empirical evidence for the propositions of analytical psychology is the reporting of case material. Our studies are also based on case material but the critical demarcation is that our studies are structured as investigations to examine the propositions of analytical psychology by subjecting them to tests of naive falsification. The reports on case material, which appears in the literature on analytical psychology, are set forth as evidence of some concept or proposition of the theory. These accounts are offered as verifications for either the existing theoretical propositions or as amplifications and refinements of the theory. There can be no discounting the value of such contributions; however, they cannot be viewed as severe tests of the theory.

My position that a more severe test must be applied to the propositions certainly reflects the influence of an academic culture. But this should not be a basis for a disjunction in our dialog, rather a further reason for a dialog.

Thus our research program involved more than just examining what was taking place in a small group in order to describe the dynamics in a coherent manner; our project has been to test the explanations of what our observations appeared to indicate was occurring in the group. Our observations were descriptions but it is also the case that most descriptions are in one form or another explanations. Descriptions come about as an interplay between the conceptual perceptions we bring to the situation and the autonomous dynamics that are structuring the trans-actions. That relationship was spoken to by Popper (1959) when he observed that it is inconceivable to assume we can view an event without bringing to it some prior preconceptions. To be able to move back and forth between one's conceptual framework and the autonomous features of events which are being observed generally takes a good deal of time. This statement simply recognizes the fact that it takes a period of study to become aware of and knowledgeable about a particular area of exploration. There was a period of three years before I undertook any investigation or encouraged any of my students to propose a dissertation in this field of study. Following that period, the task that then confronted us was: How do you go about doing such tests?

There is implicit, if indeed not a fairly explicit, criticism that reports of case material are not legitimate evidence for the testing of propositions. There is no question that case material, if accurately reported, is one form of evidence, but that is not the issue here. What is before us is the problem of determining what evidence can be accepted as the basis for the justification of an explanation. Are explanations justified on the basis of accumulated case material? Such an approach is built upon induction and explanation founded upon induction has been repudiated as a method of scientific explanation from the time of Hume (1748). More recently Popper (1959) has taken the argument against induction further and has advanced the method of falsification. In brief, this method argues that proof can not be achieved by the accumulation of supportive evidence because it is impossible to establish the point at which an exhaustive body of evidence for any given explanation has been reached. Thus evidence that supplies proof may or may not be advancing the truth value of an explanation. There is no criterion by which to judge its truth value other than the questionable process of ac-cumulating such supportive evidence. But this approach can be thrown into serious jeopardy by only one piece of evidence that disconfirms the explanation regardless of the quantity of evidence supporting the ex-planation. Why not then begin by looking for disconfirming evidence? In Popper's term scientific discovery requires the investigator to set up in advance an explanation such that, if the results contradict the explanation, it then has to be given up.

This is a stark assertion and it needs some amplification in view of recent dialogs on Popper's original dogmatic falsification (Feyerabend, 1975; Lakatos, 1970). There is some agreement now that an explanation which has been falsified should not be discarded out of hand. It is certainly highly suspect. Further research may be in order but such a decision must be made on a case by case basis. At such times, there are not only the considerations related to the method employed in the investigation but also the historical, cultural, and political forces and influences at work. For example, the initial rejection of Freud's ideas, and the labeling of Jung's works as mystic writings, were fundamentally evidence of the cultural forces at work rather than the expression of disputes over scientific content. Where such forces are at work, the decision may be too readily accepted to reject and abandon a particular line of research (Feyerabend, 1975; Kuhn, 1962). The tendency to reject unpopular explanations must be always considered and taken into account; however, Lakatos (1970) argues that the method of falsification is a surer way to the truth value of an explanation than can possibly be asserted for the method of induction, but dogmatic falsification must be given up for the more tentative rejection of a theory set forth in the methods of naive and sophisticated falsification.

It is not my intention to pursue the many issues which are raised about Popper's theory of the logic of scientific discovery, but I cannot leave the discussion at this point without one further observation. I am indebted to an Australian colleague who brought to my attention that in the final analysis Popper's position is also an inductive method. In the long perspective of a research program this is true, but not to see a fundamental and critical demarcation between the methods of falsification and induction is a failure to understand the principal issue of valuation. Falsification invites criticism and induction seeks certainty (Dewey, 1929).

We have framed the conjectures set out in our research program as assertions to be falsified. The design of the research studies has been structured in ways that have attempted to find disconfirming evidence. This approach may not always be clearly evident in the chapters as the focus of these writings was primarily on conceptual content rather than on the reporting of research procedures.

The conjecture is the point at which a research program formally begins. There is always a psychological dimension to the explanation of why one particular conjecture is set forth rather than another among an array of conceivable conjectures. This dynamic is important in the mix of things because it puts on notice the cluster of biases that add both prejudice and, what is too often discounted because of an over concern for controlling prejudice, the virtues of intuition. The conjecture itself is the directive focus, however, in the formal structure of a research program.

With the conjecture stated, the question arises: How do we go about testing the conjecture? It is not my intention to describe the specific steps which are taken in conducting our research program but I do want to speak to what may be called the logic of our method.

A conjecture is an assertion that certain relationships exist among a specific set of concepts. For example, the conjecture is proposed that the negative anima is confronted or given no place in the life of the group when the social system of the group is in the developmental phase of the Good Mother. I would like to point out in passing that the conjecture contains the condition for disconfirming evidence, namely that if there is no evidence that the negative anima is confronted or ignored then the conjecture is falsified (not dismissed out of hand, however, on the basis of this one test). It is an immediate realization in viewing any conjecture that we are unable to come to any firm understanding of its meaning until there is a sufficient specification of its language. What is meant by the words 'anima', 'Good Mother', 'confronted', etc? The task is to specify these terms in such a manner that they can be experienced in such a way that they can be differentiated from other experiences.

I want to stress the significance of 'specify' and 'experience'. I have avoided the word 'define' because it connotes a definitive quality which assumes the task to be that of determining a phenomenon by language rather than comprehending it through experience. Scientific exploration is not advanced by pushing at more and more precise definitions but by exploring and testing relations. It is sufficient to establish a firm set of specificiers through experience in demarcating a concept in order that it be a functional element in the statement of a proposed conjecture. Thus we develop experiential specifications as the way to come to a firm understanding of what is intended by a given concept. The specifications are not exhaustive but they are sufficient to demarcate the concept from other concepts and to allow us to place it into a conjecture within which it has its specific or particular meaning.

Even more critical than the notion of specification of concepts is the role that experience plays in our research program. As indicated above, there is an inseparable relationship between specified concepts and experience. Concepts do not exist apart from experience. You cannot perceive a concept that you cannot experience. To those who do not know the concept of anima yet experience its manifestations in their behavior, they may attribute its presence to projection or in even a more naive state of self-knowledge to some unexplainable emotion. The concept has to be made known to the individual by means of the specifiers but words alone will not make the concept meaningful unless it is experienced subjectively. This is a learning task whereby the information in the form of the concept's specifiers come to be understood in terms of the individual's experiences. The one is placed meaningfully in the context of the other.

As stated earlier this is not the occasion for a detailed discussion of the specific ways our research program was conducted; however, a few words concerning our procedures need to be made explicit in light of what has been spoken to. Our research program uses coders to identify the evidence needed to test the conjecture. Coders are persons who have been trained to identify the concepts under study. That is to say, they have come to know the concepts that are being studied experientially. They are knowledgeable persons in terms of the theory and concepts but generally they are not informed about the nature or problem of the study and this is particularly the case where such knowledge might conceivably influence their observations. Certainly as intelligent individuals they have hunches as to the problem being examined but special procedures are taken to check for possible biases in their observations.

The groups are videotaped and these videotapes are the raw data for our studies. The coders observe these as they would a play. They must bring themselves to the ongoing dynamics as they unfold in a way identical to the involvement a playgoer has in taking part or in being with the actors living out the drama. For example, the audience enters into the turmoil that Hamlet is experiencing and it becomes an experience shared by the audience which identifies and becomes one with his turmoil. As a member of the audience we experience the turmoil and know it in the experiential sense of the word 'know'. In an identical manner the coder experiences the members' struggle with the Great Mother, her good and terrible qualities. This experiencing does involve a firm knowledge of the concept's specifications but it is the logic of the soul, that Christou (1976) discusses, which establishes the meaning of the experience.

The complexity of human experience must be taken into account in our attempts to focus on a particular dynamic. For example, in observing the member's anima, the coder's shadow may come into play making it difficult if not impossible for the coder to record the events from the perspective of the anima. Relating this again to the analogy of a play, we may fail to see Willie's anguish in Arthur Miller's play *The Death of a Salesman* because we are viewing him from the perspective of his son. It is because of this complexity of human experience that our research program calls for more than one coder and that checks are frequently made to see that the coders are experiencing the drama in terms of its story and not solely from their own personal dilemmas. I used the word 'solely' and I wish to stress my reason for doing so. The logic of the soul involves being-in-the-world which can not thereby bracket off some part of our being. What is required of a coder is that she/he be aware to the fullest extent possible of the existence of those personal dynamics which may color the experiencing of the event. This is not always possible and hence the need for other coders. The basic point must not be lost sight of, however, by an over concern for intercoder reliability. Any attempt to understand the dynamics of small groups must be based on the sanctity of experiencing the drama that is unfolding in the group. It is understandable in light of this approach why we use such phrases as 'the group appears as if' or 'there is a sense that'. As an observer we become part of the drama and only in this way can we experience what is taking place.

A drama is experienced symbolically; it can never be conveyed in a literal language. Any attempt to describe a drama in literal terms would be to put into its stead an account or a report. Symbolic language expresses the vital integrity of the drama. A myth, as one form of symbolic language, is able to express experientially the essence of a human dilemma – a drama – as no literal description, no matter how extensive, could convey. Thus any conceptual framework which attempts to seize an experience in a language form must attempt to do so by specifying the experience in symbolic language. The Matrix Model, which is presented later in Chapter One, is a conceptual framework that examines the dramas in a small group in symbolic language. It provides provisional ways – conceptual structures – to derive meanings from the group's transactions. They are not the sole prescriptions of meaning. The autonomous nature of the transactions challenge as well as confirm the validity of the concepts to give meaning to the drama. But there is also the extraperceptional and creative input of the transpersonality – the universal soul of the collective unconscious. The transpersonality reaches out from the individual personality and intuits the existence of unusual and primal patterns of behavior and meaning. Symbolic language transcends the immediate here and now, but as a bridge through time, links the immediate with primordial experience heading toward a transcendental consciousness. If an observer is to experience and understand the symbolic drama evolving in the group then the meaning of the drama cannot be left to the sole employment of a conceptual framework if the drama is to maintain its integrity, for the integrity of the drama demands that all three elements must be involved and in dialog.

The practical import of this logic is illustrated in our experiences in training coders. Some coders are unable to experience, for example, the Great Mother in a small group. They take the specifiers for the Great Mother and employ them as definitions. They look for behaviors of nurturing, protecting, support and in doing so completely miss the drama. They have difficulty seeing the symbolic qualities of the specifiers and are trying to make these symbolic specifiers literal descriptions. Such individuals cannot be employed as coders because they are unable to break out of the confinement their egos are imposing on their personalities. They are unable to experience consciously the drama of the group, but only the apparent interactions among the members. Our method requires a sound knowledge of the conceptual framework, the openness to experience the symbolic drama of the evolving group and the integration of the transpersonality, all in an exploratory dialog.

Much of our work has been pushing at the edges of the existing theories in analytical psychology. When any group of investigators is exploring new or only recently discovered ways of understanding it is most likely that differences arise among them. These differences give evidence of the insights, the knowledge, and the questioning which enriches and furthers their research. The chapters in this volume reflect that tradition.

To this point the research program has been the focus of the discussion. It is understandable that a reader would conclude that the research program has been our major agenda. It has been a major concern but not by itself – solely as the search for truth – for it has always been a part of an educational project. The research program has been motivated without question by a primary curiosity to know but it has also been motivated as a challenge first to demonstrate and then to engage those skeptical colleagues who cling to various disguised forms of logical positivism. Paradigms that claim to be empirical must be subject to critical scrutiny in the open market place of free enquiry. This aspect of our work has been a part of our educational project. But there is another aspect more consequential than the dialogs on the scientific soundness of analytical psychology and this is the contribution analytical psychology can make by being used to develop fundamental changes in the ways educative processes are conceived and employed.

Schooling in western societies has taught that we can think our way out of difficulties. That is to say, the reflective processes, properly managed by the ego, are the means to a constructive and productive way of handling the problems encountered in life. To some extent there is validity to this position but its failure to take into account other components of the psyche creates an incomplete if not a distorted picture. Our investigations of personal transformations in small groups have attempted to demonstrate how, in educational settings, it is possible to encounter and have these other psychic components be part of the dynamics in a learning community as we have envisioned the small group.

Transformative education (Boyd and Myers, 1988) recognizes the polarity of good and evil in human nature. The struggles involved in working through the problems arising from the polarities in our human nature are the source of our personal growth and our movement toward personality integration. When we fail to help a person to know that these polarities exist as givens, too often the learner assumes a guilt for what she/he considers an aberration of personality. Today a serious condition exists in most societies where these polarities in the human psyche are no longer under religious or cultural control and are freely expressed, threatening the very fabric of the society. I am not advocating a new system of social control or a return to previous forms of social or religious controls, quite the opposite. Teachers must help learners to recognize the existence of polarities, such as good and evil, in the human psyche, and within a learning community develop ways to accept and work through a more integrative relationship with the counter elements of the polarities. This is one way of viewing a personal transformation, and one of the ways we have studied in the research program reported here.

One final observation: I find it perplexing and disturbing to see how little awareness there is of analytical psychology in education. It is impossible to pick up a representative work in analytical psychology and fail to see the implication it has for education. Its acceptance in religious ministry is clearly evident and crosses many denominations. It has been used as a conceptual structure to more fully understand literature, dance and the dramatic arts. But analytical psychology, as yet, has a very limited audience in education. It is our hope that our efforts may in some way increase the audience.

An overview of the content of the chapters will reveal the organizational structure by making explicit the relationships among the various topics presented in the book. The chapters report on a set of related study areas which are part of the research program of the Laboratory for the Study of Group Dynamics at the University of Wisconsin-Madison. The research program is involved in investigating the development of collective consciousness in the social and cultural systems of the small group in relation to the processes of personal transformation being worked through by members of such groups. Except in cases where the narrative required it, there are few cross-references among the chapters. The interrelationships among the studies, however can be readily perceived. They are all part of a whole.

Chapter One presents the Matrix Model which serves as the conceptual framework for the research program. It views the group as being composed of three interacting systems – the social, cultural and personality systems. The interactions among these three systems are examined from six points of view. The six points of view are the structural, developmental, adaptive, content, transactional, and gestalt. The group-as-a-whole must be viewed as a matrix where systems of structures and dynamic forces, represented in the points of view, are reflected in our explanations.

The second chapter moves us directly into the presentation of our research methodologies. The task before us was to take the framework provided by the Matrix Model and combine it with the theories of analytical psychology. Central to our research program was the investigation of the development of consciousness. Such studies were seen as the very core of investigating personal transformations. It would appear therefore that we would immediately start on the development of methodologies that would provide data on individual personal transformations. This was not the initial direction we took. Our previous studies had shown us the critical and focal role the social system plays in the lives of group members. On the basis of this knowledge, we began with first looking at the social system. Accordingly we constructed a methodology by which to examine the development of consciousness as it occurs in the social system. This work is reported in some detail in Chapter Two. The chapter concludes with a discussion of key issues related to the conduct of empirical studies.

The development of consciousness in the social system is affected by many variables but high on the list of such factors is the influential group member. The influential member has long been recognized as a prime mover in the life of a small group. It was important to us to understand in what ways the influential member contributed to or hindered the development of consciousness in the social system. We proposed the concept of the focal person and then proceeded to develop a methodology by which to identify and investigate the focal person's roles in the social system. Chapter Three presents this methodology. Several significant questions were raised in this part of our research and those which were central to this enquiry have been identified in the chapter.

The focal person often plays a key role in the movement of the social system from one phase to the next phase of development. But the question remains: What processes are involved in periods of transition? An extensive body of research supports the notion of phase development in small groups but little hard evidence exists to explain the phenomenon of transition from one phase to the next. Having such knowledge is critical to fill in our account of the development of consciousness as it occurs in the social system. A transition period has many qualities which are similar to experiencing a loss or accepting a new reality. An analogous relationship could be argued between what occurs in a transition period in a small group and a personal loss experienced by an individual. The processes of grieving appear to characterize both situations. The notion of social grieving was proposed and a methodology was developed to test the notion. In Chapter Four a systematic account is provided which traces the development of the notion. The methodology is described and illustrative case material is also included.

Chapter Five presents the concept of episodic themes. This concept forms a bridge between the group-as-a-whole and the individual members. The group provides the context for a drama to be worked out and to the extent that the individual accepts the possibilities which exist in the drama of the group, then to that extent she/he realizes the potentials and works on her/his individuation. The chapter contains a description of the methodology and case material.

The internal dialogs which episodic themes initiate involve the manifestation of different psychic elements. In Chapter Six we examine the roles that the anima and animus take in intrapersonal dialogs and the influence they have upon behavior at the unconscious level. To investigate these influences we first had to conceptualize the anima and animus at the various stages of an individual's personal development. From that point we then could develop sets of specifics which made it possible for observers to identify the presence of the anima or animus in the behaviors of an individual group member.

Chapter Seven presents case material on an individual group member. The chapter attempts to achieve an integration between conceptual content and concrete observations. The case material is both an exposition and an explanation of the notions and concepts presented in the Matrix Model and in our methodologies which reflect our research program.

The educational impact of Jung's work is often missed and it has certainly received minimum emphasis. That is a serious shortcoming that needs to be addressed. The last chapter is a start in correcting that condition. In Chapter Eight the question is addressed of what the leader is doing while all these things are taking place. What does the leader do to facilitate the expansion of consciousness? The question is answered by presenting a systematic examination of approaches which have been shown to facilitate not only interpersonal dialogs but more critically, intrapersonal dialogues toward the expansion of consciousness.

Robert D. Boyd

References

Bion, W. R. (1959). *Experiences in groups.* New York: Basic Books.

Boyd, R. D. (1966). An interaction model applied to supervision. In J. Raths and R. R. Lepper (eds). *The supervisor agent for change in teaching,* Washington, DC: American Society for Curriculum Development.

Boyd, R. D. (1975). A dynamic model for the study of the small group. Unpublished paper.

Boyd, R. D. (1983). A matrix model of the small group, Part I, *Small Group Behavior, 14* (4), 405–18.

Boyd, R. D. (1984). A matrix model of the small group, Part II, *Small Group Behavior, 15* (1), 233–50.

Boyd, R. D. and Myers, J. G. (1988). Transformative education, *International Journal of Lifelong Education, 7* (4), 261–84.

Boyd, R. D. and Wilson, J. P. (1974). Three channel theory of communication in small groups, *Adult Education, 14* (3), 167–83.

Christou, E. (1976). *The logos of the soul.* Dallas, TX: Spring.

Dewey, J. (1929). *The quest for certainty.* New York: G. P. Putnam's Sons.

Erikson, E. H. (1950). *Childhood and society.* New York: W. W. Norton.

Feyerabend, P. (1975). *Against method: Outline of an anarchistic theory of knowledge*. London: Verso.

Freud, A. (1937). *The ego and the mechanisms of defence*. London: The Hogarth Press.

Hartmann, H. (1958). *Ego psychology and the problem of adaptation*. New York: International University Press.

Hume, D. (1748). *An inquiry concerning human understanding*. New York: Open Court (reprint 1949).

Kuhn, T. S. (1962). *The structure of scientific revolutions*. Chicago: University of Chicago Press.

Lakatos, I. (1970). Falsification and the methodology of scientific research programs. In I. Lakatos and A. Musgrave (eds), *Criticism and the Growth of Knowledge*. London: Cambridge University Press.

Murphy, L. (1960). Coping devices and defense mechanisms in relation to autonomous ego functions, *Bulletin Menninger Clinic, 24,* 144–53.

Neumann, E. (1954). *The origins and history of consciousness*. Princeton, NJ: Princeton University Press.

Popper, K. R. (1959). *The logic of scientific discovery*. New York: Harper & Row.

Slater, P. E. (1966). *Microcosm: Structural, psychological and religious evolution in groups*. New York: John Wiley & Sons.

Stock, D. and Thelen, H. A. (1958). *Emotional dynamics and group culture: Experimental studies of individual and group behavior*. New York: New York University Press.

Chapter one

The Matrix Model
A conceptual framework for small group analysis

Robert D. Boyd

The small group from six points of view

I take my place at the circle of tables. Shortly I am joined by other men
and women who have entered the room and make their way to one or
another of the ten empty chairs arranged around the tables. Some stop to
exchange greetings, others engage in light conversation before sitting in
the chair that they have selected. After a few minutes all have taken their
places at the tables and an acknowledged hush falls over the group. I
look about me catching the accepting smiles of some members, noting
the poker faces and the preoccupied expressions of the other members.
I am once again in the chair of the leader. I am being looked to as one
who, by designated position and expectations based on cultural
socializations, will guide, instruct, support and, counsel the group and
the members. The dynamic field of the group remains uncompleted until
my part as leader has been entered as a dynamic within that field.

The initial question would appear to be: How do I define my role in
the group? As critical as this question is, there is a more fundamental
question that must be answered. In order to address the question of what
a leader's role might, could or should be, it is necessary to have clearly
in mind how you, as a leader, are conceptualizing the nature of a small
group. My interventions to guide, instruct, support and counsel both
members and the group are structured upon my conceptualization of the
small group. The first task of any leader is to have clearly in mind a
conceptual metaphor, model, or paradigm which gives some understanding to the complexity of the phenomena that are being rapidly
played out and to which the leader's interventions must contribute
insights and guidance. The direct relationship of grounded practice to its
operational framework is recognized by any thoughtful practitioner and
needs no further argument here.

Many conceptual frameworks have been put forward (Cartwright and
Zander, 1968; Mullen and Goethals, 1987). They have all been supported by empirical studies of one form or another, or case studies that
are offered as documentation or as an argument for their operational

14

validity. They are different ways of making sense of the complex and complicated phenomenon we speak of as the small group. The frameworks can be differentiated by examining the sets of assumptions upon which the frameworks are based. From a more global perspective, these different ways of explaining this phenomenon are a function of the observer's *Weltanschauung*. Investigators and practitioners make their most meaningful contributions as they live in good faith with their *Weltanschauung*. Such a statement may strike those who are looking for a more unified social psychology as a tolerant position to hold but one that is entirely unacceptable and at best a disappointing state of affairs. But at this point in time, we are a long way from arriving at one accepted conceptual paradigm by which to explain the dynamics of the small group. There is a more fundamental fallacy in such an expectation, for it reflects a serious lack of understanding. It fails to realize that the phenomenon of the small group can be viewed from the perspectives of different questions and frames of references. Any unity that may be achieved will not be by insisting upon a universally accepted paradigm but by acknowledging the various aspects of the *Weltanschauungs* that have played a part in structuring our views of the dynamics of the small group. Thus what unity we may find will be a function of the question we ask.

The literature on small groups contains many conceptual frameworks which describe and explain the nature and dynamics of the small group. It is not my intention to review this literature but that is not to say that I will ignore it. This chapter presents my Matrix Model. In the presentation of my work there will be many occasions when I will note my indebtedness to other investigators whose work I have built upon or whose work has clarified points upon which there are clear differences.

I propose that any conceptual framework of the small group must attempt to deal with six points of view. They are, the structural, adaptive, developmental, transactional, Gestalt, and content points of view. Each of these are important in order to perceive the nature of the small group and critical to an understanding of the Matrix Model. They form a general framework within which to conceptually view the small group. Collectively these six points of view constitute the Matrix Model. Each point of view will be explained in turn, thus building the framework of the Matrix Model as the discussion progresses. The reader may find it helpful in reading about the six points of view to refer to Figure 1.1 (page 22) which presents the Matrix Model in diagram form.

The structural point of view

Individuals compose small groups and most paradigms focus only on the individuals, the roles they take, the status they have in the group, and

15

their patterns of interactions. To explain what is happening in the group by observing individual members is not only an accepted mode of investigation but a very instructive one. But from the structural perspective the individual member is only one component system. There is also a social and a cultural system. For the present, a discussion of the cultural system will be set aside in order to first illustrate the existence of the social system, which is evident in the following incident.

The setting is a seminar for psychology majors. Different members over the course of the last two sessions have suggested agendas that the group could work on but none of these have been adopted. When they were put forward they were explored politely but no commitment was made to adopt them after they were briefly discussed. It appeared that the members could not come to any consensus. A general sense of apathy was present among the membership because, in their view, nothing had been resolved. Some members pushed their chairs back from the table and appeared to have physically withdrawn from the group. Other members looked apprehensive while others looked bored. A silence fell on the group. At this point a member whose agenda had not been accepted moved his chair back to the table and said, 'I think we are waiting for Dr B to step in and lead us. I think we have abdicated our autonomy and this makes me damn angry.' An immediate upsurge of energy can be felt in the situation. There is a rush of agreements and denials. Members find it difficult to break into the rapidly moving discussion. It is difficult to conceive that this is the same group of some ten minutes earlier.

How can we describe this phenomenon other than to posit the existence of some entity different from the individual membership in the group? What was observed was not the summation of that membership but the expression of a structure that has its own existence. Groups are frequently described as manifesting a sense of trust, while at the same time, it is recognized that the trust that exists between members can vary within a wide range from little to a great deal. The illustration above is offered as evidence that, in addition to the structure of membership, there is the structure of a social system. Viewing the small group as a social system does not replace or discount the view of the group as involving interactions among individual members. Small groups can be examined in terms of the interactions among members or personality systems, but the small group can also be viewed as a dynamic entity – as an existing social system.

The social system, unlike the individual who brings historical content into the small group, comes into being at the initial period of the small group's formation. Its unique identity is developed in the course of the group's life. The social system comes to have its own history. As a dynamic structure it asserts itself on other structures within the small group and expresses its own nature in the life of the group. It is a proactive and reactive system from the initial moments of the group to that moment when the group terminates. It is a system entirely defined in a specified time – the span of the small group's existence. In that sense we may speak of it as a system which is focused on the here and now and recognizes nothing other than its own history as being pertinent and valid.

To the personality system and the social system we add a third structural entity – the group's cultural system. Unlike the social system which comes into existence and is terminated within the lifespan of the small group, the cultural system, like the personality systems, can trace a continuity before and after the group. The small group exists in a cultural context; it is an entity within a given society. The group is directly affected by the cultural structures and patterns of the society in which the group exists. This is evident in the pattern of relationships between members and the designated leader, in the values that are expressed in the group, in the numerous mores and rituals that get played out in the group. The influence of the cultural system can also be observed in the ties that members seek between the group and the larger society. The following statements are frequently heard in small groups. 'In what ways is this group like the ones I work with?' 'I can't see how what we are doing here can be used in the groups we work with.' 'What we are doing here is so unreal.' It is evident in these remarks that a group is always linked to a larger context even when the relationship is not made explicit. The culture of a society is every bit a part of the group's structural framework as are the personality systems of the members who compose the group.

The impression should not be left, especially at this point in time, that we may look for only one predominant culture which serves as the formative structure of a small group. A small group may be drawn from two or more cultural publics within a given society. In such cases there exists the potential for growth as well as the basis for serious conflict. In so far as the difference among cultural publics may serve as the potential for growth, we have an example of the formula of polarity to which Jung so frequently spoke.

In summary, a small group can be conceptualized from a structural point of view as having three interacting and dynamic systems: the social, personality, and cultural systems. Each is concurrent in the life of the group yet unique in both the matters it deals with and the manner in which it functions. Each system is autonomous in that it can be viewed as having its own agenda in dealing with the primary tasks to be encountered and resolved. The manner in which these tasks are handled and resolved comes to define its own identity in the sense that its unique development can be described. These qualities of the structural systems will be treated in greater detail as we examine the other points of view.

Robert D. Boyd

The developmental point of view

There have been a number of studies which describe the small group from the developmental point of view. Notable among these contributions have been the works of Bales and Strodtbeck (1951), Bennis and Shepard (1956), and Tuckman (1965). Hill and Gruner (1973) reported on over 100 papers written on small group development. These studies describe the group as a whole progressing through phases of development. Here, there is a fundamental difference between these studies and our studies which lead to the formulation of the Matrix Model. The Matrix Model views the small group as a collective concept constituted by three systems, the social, personality, and cultural, which are the dynamic components of the small group. Unlike previous investigations of group phase development, I propose that each of the three systems progresses through its own phase of development. The concrete formulations of the developmental phases for each of the systems will be presented in the following section. In focusing upon the developmental point of view we must continue to recognize that all six points of view are interconnected and interrelated; however, the developmental and the adaptive points of view are tied conceptually in the way they are formulated at the observation stage. It is because of this relationship, that a more meaningful discussion of the developmental point of view can be presented in conjunction with our explanation of the adaptive point of view.

The adaptive point of view

The adaptive point of view describes the ways in which the three systems encounter and work at three primary tasks. Each system faces the tasks of (1) *defining* the nature of its identity, (2) *establishing* modes of relating, and (3) *developing* means to relate to reality-adaptive demands. The three tasks are discussed immediately below and illustrative examples from group observations are given to show how each system may deal with these tasks, which may provide some concreteness to our treatment of these primary tasks.

The social system without some definable form of an identity cannot be related to and, accordingly, would have no meaning for the members. It is not uncommon to hear expressed in the initial sessions of a small group, 'I don't know what this group is. I don't know whether I can trust this group or not.' For a group that has been developing a sense of its identity we hear very different expressions. 'I have good feeling about this group. I don't think we are clear yet about what we are about but there is commitment here.'

The task of establishing identity is fundamental to the personality system. Individuals can be observed working at establishing their identity in the group: as a person to be trusted, a person who can be counted on to help make decisions, as a person who is not afraid to work. Some can be observed reworking their identities. For example, the social system is struggling with the issues of control and authority and a member identifying with the conflicts these issues raise for him/her personally, can be observed struggling with his/her personal crisis of autonomy. 'I have often found it difficult to accept authority figures and I am beginning to see how this has sometimes prevented me from relating to others in a positive way.'

The cultural system works at establishing its identity when it focuses attention on the development of and adherence to mores, roles, norms, and group values. These serve to set the boundaries of the group's unique cultural structure and how that structure is to relate to the other two systems as well as to the larger society.

The second primary task is the establishing of modes of relating. Specific modes of relating become dominant in the social system at different times in the life of the small group. At a given time there is a sense in the social system that aggressive behavior is acceptable and even appropriate. At other times the social system's *emotionality* may be one of dependency which is directed toward the leader. This mode of relationship may be clearly descriptive of the social system although, simultaneously, it is possible to observe certain individual members who do not overtly subscribe to the dependency *emotionality* being expressed in the social system. Our reading of the social system is not based on the summation of the members' behaviors, a point that has been emphasized earlier, but on the general sense of the social system itself. To explain these modes of relating expressed by the social system we have turned to the contributions Bion (1959) has made in his studies of emotionalities in the small group. He has described the emotionality of dependency, as illustrated above, as a basic assumption culture of the group. Stock and Thelen (1958), Thelen (1959), and Slater (1966) have extended Bion's work and have also contributed corroborating evidence to Bion's original work.

Since the structural perspective views the social system as an entity, metaphorically as an organism (Thelen, 1959), it must out of necessity develop specific modes of relationships to deal with other entities that it encounters. For example, the social system develops specific ways of relating to the leader as its agenda changes. A member who is radically out of step with the social system's mode of relating can be viewed as obstructing, acting in conspiracy or withdrawing.

The interpersonal relationships of individuals has long been a focus of research and an extensive body of literature reports on the modes of relating employed by members of small groups (Penland, 1974). At any time in the life of the group, members can be observed working at developing or avoiding relationships with other members, as well with the social or cultural systems. Every member is faced with the primary task that involves the decision whether to approach or avoid a relationship and how this is to be done.

The cultural system also encounters the task of relating to other entities and issues. The cultural and the social system are frequently observed as being at cross purposes. For example, the cultural system may have an agenda of furthering a particular norm – personal boundaries must be respected – while the social system is striving to establish trust in the group. The cultural system may resist a confrontation through flight. In another sphere the question is raised in the group, what is the relationship of the group to the larger society? Here we are observing the cultural system struggling with the primary task of evolving a mode of relating.

There is a third primary adaptive task that all three systems must face and handle – developing means to more fully deal with reality-adaptive demands. Although in a later section we will go into some detail describing the nature of these reality-adaptive demands, a few words of explanation are needed to clarify what is meant here by 'reality-adaptive demands'. Its meaning is framed within analytical psychology. There are three constituent parts to what we call reality and these are manifested in the three existential dynamics, the social, personality, and cultural systems. Each interrelately shapes and is shaped by the projections put on the active environment which is encountered and which confronts the three systems. Thus reality is constructed from those evolving transactions. It is necessary if each system is to function in this reality to work through some form of resolution to the demands which arise in these transactions. These are the experiences which lead to the expansion of consciousness, which in turn effect and lead to a greater integration of personality, a more fully functioning social system, and a richer and more flexible cultural system.

It is readily accepted that individuals must learn to deal with the world in which they find themselves. What has been presented above concerning the reality-adaptive task can be seen as a task individuals face every day. The interactions an individual has with every aspect of his/her environment confronts the individual with demands of one sort or another which play an active role in forming the individual's projection of the world.

In the reality-adaptive sphere the social system is manifested in a sequence of archetypal symbols (for example, the Great Mother) which herald a body of unconscious content. For the social system to progress through this sequence, each archetypal element has to be encountered, confronted, and resolved. These are the demands of the reality-adaptive task and the ways in which these demands evolve define this dimension of the social system. As I will discuss in greater detail later, the social system must struggle through the stages from the Great Mother to the Birth of the Hero. These are the unconscious content that is projected into the life of the group.

The situation is similar for the cultural system. In analytical psychology the concept of collective consciousness is used to describe what are the active adaptive processes at work in the cultural system. These adaptive processes may prove to be destructive as was the case with National Socialism in Germany (Jung, 1959). When a cultural system is adaptive it is encountering the task; the resolution is a related but also a separate issue.

Thus far three points of view have been spoken to. The structural point of view posited the existence of three discrete, autonomous, concurrent, and interrelating systems, the social, personality, and cultural. The developmental perspective described the systems as dynamic and evolving components of the small group. The adaptive point of view identified three primary tasks which each system must work at: defining the nature of its identity, establishing modes of relating, developing means to relate to reality-adaptive demands. At this time it may be instructive to present the Matrix Model in the form of a diagram. Figure 1.1 presents a visualization of the three points of view as they have been described. The three primary tasks are set to the left of the cube. The developmental perspective is shown along the side of the cube progressing from the face of the cube upwards. The intent here is to picture the time dimension. The three systems are listed at the top of the cube. The three remaining points of view will be discussed in the following text.

The transactional point of view

There are three points of view that have not as yet been discussed. We will now consider each in turn starting with the transactional point of view.

The transactional perspective asserts that whatever is happening in any constituent part of the matrix affects in some manner what is happening in the other parts of the matrix. This does not mean that a particular act or a specific transaction is to be identified exclusively to one cell of the matrix and any repercussions are to be noted if they are observed occurring in other parts of the matrix. The basis for such a misinterpretation may be readily appreciated when we recall that coding schemes in social psychology demand an exclusive categorizing of behavior. Were this approach to be employed to make the Matrix Model operational, a given behavior or event would be seen as a discrete

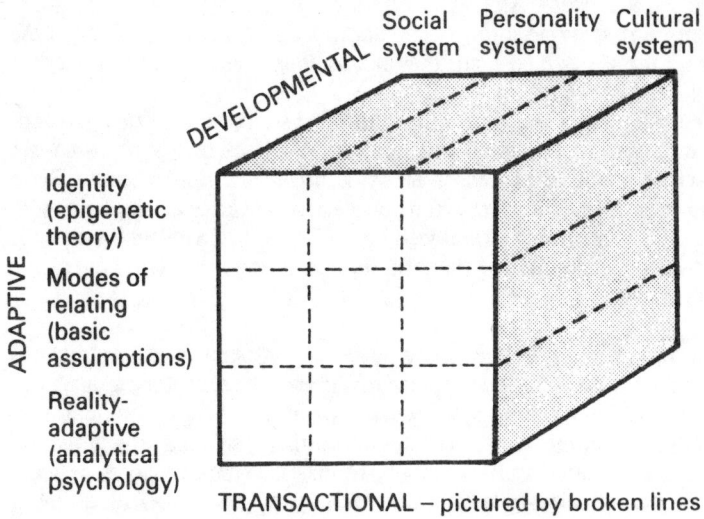

STRUCTURAL

Social Personality Cultural
system   system   system

DEVELOPMENTAL

ADAPTIVE

Identity
(epigenetic
theory)

Modes of
relating
(basic
assumptions)

Reality-
adaptive
(analytical
psychology)

TRANSACTIONAL – pictured by broken lines

DYNAMIC – unique resolutions of relationships
developed in cells

Figure 1.1 Matrix Model showing points of view and theoretical frameworks

phenomenon matching the specifications of one and only one cell of the matrix. For example, an observation would be coded into the Social System–Identity cell. This would completely miss the rich meaning imbedded in the word 'transactional' which conveys explicitly the trans quality of effect.

At this point a question may be raised: If, as it appears to be proposed here, a behavior should not be viewed as a discrete form or type of behavior, codable to a specific category of acts, why, then are specific cells identified in the Matrix Model? The answer, quite simply, lies in the notion of the transactional nature of experience. A behavior is codable to a given cell but its meaning transcends its coded designation. A definable behavior, such as a member speaking about his/her difficulty in expressing intimacy, may be treated empirically and accordingly coded as an act having the primary intentionality of dealing with self-identity and therefore coded in the Identity–Personality cell. But, in addition, it may be directed to and be reflected from the issue of intimacy being worked through in the social system. The transactional point of view enables us to place the meaning of a lived experience within the matrix as it affects the group-as-a-whole. This realization brings us to the next point of view.

The Gestalt point of view

Viewing the group-as-a-whole is critical to an understanding of what is taking place in the group. One way to conceptualize the small group is to view it metaphorically as an organism (Thelen, 1959). There are different levels of empirical evidence that support taking the Gestalt point of view. One common observation of a small group is the change which occurs in the dynamics of a group with the change of its membership even if that change only involves one person. Another observation supporting the Gestalt perspective is the noticeable change which occurs when different cultural norms or values are introduced. It is not only the cultural system that looks different, but different observable transactions related directly to these norms and values can be seen occurring in the social and personality systems. A case in point is the introduction of the norm which asserts that what does not appear to be an honest answer can be confronted. Frequently, when such a norm is introduced as a construct of the cultural system, the social system initially becomes more dependent upon the leader for there is a fear that confrontations may get out of control. For some members this norm allows them to begin to explore personal feelings and even to begin to deal with unconscious content. Other members are obviously frightened by what may happen and become silent or even withdraw as active members of the group.

Any one of the three systems affects the group as a whole. The group is also a different entity as it focuses on a given task and as it moves through different phases of its development or as it evolves as a unique entity. Most of the time it is understandable why we focus upon particular aspects of a group we are observing; however, to lose sight of the wholeness of the group has the serious possibility of distorting our understanding of what is taking place in the group. An intervention that is made to help a group deal with a particular issue or problem should be first considered, as far as it is reasonable, with the group-as-a-whole in view. An intervention directed at one aspect may be the result of focusing on a particular system or task, and the consequence may prove to be confusing if not disruptive to the group.

The content point of view

Finally there is the content point of view. Transactions which take place in the context of a small group can be delineated in a variety of category paradigms. One perspective is to observe verbal inputs and to classify them into two sets of utterances, for example instrumental and socio-emotional (Bales, 1950). Other verbal category frameworks examine statements from a problem-solving model. Certain clinical models identify the various types of verbal utterances using category systems that yield evidence on such psychological factors as mechanisms of defence, transference, and repression. Other content frameworks focus only on behaviors and classify them into particular sets of categories depending on the conceptual framework of the investigator. One such framework employs approach and avoidance categories. Examples of these various category systems have been reported by Hill and Gruner (1973), Argyris (1957), and Stogdill (1959).

Content refers to the forms the transactions take in the life of the group. This point needs to be emphasized because it is so often assumed that only individual members engage in and originate transactions in a group. Transactions are not simply the interactions between members: they describe the actions of all three systems. There are observable transactions within the social system itself, as it struggles to evolve from one phase to the next. And similarly in the case of the cultural system as new values are adopted and old ones are discarded.

In the Matrix Model we observe symbolic content and categorize transactions which occur within all three systems from that perspective. Symbolic content makes use of the subject matter of manifest content but examines it with the question: Is there a message behind the literal message? In other terms, the task here is to discern what is the symbolic meaning of the experience. Bion (1959) made an important contribution to the empirical study of symbolic content by phrasing the observation of symbolic phenomena in the terms 'as if' in describing the sense of the transaction he was attempting to identify. For example, in describing the basic assumption culture of Fight/Flight, where the culture of Flight was dominant, he spoke of it 'as if the group were flighting from some enemy it was unable to confront'. Symbolic analysis of transactions frequently makes use of such images because they capture the essence of the meaning that is embedded at one basic level of the transaction.

Symbolic content is set out in descriptive terms totally unlike the variety of terms used to describe rational content, such as literal, conceptual, practical, and propositional. Symbolic content is different in that it is not subject to delineated specifiers and fixed definitions, but is extremely variable because its meaning is grounded in the experience that it portrays. For example, aggressive, attacking, criticizing, and opposing forms of behavior may in one situation be seen as expressing counterdependency while in another situation the symbolic content of these behaviors is the expression of Fight. The difference between these situations is the meaning these behaviors have in the context of the group's life – that is to say, in the symbolic nature of the transaction. The point here is not to criticize the use of the other forms of content as legitimate bases for the study of transactions within small groups, but rather to differentiate the nature of symbolic content as it is used here in the study of transactions within the small group.

In the section which follows, symbolic content is the focus of our observations because it reveals a depth perception of the existence of the three primary tasks (identity, emotionality, reality-adaptive) which the three systems (social, personality, cultural) work at during the life course of the group. The central role given to the tasks is readily explained in that the account of a small group's life is organized around the three tasks, and a discussion of the tasks is a functional approach by which to bring together all six points of view. In following this plan, the developmental and transactional points of view are woven into the discussion which explains the ways in which each of the three systems works on the basic tasks. The Gestalt point of view becomes evident in the picturing of the interrelationships which reveal the wholeness of the group as an existential entity.

The three primary tasks

The small group is an existential entity. It is recognized as an entity only so long as these systems continue to work on the primary tasks. It is in that sense that the small group is described in phenomenological terms as an organism. This view of the group reintroduces the adaptive point of view. As was proposed above, the adaptive point of view serves as a dynamic perspective through which the other points of view may be explained in the course of a group's life. Thus an understanding of the adaptive point of view is critical. This means that if we are to gain a working knowledge of the small group based on the adaptive point of view, it then will be necessary to identify and set out conceptual schemas that operationalize the three primary tasks which are the adaptive perspective. Earlier, in our discussion of the adaptive point of view, three primary tasks were identified: (1) define the nature of the system's identity, (2) establish modes of relating, (3) develop means to relate to reality-adaptive demands. Although in our earlier discussion there were general descriptions of the three primary tasks, these are not adequate to serve as the basis for a systematic observation of these tasks. It is necessary to move to a more specific descriptive level of these tasks if studies on small groups are to be undertaken. Thus the critical question arises, for example: How do you observe an individual, a social system, or a cultural system working at defining its identity? Also, is there a different schema for each of the three systems? A number of other questions arise when considering what has to be done to move our initial observations first into more careful and systematic observations and when to determine if an explanatory conceptual framework exists.

It would appear from what has been set out above that the conduct of empirical studies proceeds in a very logical and systematic fashion. That may well be the situation in some cases but it was not quite the case in the development of the Matrix Model. There were many explorations, some on the main route and others somewhat tangential to the development of the Matrix Model. It is not my intention to chronicle its development here; however, some reference to its history may provide the reader with a better understanding and give helpful insights into our work. Therefore, in explaining and discussing the frameworks used to operationalize the primary task, I will present the material as a historical account, for the most part; however, I will deal only with the investigations that pertain to the topic at hand.

Identity

Each system, the social, personality, or cultural, has the task of defining its boundaries, demarcating itself from the other whether the other is an item or agent within or between systems, establishing its unique characteristics, and furthering its developing qualities as a functioning entity. These components of the identity task may be illustrated by examining trust development (Gibb and Gibb, 1978), problems of dependency and interdependency (Bennis and Shepard, 1956), and boundary awareness (Slater, 1966). The social system of a small group evolves its own identity. It is described in specific ways by its members: 'This is a hard working group.' 'I see this group as very different from other groups I belong to.' What has been observed occurring within the social system can also be observed with individual members who can be seen reflecting on values they hold, the kind of person they are, and not infrequently, the kind of person they would like to be, as well as the personal goals that are shaping their lives. One of the major contributions that a small group can give to its membership is the opportunity to rework aspects of their identities, moving these aspects to a more favorable and constructive resolution. More will be said on this subject later. Finally, the cultural system, as is the case for the social and personality systems, must work at defining its identity. From its initial session onward the small group is involved in clarifying and evolving commonly held sets of mores, values, expectations, and norms which define the dynamic identity of the cultural system. For example, in a managerial team, it is tacitly understood that openly hostile confrontations between members are not acceptable behavior: this is a norm that defines one identity aspect of this group's culture.

Erikson's (1950) epigenetic theory was used as the framework to conceptualize the task of identity for each of the three systems. The decision to employ this theory was initiated by an insight that came to me as I was consulting with a small group of managers who were exploring ways of working more harmoniously together. Watching them struggling with identity issues, the thought struck me that there perhaps was a similar pattern to group phase development as there was to the stages of ego development. At the same period I was deeply involved in an area of research in which I was employing the epigenetic theory in a study on motivation. My other project at that time was focused on studying small groups in which I was attempting to get a more comprehensive picture of a small group than were offered by those conceptual models then available in the literature.

I had developed a methodology (Boyd, 1961) based on Erikson's ego stage epigenetic theory by which I could code verbal utterances into the eight stages. This methodology was used to examine the conjecture that the social system of a small group goes through identity phases analogous to those stages in ego development. Davie (1971) analyzed the complete protocol of a small group that extended over fifteen weeks, some 37 hours. The data showed that the social system had a general configuration that paralleled the predicted sequence. Although the results were seen as encouraging, if not entirely supportive of our thesis, it was not until later that we realized that we had employed an inappropriate method in this study. At the time it was quite understandable why we coded individual utterances to get a reading on the group as that was the approach employed by other investigators whose empirical methods we took as models (Bales, 1950; Stock and Thelen, 1958). Although well aware of the teachings of Field psychology, I failed to heed them in the guidance I gave Davie in applying my method to the study of the small group. The sum of the parts generally does not give an accurate picture of the whole: coding individual behavior may provide some insights as to what the social system is about but it may also completely misrepresent what is occurring in the social system. If either the social or cultural system is the focus of study then it must be viewed as an entity – a method of study that had been set out earlier by Bion (1959).

The task became, in light of these realizations, to develop a method to observe the social system based on the epigenetic theory. Instead of describing individuals confronting the epigenetic crises, the task was to describe a social system as it encountered the sequence of crises analogous to those which evolve in individual epigenetic development. We will not examine here the epistemological issues which may arise in the minds of some readers on the question of translating a theory explaining individual psychology to a schema explaining phenomena in social psychology. For the present we refer the issue to Erikson's writings where he relates the epigenetic theory to both the social and cultural domains (Erikson, 1959). My initial insight was realized after much labor. A methodology to observe and code social system phenomena into identity phases was developed from extensive studies on both ongoing and video-taped groups.

This methodology has been used in a number of studies (Boyd et al., 1980; Kushel, 1980; Myers, 1986; Ullrich, 1987; White, 1976). On reflection, it is not difficult to see the appeal of Erikson's work in providing categories for the social system's phase development. It is well documented (Bradford, 1978) that the social system first struggles with the problem of trust and mistrust. After it has developed some form of resolution between the polarities of trusting and mistrusting, it moves on to the next phase – encountering the issues clustered around the crisis of autonomy. When the group has come to realize and to accept the exercise of its autonomy, it proceeds to assert its initiative, which is quickly blended with work activities. The carrying out of these work activities leads to a sense of a 'group identity' in that the social system expresses clear evidence of the goals it is seeking and values that define and support its identity as a group. Once this phase has been firmly established a transition occurs that moves the group into less of a 'work-conscious' group and noticeably more of a group that openly accepts and readily fosters intimacy. The sense of intimacy in the group comes into conflict with expressions of isolation which is manifest in a variety of symbolic content. For example, the sense of isolation is felt in the uniqueness of this group compared with other groups. The intimacy in the group seems impossible to convey to others with whom one is intimate in the world outside of the small group. On the one hand there is a feeling of intimacy in the group but this intimacy can, on the other hand, give a sense of isolation with the world outside of the small group. In addition the social system faces other concerns, including sexuality (Slater, 1966) and problems of boundary definitions (Gibbard and Hartman, 1974). Following the resolution of intimacy vs. isolation phase, the social system begins to address its relationships with and its contributions to the larger society. This phase corresponds to Erikson's Generativity stage. The final phase – the phase of integrity – frequently consumes the total time of the last meeting of the small group. In this session the worth of the social system, or what Erikson speaks of as the stage of Integrity, is examined as the final phase of the social system. Individual members become the spokespersons for this phenomenon. 'Was all the struggling worth it?' 'There was a good deal of grief in our life together, but I will miss it when it is over.' It is not uncommon for food to be brought into this last session. Slater (1966) very ably labels this phenomenon as the 'Last Supper'. The symbolism of the food at this point in the life of the small group would clearly support this interpretation. The sense that one has in being a part of this event further corroborates this interpretation.

The epigenetic theory was initially proposed as an explanation of identity development in the course of an individual's life. Thus it is unnecessary to argue for its application to the personality system within the Matrix Model. Individuals bring into the small group the resolutions of ego stages through which they have passed as well as the phase specific crisis that they are working on at the present time. For example, in a group of twelve adult members ranging in age from the late twenties to the mid-forties, it can be expected that the ego stages of Intimacy and Generativity will be the psychosocial crises these individuals are confronting. Even though these concerns are the focal ego crises for these members, at the time these individuals join the small group, the nascent social system will effect a retrogradation of these members' ego identity concerns, moving the focus of their concerns to the phase that it is at in its own development. We observe the members struggling with issues of trust vs. mistrust. The retrogradation is not to be understood, in such contexts, as a return to that earlier period of one's life (regression); it is movement on the horizontal plane and not a downward movement, back to that period when the crisis was phase specific. A specific case may illustrate the point being made here. A male member is working through the ego crisis of Generativity which is then identified as being phase specific (VII-7) for him. He finds himself in a social system that is working through issues of trust and mistrust: the first crisis a group confronts in establishing its identity. His involvement in this work, as an active member of the group, also affects him as a person for the experience of being actively involved with the group's struggles of trusting and mistrusting awaken his reflections on how he, personally, relates to issues of trusting and mistrusting. He considers these reflections within the context of his own ego development, thus trust vs. mistrust are experienced within the stage of Generativity (VII-1). That is, the problems involved in trusting vs. mistrusting in the social system will be viewed from the perspective of his current ego stage crisis. As the social system moves from one phase to the next, members will progress horizontally in step with the social system's phase development and toward their current phase specific stage.

Erikson's epigenetic theory serves also to conceptualize the identity formation of the cultural system. The question may again arise as it did with the social system: On what basis can one justify the use of a theory explaining individual development to explain the development of a cultural system? As in the case of the social system we turn again to Erikson's (1959) position on this matter. He posited that the critical phenomenological issues facing a culture are identical in nature – if not in scope – to those phenomenological crises facing an individual. A cultural system is a reflection of human nature while at the same time, the culture is reflected in the individual. There is a transactional relationship through which each is shaped by the other. The cultural system is not something apart from the individuals for they manifest its existence and find their being in it. If the person struggles with the crisis of Trust vs. Mistrust then we can expect to find and look to see how the cultural system confronts, defines and resolves the conflict of trusting vs. mistrusting.

The cultural system is carried into the setting of the small group by the members who compose it. It is the members who in portraying their existential culture come to experience it as defined within the context of the small group. In our present society with its mix of publics, it cannot be assumed that a common culture is shared by all group members. Particular values, norms and expectations are frequently held in common among the various subpublics within a given society and it is upon that seemly reasonable assumption groups work on developing their culture systems. Whether there are common traditions or not the cultural system wills a life of its own. This phenomenon can be observed in groups composed of international negotiators, in managerial groups, community action groups, therapy and learning groups.

The cultural system, like the social system, makes its own demands felt in the life of the group. For example, early in the life of a small group there are attempts on the part of group members to relate their particular group to some larger scheme, program or enterprise outside of the group. This may serve the purpose of helping some members justify their involvement in the group when the group experience in itself fails to provide such meaning, but it can also be observed that the existence of the group perceived as a cultural entity demands its own meaning in the scheme of things. This search for meaning not only gives the individual cause to participate but it also evolves the particular cultural system of the group. Erikson (1959) noted this phenomenon when he described a culture as having an initial problem of establishing cosmic order as opposed to chaos: an observation also made by Neumann (1954) from the perspective of consciousness development. The struggle to establish cosmic order in the cultural system of the small group can be readily observed. This is illustrated in the case of the 'designated' leader who provides no stated structure for the group (invariably experienced as chaos) which awakens in the members not only psychological anxieties but demonic images and powerful feeling-tones. When the cultural system is experienced as being in chaos, while at the same time the social system is working through the phase of trust vs. mistrust, there can be little wonder why some members drop out of the group and why many of those that stay, frequently express puerile frustration and explosive anger.

Similar to both the personality and social system there is a sequence of eight identity phases through which the cultural system may progress. Unlike the ego stage development of an individual, as set out in Erikson's writings, there is no bio-psychosocial clock in the cultural system that propels it onwards to the next phase whether it be ready or not. The crises are sequential but while one may be focal, evidence of other crises may be observed in the cultural system of the group. The content of these crises parallels those of the personality and social systems: (1) cosmic order, (2) law and order, (3) ideal prototype, (4) technological elements, (5) ideological perspectives, (6) patterns of cooperation and competition, (7) currents of education and tradition, and (8) cultural wisdom. Space does not permit a discussion on each of these crises but in a general way, the sense of each of the phases is identified in their naming.

Emotionality

The conceptual framework set out in a comprehensive collection by Bion (1959) was extended by Thelen (Stock and Thelen, 1958) and his students from Bion's earlier published articles. It was this extended framework which was incorporated into the Matrix Model to explain modes of relating. All three systems must employ ways of relating to other entities and modes of relating within their own system. The selection of Bion's conceptual scheme was made primarily on the basis of its explanatory power. Anyone who has worked with small groups and has even a moderate acceptance of depth psychology cannot fail to appreciate the contribution Bion has made in giving us such clear portraits of the basic emotional states of the group's social system. There was also a personal and a subjective influence in the selection. With the goal of keeping the Matrix Model grounded in depth psychology, I was not about to mix apples and oranges either ontologically or epistemologically. It is difficult enough to understand the dynamics of small groups without superimposing on the project the additional task of resolving conflicting assumptions. It also happens to be the case that depth psychology gives us a more inclusive and integrative picture of the human experience than other current paradigms can offer.

A detailed presentation of Bion's theory of Basic Assumption Cultures is assumed to be unnecessary as it has been so widely discussed in small group literature. We review it here briefly, only to place it operationally within the Matrix Model. The works of Thelen and his students at the University of Chicago may be somewhat less well known and therefore may need a more extensive explanation.

The social system can be observed at different periods in the life of a small group expressing different emotionalities, that is to say, being in different basic assumption cultures. In our work at the University of Wisconsin-Madison, we have observed that the vast majority of groups start out in BaC (Basic assumption Culture) of Dependency, then move on to Fight/Flight and come next to Pairing. We are aware that other investigators report a different sequence (Slater, 1966). I do not see this theory proposing a strict developmental sequence as was the case with the epigenetic theory; however, because of many factors, for example cultural factors and the symbolism of family, a Dependent BaC seems highly probable as the first emotionality state. Basic assumption cultures may also be cyclical during the life of a small group. This occurs frequently when major transitions are encountered. A social system may move between two BaCs for an extended period of time and during such periods it may never manifest the third type of BaC. These various patterns do not necessarily indicate that the social system remains at the same level of emotionality. Although a BaC of Dependency always has the quality of its basic emotionality, it may become more subtle and convoluted at later stages of a social system's life.

I drew upon the Chicago group (Stock and Thelen, 1958) to conceptualize the emotionality expressions of the personality system within the Matrix Model. Their investigations revealed six types of emotionalities that individuals express in their relationships in small groups. They are: (1) dependency and (2) counterdependency; (3) fight and (4) flight; (5) pairing and (6) counterpairing. Each of these six valencies of emotionality were further delineated into three forms, positive, neutral, and negative, according to the effect they had upon transactions. This schema provides an inclusive and an exhaustive set of categories which make possible careful observations of the modes of relating individual members' use in their relationships.

The cultural system is also active in establishing and maintaining specific modes of relating. As is the case with the social system, the cultural system expresses three forms or types of relating, dependency, pairing, and fight/flight. The type of emotionality that the cultural system manifests initially is determined by the larger cultural milieu in which the small group has its context. For example, the cultural system of a group of college students meeting with their professor would be generally structured on the emotionality of Dependency. The norms, expectations and rituals would express this relationship mode. Small groups form their cultural emotionalities based on the fundamental prototype to which the members see the group belonging. In education there is clearly a dependency on the teacher as a guide, a resource person, a helper, and in some situations as a beneficent or a castigating sovereign. All small groups are drawn from or are directly responsive to a larger cultural body which could be a specific public, institution, movement, organization, or corporation. Both Freud (1922) and Bion (1959) discussed the basic emotional states of the Army and the Church and Bion specifically related these to the basic assumption cultures. He did not, as I have done here, differentiate between the social and cultural systems, clearly because he did not hold such a structural view of the small group. This point may be more fully understood in the case of the

Army which may be used to illustrate the emotionality states of both the cultural and social systems as viewed from the Matrix Model. The Army, as both Freud and Bion recognized, is founded on the cultural prototype of Fight/Flight, but it functions most effectively and efficiently at the platoon level when, as a social system, it employs the BaC of Pairing. The recognition of the cultural system's and the social system's emotional states explains why observers are aware of two co-existing emotionalities in the life of a small group. It is of some interest to note that Bion was also aware of the existence of underlying emotional states in the group and described this phenomenon as proto-mental states of emotionality. It is beyond the scope of this chapter to examine his interpretation against the explanation set out here. It is apparent that the context in which the small group has its existence must be taken into account in some functional manner as the need to do so is pointed out in the above discussion.

The following account of a segment in the life of a small group will illustrate the ways in which the three systems express modes of relating.

A psychiatric team has been examining, with the help of an outside consultant, the manner in which it has been operating as a team. The third meeting began in much the same manner as the previous two sessions with no clearly stated agenda but with the sense that the group was waiting for the consultant to take a leadership role for the group. He had informed them that he would provide whatever insights he believed would be helpful to the group but that the work of resolving issues was up to everyone and that he could not provide solutions to the problems the team was encountering. These points had been made on more than one occasion during the group's sessions; however, there was a clearly observable sense in the group that it was waiting for the leader to offer ready-made solutions to its difficulties. A few minutes into the third session, John, one of the two male psychiatrists, spoke up. 'We're getting nowhere fast. Perhaps we will have to face up to the fact that there is a hierarchy of responsibility and this in turn dictates the structural nature of our organization as a team.' Mary, the head nurse, immediately confronted him. 'Perhaps that's what you have always wanted.' 'Nonsense, I feel all the wasted affect in our relations comes about because there is no agreed upon structure.' Mary: 'What you mean is an organization based on status.' John looked down at his folded hands and did not reply. A period of silence followed. A psychiatric social worker spoke next in what appeared as an intentionally quiet voice. Janet: 'We came together because we all are committed to improving what we are doing.' Another period of silence. Janet added, 'As we agreed, when we started, the delivery of good care is what is before us.' Mary turned to Janet, 'That's right but we're not going to get there unless we can be honest with each other.' John: 'And I am not being honest?' Mary: 'It's not a case of you being honest but whether we are honest with each other.' John: 'That doesn't make sense.' Before Mary could answer, Anne, a staff nurse, spoke up.

I am beginning to feel very uncomfortable and I really don't understand where we are going. And I also agree with Janet that we came together to work together, to share with each other and to be a better team by finding ways we can support each other. For three sessions now we haven't done that. We just seem to get together to express our frustrations.

Henry, the psychiatric resident, appearing to agree with Anne added, 'It appears that we have one set of stated norms but another set which we really operate on.' The leader then raised the observation, 'Perhaps the rules the family has given itself are preventing the family from dealing with itself as a family in the here and now.'

The social system is expressing the BaC of Fight/Flight. This is evident in this brief account of the group in the sense that there is some basic matter that is working against the resolution of the team's problems, thus in Bion's terms 'appearing as an enemy to the group'. But the group is not organized against it and thus finds itself in Flight. When we examine the small group from the point of view of the personality system, three valencies can be identified. John and Mary are relating to the situation on the valency of Fight. Janet is attempting to express the valency of Pairing, while Anne is employing the emotionality of Dependency. The emotionality modality of this group's culture is Dependency. The sense of this culture is reflected in symbolic meanings manifest in the statement made by John, Mary and Anne. This finding is not unexpected in that, for this team, the larger context is a hospital setting which is generally structured as a hierarchical culture, where status and authority are institutionalized.

This brief outline of emotionality as manifested by the three systems provides only the barest of introductions to these dynamic forces in the life of a small group. It is critical in terms of what is proposed here to remember that all three systems are expressing modes of relating simultaneously, otherwise we may fail to perceive certain critical dynamics which are shaping and directing the life of the group.

Reality-adaptive

The third primary task I have identified as the reality-adaptive task. Such a label is in immediate need of being defined for as it stands it may mean a number of different things to a variety of people. To carry through with the conceptual premisses that I have adopted places immediate boundaries on the possible meanings of the reality-adaptive task. It is defined within the framework of depth psychology – specific-ally, analytical psychology. Its content is examined at the symbolic level. As is the case with the other primary tasks, the developmental, transactional, and Gestalt points of view describe the functional per-spectives of the reality-adaptive task.

The realization of this primary task evolved over many years of working with small groups and attempting to explain what I was observing. Initially I formulated my observations in terms of problem-solving behaviors. The group defines the problem before it, differ-entiates what is involved and works through the structuring of a solution to the problem. This approach is widely used in the study of small groups in education, commerce, and academic psychology. This approach puts the reality-adaptive task off by itself as it fails to directly relate it to the affect in the group and also to the group's task of defining its boundaries (identity). Bion's (1959) concept of work, which I then adopted, had a distinct virtue over the problem-solving framework in that it related work and affect (emotionality). His notion of work was very limited because it was a binary concept – there was a sophisticated group or there wasn't. The Chicago group (Stock and Thelen, 1958) delineated work into four subcategories. This step did provide a more detailed observation of the group as it works on the reality-adaptive task and it was one we made use of in our research at Wisconsin. It also had the conceptual integrity by keeping the category systems within one theoretical framework. The four categories of work were helpful in understanding certain aspects of the group's life but they did not account for other phenomena within the group which I experienced but could not explicitly describe. After many months of observing video tapes and finding no acceptable resolution to my dilemma I turned to my library for whatever help I might be able to find. A rereading of Slater (1966) alerted me to a reference on the works of Erich Neumann (1954), whose research Slater did not however incorporate into his own work, probably because of his psychoanalytic leanings. I found and read Neumann's *The origins and history of consciousness.* Doors flew open and for the next year I immersed myself in the reading of Jung and analytical psychology. What I had experienced both as a member and as an observer of a small group, but had not been able to express, now slowly yet distinctly became clear to me. The reality-adaptive task is the expansion of consciousness.

The theory of the development of consciousness can be used to explain what each system faces in dealing with its unique encounters with the sphere of experience that I have here called reality demands. We will begin by first observing the social system.

In the initial meeting of a small group, the social system is ex-perienced as an evolving entity. Some members immediately strike out at this situation that they sense, asserting their individuality in one of a number of ways. Their fear, explicitly conscious or not, is that they will be swallowed up by this entity; that their unique individuality will be denied to them in this situation. This phenomenon occurs in a range of groups we have observed and we therefore assume it is common to all small groups. It is the initial phase of the social system as it comes into existence when viewed from the reality-adaptive perspective. Here it is in the Uroboric stage of consciousness development, the Great Round, as Neumann describes it, a most apt description for this initial phase of the social system. To most members, the group is experienced as a circle that contains and defines. It is this sense of the group which arouses anxiety in some members and a primary feeling of security in other members. It is the first reality-adaptive task encountered by the social system and one that it must work through to move on to the next phase in the expansion of consciousness.

When the group moves out of the Uroboric phase, it is then experienced as the Great Mother. Such polarities as caring and abandoning, feeding and devouring, nurturing, and denying are manifest in the group as it struggles to find its way. These are the symbolic content expressed in the life of the social system and reflected in the behaviors of members as they relate to the social system. A variety of statements made by members give witness to this fact. 'I feel that we have come to be a caring group.' 'Initially I was uncertain that this group could hear what I was needing, now I feel relaxed about that.' 'I feel as if this group, and I don't mean any one member, could leave you out there to dangle in the wind, if you didn't agree to do a certain thing the group wanted.' There is an overwhelming impression that the group at this phase has taken on the image of the Great Mother when viewed from the perspective of analytical psychology. In a later chapter, the Great Mother as an image of the social system is discussed in detail.

There are three phases of the Great Mother, the Uroboric Great Mother, the presence of and the encounter with the Good and Bad Mother, and the resolution that leads to the dominance of either the Good or Bad Mother. Although a general pattern of progression can be observed to these phases, it can also be observed that often there is a back and forth movement to these phases. Finally there will be a resolution that establishes the group as being either predominately a Good or Bad Mother. The dominance of the Bad Mother results in the stagnation of the group, while the ascendancy of the Good Mother leads to a forward movement of the group. Moving out of that resolution the group encounters the separation of the Great Parents. The Great Father then joins the Great Mother and becomes the principal element of the social system and thus the critical content of the reality-adaptive task. The group then confronts the Good and Bad Father and again must resolve the choice between them. If the Bad Father comes to characterize the social system, the group stagnates and often regresses. The Good Father is the phase in the life of the group that leads to the subsequent phase of the hero journey – the developmental phase described as interdependency (Bennis and Shepard, 1956), the New Order (Slater, 1966), and the Transformation Myth (Neumann, 1954).

The individual adult member of the group struggles with the stages of consciousness development as he/she experiences them in the social system of the group. It is generally the case that members are aware of some struggle going on but would not be aware of it in the terms in which we have described it above. For those members who are aware and accept the concept of the unconscious, its meaning is frequently restricted to repressed material. Few have a knowledge of the concept as set out in analytical psychology. Whether there is a conscious awareness or not, all members are confronted with the archetypal content of the social system as it evolves through phases of consciousness development. As illustrated above (Uroboric phase) some members feel threatened by the group because it may swallow them up and destroy their individuality. In the phase of the Great Mother some members speak of relationships with their personal mothers as this helps them to understand some of the feeling which they are experiencing in the group. Later their struggles with autonomy – with the Great Father – are projected onto the leader's behaviors. It is apparent in observing the members that they are revisiting and not infrequently restructuring aspects of their consciousness development. To the extent that members commit themselves to the welfare of the group, and are willing and able to examine their own psychic development, is the ground prepared for personal transformations.

Neumann (1954) documented the stages of consciousness development in human cultures. His studies uncovered a pattern of development outlined above in the discussion of the social system. Thus every society can be examined to determine which stage the culture is at in its development. This information is critical to an understanding of what is taking place in a small group. The culture of the society within which the small group exists is brought into the group by the members and is experienced as a dynamic force within the matrix of the group. Major aspects of the content which compose the developmental stage are the directive forces in the society's collective consciousness. These several points may be illustrated in the following observation.

An advance seminar of graduate students in a Midwest university has been formed to examine the criminal justice system in United States. The ten men and women, who are unknown to each other, are meeting for the first session. The professor after a few words that sketch the broad issues, asks the members to view the group as a learning community in which everyone should feel equally responsible for the direction of their enquiry. There is a sense in observing the group that the individuals have been thrust into a type of social system to which they have little familiarity. Out of an initial feeling of chaos the image of the Uroboric arises. Concurrently, other dynamics are observable. The group struggles to identify and define an agenda but with the professor remaining quiet during this period, they appear unable to make any decision. It appears the class members are waiting for the professor to give them guidance. The members have brought into the cultural system of the small group the cultural dynamics of the educational institution and also of the larger society for both share in the predominant archetype – the stage of the Great Father. Both the institution and the American society manifest the patriarchal culture. The social and cultural systems of this small group are out of phase with each other and it is this situation, so often observed in small groups of various types, that is one of the major conditions which produces miscommunications and misunderstandings in these early sessions. The group is encountering the Great Mother in the social system while it is trying to conform to the Great Father in the cultural system. In such groups where the designated leader does not step in and confirm the Great Father and define the Great Mother, it can be expected that turmoil as well as the opportunities for personal transformations will be present. To realize these opportunities the patriarchy must be put aside and the matriarchy allowed to be expressed in the cultural matrix of the group and experienced by the members.

The cultural system's stages of development parallel those of the other two systems, but, as has been illustrated above, the sequence may be out of phase in the initial sessions of a small group.

A concluding statement

The small group is viewed here as an entity-in-process. The points of view which constitute the Matrix Model are the places where one may stand in order to gain some understanding of this entity-in-process, a phenomenon that we speak of as the small group. There are different levels upon which these perspectives can be structured. Here theories from depth psychology have been chosen as the framework for these perspectives. The firm ground upon which any structure is built must be the meaning of the experience as lived. This is the tenet of our empirical research. The validity and integrity of the Matrix Model in turn rests upon empirical enquiries.

Empirical studies in the social sciences require the development of data-gathering empirical procedures. These are the methodologies by which we explore and test our hunches and conjectures. Social sciences are dependent upon methodologies in the same way that the physical sciences of physics and astronomy are dependent upon the invention of instruments. Methodologies in the social sciences are analogous to the instruments the physical scientists use in their research. Our purpose was to subject our theories to empirical tests. Therefore the task before us became one of developing appropriate methodologies by which to subject our theories to empirical tests. The chapter which follows reports on a methodology which examines one dimension of the Matrix Model – the social system in the reality-adaptive domain.

The methodology allows us to examine the five points of view set forth in the Matrix Model in combination with the theory of the development of consciousness as described in the works of Erich Neumann. The Matrix Model provides a dynamic and structural framework for the methodology. Neumann's theory defines the content for the observational categories of consciousness. As will be shown in the following chapter, the combination of the two frameworks was the basis for the development of empirical procedures. This methodology provided the way to study the development of consciousness in small groups and to test our conjectures concerning these developments.

References

Argyris, C. (1957). *Personality and organization.* New York: Harper & Row.

Bales, R.F. (1950). *Interaction process analysis: A method for the study of small groups.* Reading, MA: Addison-Wesley.

Bales, R. F. and Strodtbeck, F. L. (1951). Phases in group problem solving, *Journal of Abnormal and Social Psychology, 46,* 485–95.

Bennis, W. G. and Shepard, H. A. (1956). A theory of group development, *Human Relations, 9,* 415–37.

Bion, W. R. (1959). *Experiences in groups.* New York: Basic Books.

Boyd, R. D. (1961). Basic motivation of adults in non-credit programs, *Adult Education, 11,* 92–8.

Boyd, R. D., Bressler, D., Dirkx, J.M., Fullmer, R., Levenson, E., Kushel, C. K. and Ullrich, W. (1980). *A report on the Evaluation Study of the Group Dynamics Traffic Safety School, State of Wisconsin.* Madison: Department of Transportation, Wisconsin.

Bradford, L. P. (1978). *Group development.* San Diego: University Associates.

Cartwright, D. and Zander A., (1968). *Group dynamics: Research and theory.* New York: Harper & Row.

Davie, L. E. (1971). *Eriksonian ego stage theory applied to small group phase progression.* Unpublished doctoral dissertation, University of Wisconsin-Madison.

Erikson, E. H. (1950). *Childhood and society.* New York: W. W. Norton.

Erikson, E. H. (1959). Identity and the life cycle, *Psychology Issues, I.* International University Press.

Freud, S. (1922). *Group psychology and the analysis of the ego*. London: Hogarth.

Gibb. J. H. and Gibb, L. M. (1978). The group as a growing organism. In L. P. Bradfords (ed.), *Group development*. San Diego: University Associates.

Gibbard, G. S. and Hartman, J. J. (eds) (1974). *Analysis of groups: Contribution to theory, research and practice*. San Francisco: Jossey-Bass.

Hill, W. F. and Gruner, L. (1973). A study of development in open and closed systems, *Small Group Behavior, 4*, 355–81.

Jung, C. G. (1959). The archetypes and the collective unconscious. *Collected Works of C. G. Jung, Volume 9, Part 1*. Princeton, NJ: Princeton University Press.

Kushel, C. M. (1980). *A study of the cultural phase development of two small instructional groups based on Eriksonian theoretical framework of individual psychosocial development*. Master's thesis, University of Wisconsin-Madison.

Mullen, B. and Goethals, G. R. (eds) (1987). *Theories of group behavior*. New York: Springer-Verlag.

Myers, J. G. (1986). *Grief work as a critical condition for small group phase development*. Unpublished doctoral dissertation, University of Wisconsin-Madison.

Neumann, E. (1954). *The origins and history of consciousness*. New York: Pantheon.

Penland, P. R., (1974). *Group dynamics and individual development*. New York: Sara Fine.

Slater, P. E. (1966). *Microcosm: Structural, psychological and religious evolution in groups*. New York: John Wiley.

Stock, D. and Thelen, H. A. (1958). *Emotional dynamics and group culture*. New York: New York University Press.

Stogdill, R. M. (1959). *Individual behavior and group achievement, a theory: The experimental evidence*. New York: Oxford University Press.

Thelen, H. A. (1959). Work-emotionality theory of the small group as organism. In S. Kock (ed.), *Psychology: A study of a science, Vol. 3*. New York: McGraw-Hill.

Tuckman, B. W. (1965) Developmental sequence in small groups, *Psychology Bulletin, 62*, 384–99.

Ullrich, W. (1987). *Will and circumstance in a small self-directed seminar. Orientation to authority, coping/defense, and their relationship in the development of reflective student teachers*. Unpublished doctoral dissertation, University of Wisconsin-Madison.

White, S. W. (1976). *The relationship of small group members' ego-identity concerns and their employment of mechanisms of coping and defense*. Unpublished doctoral dissertation, University of Wisconsin-Madison.

Chapter two

Methodology for the study of the development of consciousness in the small group

Robert D. Boyd and John M. Dirkx

The Matrix Model described in the previous chapter provides ways to conceptualize the dynamics of small groups. This chapter reports on a methodology that has moved our work from a conceptual to an empirical level. Specifically, the purpose of this chapter is to present a systematic methodology for studying the process by which small interactive groups evolve from a condition of near fusion of the members to one in which individuality is more freely manifested and expressed. This process is viewed from the perspective of Erich Neumann's (1954) theory of the evolution of consciousness, as he described it within the context of a cultural system, and Boyd's (1983, 1984) Matrix Model of the small group. This methodology focuses on the social system of the small group and how the group-as-a-whole develops an increasingly sophisticated and differentiated process for meeting reality demands. Distinct mythological motifs or archetypal themes, attributed to the social system manifest the process of an emerging and identifiable character of the social system.

The chapter is presented in four sections: (1) The rationale for studying the small group from the perspective of analytical psychology; (2) The theoretical basis for the framework presented in this chapter; (3) A description of the categories used to identify the manifestation of archetypal themes in group interaction; and (4) A description of the procedures used to identify archetypal motifs in group interaction.

The small group from the perspective of analytical psychology

Analytical psychologists have generally avoided theoretical or clinical application of the principles of analytical psychology to social con- texts, such as families and interpersonal or small group behaviors. Empirical studies which make use of this conceptual framework have been based for the most part on the clinical experiences of therapists with individual patients, with a focus primarily on psychic phenomena as they occur in the individual personality. Much of this research is devoted to developing or advancing the theoretical basis for psychotherapy founded on the postulates of analytical psychology.

The predominant focus on the psychological implications of Jung's work is a curious characteristic of the field, given the profound social foundations of this school of thought. As Progoff (1973) has clearly demonstrated, Jung's interpretation of the psyche is based on a social conception of the human being. Individuality, rather than a given in our lives, is actually derived from a more fundamental notion of society. The relationship of the individual to the group is also inherent in Jung's notion of the unconscious (Fordham, 1957). For Jung, 'the social is essentially the unconscious, and, more particularly, the deeper layers of the Collective Unconscious' (Progoff, 1973, p. 143). From the social, or the unconscious, the individual emerges through the processes of differentiation and individuation. Bound up with the process of individuation is the problem of how the social sources of individuality relate or contribute to the enlargement of personality. The processes of psychological development and individuation involve processes of objective relationships and careful consideration of transference relationships. Thus, at the core of Jung's social thought is the issue of the emergence of personality from society.

Given the social nature of the human being inherent in Jung's thinking, it follows that individuation does not occur independent of or isolated from social relationships. It is a process that goes on, whether we know it or not, within the social contexts of our natural, everyday lives (Jung, 1968). Individuation is intimately bound up within these relationships and inseparable from them. Social contexts often serve to precipitate or mediate the crises of the individuation process. As Ulanov (1971) stated, 'Individuation is not a private affair but is indissolubly bound up with the relation to a partner and to society' (p. 273). The relatedness of one's self to another represents yet another of the polarities that are so critical to the individuation process. Thus, in attempting to further understand the individuation process within the context of the individual in society, it is necessary to examine how social relationships contribute to the individuation process. What we need are analytical tools that will help us better understand how these intrapsychic phenomena relate to a larger social setting. The concepts, theories, and ideas of analytical psychology provide a valuable framework which may be used to further this aim.

The small group, in the form of work groups, social groups, learning groups and families, represents a very common context for social relationships in all cultures. Unlike the one-on-one or group analytic session, these groups represent potential contexts for natural, everyday transformations of personality (Jung, 1968). Several characteristics of the small group contribute to the strong social relationships that form among the members. The relationships that do form are sustained over time, usually for at least several weeks or more. During this period, members will often develop a deep sense of commitment to these relationships and to the overall goals of the group. As a result of the sustained nature of the members' involvement and commitment, these groups often develop a relatively high level of intimacy and trust among the members. Thus, a climate evolves in the group in which members are more willing, if they so choose, to engage in the personal examination and exploration necessary for individuation. Approached with the correct conscious attitude, the relationships formed in the context of the small group provide a potent source for natural transformations.

We have no reason to believe that all or even most small, interactive groups develop to this level of maturity. Yet the nature of the small group at least provides the necessary conditions for this to take place. Groups that do develop high levels of trust and intimacy allow for expression and examination of projections and identifications. Acting out is frequently observed and members manifesting such behavior receive feedback, as well as guidance and insight, from fellow group members. Members also have the opportunity to try out and test new conscious attitudes within a safe and supportive environment. Thus, small group participation provides individuals with the opportunity to work on processes of individuation who otherwise would not choose analytic or other explicit experiences to further their psychological development.

The potential contribution that participation in small groups makes to individuation, however, has been viewed by many analytical psychologists with considerable skepticism (Illing, 1957; Jung, 1968; Meier, 1948). To summarize the argument, the group promotes a state of collective uniformity with a consequent loss of individual responsibility and uniqueness. Undesirable regression is promoted and maintained within the group contexts, contributing to a false sense of security among the members. An increased suggestibility among the members often leads to conformism to the leader's direction and to dominant group ideas. Finally, ego defenses decrease in the context of a group, resulting in uncontrollable invasion of consciousness by unconscious material. Jung's basic position toward groups, reflected in this argument is that the individuals need to free themselves from the bondage and domination imposed by the group.

There is reason, however, to question the applicability of these objections to a serious study of how the small group contributes to individuation. The argument assumes that groups share many of the characteristics of a mob, crowd, or a mass of people. This is reflected in the kinds of examples that Jung used to illustrate his point, with references to 'gatherings' of people well beyond what most small group researchers would consider a 'small group'. In these examples, there seems little consideration for face-to-face interaction and for group meetings extended over a period of time. Jung's objections also reflect a practical concern with how to best further the individuation process within the context of an analytic experience, rather than a concern for furthering a depth understanding of the individual–group relationship, and the conditions within this relationship that either impede or facilitate individuation.

Many analytical psychologists have assumed Jung's position with respect to the small group and have accepted, rather uncritically, the premiss that the group remains an undifferentiated mass. Yet, as Hobson (1964) suggests, it is inappropriate to assume that this assertion applies categorically to all groups. Numerous empirical studies which have examined developmental processes in small groups have demon- strated that the small, interactive group moves through systematic and orderly phases of development (Bradford, 1978; Slater, 1966), a kind of life cycle (Lacoursiere, 1980) unique to the small group. A key characteristic of this development is a process of differentiation within the group and among the members. As the small, interactive group develops, it demonstrates movement away from uniformity and unanimity and toward the establishment of individual standards and values. In effect, the small group reflects a microcosm of the individual–society relationship, in which one observes the gradual differentiation and emergence from the society represented by the group-as-a-whole.

A growing body of empirical evidence also supports the potential contribution that the small group can make to individuation. Champernowne and Lewis (1966) have shown that participation in group therapy results, for some members, in an increased sense of personal responsibility, an acceptance of one's self and one's limitations, and an opening up to the presence of archetypes in one's life. In maintaining contact with an outer reality, represented by the small group, unconscious activity is promoted, which then allows individuals to become increasingly aware of its influence in their lives. For example, Champernowne and Lewis observed that patients were often better able to face their shadows after witnessing their own conflicts acted out by others in the group. These findings are illustrative of the attributes which also characterize an active process of individuation.

Whitmont (1964) also provided evidence for the positive contribution that the therapeutic group can make to the individuation process. In his research, Whitmont found group settings helpful in providing a basis for the reality testing of relationships. This work often resulted in more accurate and realistic perceptions of the significant relationships established within the group context. Whitmont also demonstrated that analytic scrutiny of the 'group archetype' lead to a working out of the group transference as well. Both the reality testing of relationships and the working through of group transferences furthered the aims of group therapy and processes of individuation.

Greene (1985) also identified ways in which the therapeutic group contributes to individuation. According to Greene, the group context constellates archetypes inherent in the family relationships, but which are difficult to manifest in the therapeutic dyad. This provides group members with an opportunity to identify and work on these archetypal influences which they otherwise might not readily confront. In addition, Greene argues, the group provides a supportive, psychic environment for the working through of transference relationships with the leader.

Jones (1983) identified and interviewed several analytical psychologists who regularly utilized group therapy in their analytic practice. One of the issues of central concern in her study was the extent to which group work resulted in what she referred to as 'intrapersonal learning', a term which appears to be quite similar in its operational definition to what is meant by processes of individuation. The analytical psychologists included in the study sample reported that group participation resulted in considerable intrapersonal learning for their patients, thus contributing to individuation within their individual lives.

To summarize, there is both theoretical and empirical support for the assertion that small group participation has the potential for facilitating processes of individuation, despite a pervasive reluctance among many analytical psychologists to seriously consider such a thesis. Their objections appear to assume that the small, interactive group remains an undifferentiated mass which induces dangerous regression and conformism over its members. There is little question that, if not facilitated properly, the small group can and does manifest these highly undesirable features, characteristics more appropriately attributed to a crowd or a mob. As we have seen, however, when facilitated by skilled leaders, the small, interactive group can and often does work through these constraining, potentially destructive influences. The result is a social context which enhances the potential for natural transformations to occur among the members. Given the pervasiveness as well as the potential of the small, interactive group for contributing to natural transformations, it behooves us to better understand the underlying dynamics of these groups and the way these dynamics either facilitate or impede the process of individuation among their members.

Theoretical framework

Before describing the specific categories and the procedures used to identify archetypal themes in a small, interactive group, it is necessary to first briefly describe the theoretical framework upon which the methodology is based. The components of this framework include Neumann's (1954) theory of the archetypal development of consciousness, the Matrix Model of the small group (Boyd, 1983, 1984), and notion of archetypal theme (Dirkx, 1987).

Individuation represents the process by which enlargement of consciousness occurs. Thus, in initiating a research program to study the social context of the small group as a milieu for facilitating natural transformations, it seems only logical to utilize a theoretical framework which conceptualizes small group behavior from the perspective of consciousness. Erich Neumann's (1954) theory of the cultural evolution of consciousness is ideally suited for this purpose for several reasons. Neumann focused his research on cultural manifestations of consciousness and how these expressions of consciousness change over time. It is, therefore, a framework from which to view consciousness within a given collective, rather than just an individual expression of consciousness. Neumann's theory also provides a theoretical basis for relating consciousness to deeper, more unconscious levels of a given culture. As we have seen, this relationship of consciousness to the unconscious is at the heart of the process of individuation. Neumann focused on mythological motifs as manifestations of the underlying structural relationship of consciousness to the unconscious. He identified a number of archetypes which appear to be the primordial foundations for these motifs. According to Neumann, these archetypes tend to be manifest in a stage-like fashion as consciousness evolves within a culture, with each subsequent stage reflecting an increasingly differentiated relationship of consciousness to the unconscious. Furthermore, the motifs attributed to the evolution of consciousness within cultures appear to characterize individual development as well (Neumann, 1954; Whitmont, 1982). Because of its applicability to both the cultural system and the individual, Neumann's theory provides an excellent framework from which to study the relationship of the individual to the group as this relationship evolves over time.

The methodology also makes use of the concept of the group-as-a-whole. Within the context of Boyd's (1983, 1984) Matrix Model, the small group can be viewed from three structural points of view: the personality system, the social system, and the cultural system. The group-as-a-whole is reflected in the notions of the social and cultural systems. Thus, the group is viewed as if it were an entity in and of itself. As such, the group has certain attributes, structures, or characteristics which are not simply the sum of individual structures and dynamics. Issues which involve the social and cultural systems are manifest in the behaviors of individual members but these behaviors tend to reflect patterns or relationships that are simply not seen if one watches individuals instead of the group-as-a-whole. According to this model, the cultural system of the group represents the beliefs, values, rules, and traditions that come to define roles and expectations within the life of the group. The social system is confronted with the task of developing effective means of adapting to the demand of reality. Neumann (1954) has clearly demonstrated that a culture's level or stage of consciousness mediates this process of reality adaptation.

Thus, it seems reasonable that the stage-like appearance of mythological motifs documented in individual and cultural development may also occur within the cultural system of the small, interactive group as well. Although Neumann (1954) and Whitmont (1982) alluded to this possibility, neither scholar systematically developed the idea further. In our group dynamics laboratory, we have begun to develop a systematic process for studying these phenomena in small groups. Preliminary studies have demonstrated motifs similar to those described by Neumann, including the Uroborus, the Great Mother, Separation of World Parents, and the Great Father (Dirkx, 1987). Slater's (1966) empirical study of training groups also provides evidence of the presence of these motifs in the small group context.

In this methodology, we utilize the term 'archetypal themes' instead of mythological motifs. Although the terms are intended to be synonymous, we have found the idea of themes to be somewhat less obscure than motifs when training judges to use the observational system. Archetypal themes share characteristics with other forms of themes that have been reported to occur in small, interactive groups, such as fantasy or utopian themes (Gibbard and Hartman, 1973; Slater, 1966). These themes tend to reflect group-wide concerns that transcend any one member of the group. They also tend to convey deep, emotional concerns underlying group interaction. Fantasy and utopian themes, however, may not always be latent. Indeed, members are often aware at some level that they are using these themes. In addition, fantasy or utopian themes are often based on the personal unconscious of the group members and do not truly reflect a collective theme.

Archetypal themes, on the other hand, are intended to refer to the overt manifestation of specific archetypes within the context of the small group. The themes reflect poorly or incompletely articulated beliefs or assumptions that the social system seems to be acting on. Group members are usually unaware of their manifestation. The archetypal themes represent specific concerns of the collective unconscious of the social system. The different themes which emerge in the group suggest changing structural relationships between consciousness and the collective unconscious. It is in this sense that the archetypal theme is similar to the idea of mythological motif as described by Neumann (1954) and others for the evolution of consciousness in cultures.

Descriptions of the archetypal themes

In the previous section, we indicated that a number of researchers have reported the manifestation, within small group interaction, of certain mythological motifs that closely resemble those described by Neumann (1954). Most of these reports, however, have been based on clinical observations made within the context of a therapeutic setting. Only a handful of these observations were made within learning or training groups. In addition, there has been little attempt to set forth and test conjectures that seek to explain how these motifs relate to each other over the life of a group or what they mean to the group's growth and development.

Our aim in developing this methodology was to provide a systematic basis by which researchers could reliably and validly identify the presence of mythological motifs in the ongoing interaction of a small group. With the framework and the procedures discussed in this section, it is possible to meaningfully test a series of conjectures related to archetypal phenomena in small groups. Such a research program will help us better understand the underlying processes through which groups evolve into highly differentiated entities and how, in the process, conditions are created which provide members with the potential opportunities for personal transformation. The methodology makes use of the 'category system' of observational research (Evertson and Green, 1986), with each of the categories representing a particular archetypal theme. Judges are trained to systematically observe group interaction using these categories and to identify archetypal themes as they occur within the group-as-a-whole. In this section, we will briefly discuss the development of the categories used in this methodology. Then, general descriptions of each of the archetypal themes will be provided (a more complete description of the observation schedule is available from the authors upon request).

Development of the categories

A total of twelve categories, listed in Table 2.1 comprises the observation schedule. Each of the categories in this schedule represents a mythological motif or archetypal theme that may be manifest within the group-as-a-whole. The specific themes included in the schedule were derived from a careful study of the theory of archetypal development of consciousness as described by Neumann (1954). The rationale for selecting Neumann's theory was discussed in the previous section. In his theory, Neumann identified eight archetypal stages which he believes evolve in a stage-like manner. According to Neumann, it is this stage-like succession that determines consciousness development both within cultures and individual lives.

In order to account for previous observations of archetypal themes that we have made in small learning groups, it was necessary to reconceptualize Neumann's eight stages in limited and specific ways. This reconceptualization focuses primarily on Neumann's three central myths: the Great Mother, the Great Father, and the Hero, all three of which have been observed to occur in small, interactive groups.

Table 2.1 Categories comprising the observation schedule for archetypal themes

1.	Uroborus
2.	Awareness of the Great Mother
3.	Separation of the World Parents
4.	Separation of the Good Mother and the Bad Mother
5.	Struggle with the Great Mother
6.	Fixation with the Bad Mother
7.	Resolution of the Great Mother
8.	Separation of the Good Father and the Bad Father
9.	Struggle with the Great Father
10.	Fixation with the Bad Father
11.	Resolution of the Great Father
12.	Journey of the Hero

Neumann's stage of the Great Mother was identified as having two themes – awareness of the Great Mother (category 2) and Separation of the Good and Bad Mother (category 4). Neumann's stage of the Birth of the Hero was re-labeled as the Struggle with the Great Mother. The stage of the Slaying of the Great Mother is referred to in our methodology as the theme of the Resolution of the Great Mother. There are occasions when the struggle with the Great Mother either does not materialize fully or it ends in a state of non-resolution, which we have labeled Fixation with the Bad Mother (category 6).

With respect to Neumann's description of the Great Father, again our observations lead to a further refinement of his schema. There is indeed work in the group which indicates the existence of the symbol of the Great Father in the social system. Our observations lead us to conclude that this archetype is quickly defined by two themes – the Good Father and the Bad Father. Accordingly we have added the theme of the separation of the Good Father and the Bad Father (category 8). In addition we have re-conceptualized Neumann's stage of the Slaying of the Great Father into three separate themes – Struggle with the Great Father, Fixation with the Bad Father, and Resolution of the Great Father.

Finally we have collapsed his last two stages – the Captive and Treasure, and Transformation – into a single theme, the Journey of the Hero (category 12). Once a group has successfully resolved its struggle with the Great Mother and Great Father, it is at a point in its development where the feminine and masculine principles can be equally accessed and brought to bear on reality-adaptive tasks. This work of the group is what is meant by the Journey of the Hero.

These modifications of Neumann's eight stages do not reflect a substantive alteration of his theory. Each of the themes that were added to the observation schedule are, in fact, explicitly recognized and described by Neumann. Although Neumann does not specifically label these themes as stages, his description differentiates these themes as separate issues in the development of consciousness. Thus, the twelve archetypal themes reflect separate ideas that can be readily identified in his work. An additional general category specifies the absence of evidence for archetypal themes. Judges were instructed to use this category when they found no evidence of archetypal themes in a given coding unit.

Each of the archetypal themes was defined by a set of descriptors or specifications. These specifications were derived explicitly from Neumann's descriptions of the archetypal stages. Each of the stages discussed in *The origins and history of consciousness* were examined carefully for specifications that could be used to define the stage. A list of these specifications was then compiled for each stage. Specifications containing references to archaic images found to be inappropriate to groups or making references to individuals rather than groups were reworded so that they reflected an orientation only to the social system. Care was taken in the rewording of specifications not to alter the original meaning of the specification as presented in Neumann's work. Most specifications that we had identified in Neumann's work were readily observable. Specifications which required either an unacceptable level of inference, or were not observable because of archaic images, were deleted.

After the twelve sets of specifications had been developed, they were cast against our extensive observations of and experiences with small groups. This step was taken for two reasons: first, we needed to be certain that the wording and the images used in the specifications related meaningfully to the dynamics observed in small groups; second, it was necessary to determine that the specifications used to describe the themes were observable in the dynamics of the social system. Wording and images that we found not to be meaningful were either reworked or deleted.

The identification of specific archetypal themes consists of two major judgements. First, judges need to determine if archetypal influence is even present to any significant degree in group interaction. Observation continues until such a determination is made. When judges determine that archetypal influence is indeed present, then the observation schedule is used to determine which of the twelve archetypal themes contained in the schedule is being manifest at that period in time. General specifications were developed to assist judges in determining if archetypal influence is present at a given period of time in the group. In developing these specifications, we relied on the phrase 'a sense of'. This phrase indicates an intuitive impression of what is happening in the social system of the group at the time the observation is being made. It is a phrase that has been successfully used by other investigators of group-wide phenomena as well (Bion, 1959). In addition to specific, overt behaviors, judgements are based on intuitive impressions as well.

In the remainder of this section, we will briefly describe the specifications used to determine if archetypal influence is present as well as those used to make determinations of specific archetypal themes.

Indications of archetypal influences

Archetypal influence is indicated in group interaction when there is a clear sense of the group acting as a collective entity. The group appears to be caught in the grip of something that it cannot consciously control, as if completely possessed by an issue, argument, fear, or image. Observations of behaviors appear to be characteristic or extensions of the social system rather than of one or two individuals.

Relatively high levels of emotionality within the social system also suggest archetypal influence. This emotionality may occur within the context of a relatively task-oriented process or it may be manifest in a situation where the group appears completely caught up in an emotional concern or problem. It is important to point out that the observed emotionality must be attributed to the social system and not to individuals within the group.

Another indication of archetypal influences is the symbolic use by the social system of language, ideas, or concepts. For example, discussion surrounding the role the leader is taking, as described by the members, may leave one with the sense that the group is really focusing on an examination of issues related to patriarchy. Groups under the influence of an archetype may also appear to be 'free associating'. That is, discussion seems to be random and directionless, with no clear, logical development of ideas or thought. Magical or wishful thinking may be manifest during these situations, such as planning for a re-union after the groups ends, or speculations about the group's role in a grand experiment being conducted by the leader.

If judges, using these general indications of archetypal influence, conclude that archetypal phenomena are present, then they must decide what specific themes are represented in the group interaction. In the material that follows, each of twelve archetypal themes comprising the observation schedule is briefly described.

The Uroboric theme

In the Uroboric phase, the social system is characterized by an almost complete state of nondifferentiation and wholeness, contained in some manner as if it were in an unbroken roundness. Little, if any, distinction is made among group members. Even the leader is poorly differentiated from the social system, if at all. Belonging to the group is the predominant ethos and serves to minimize important distinctions such as gender. Differences in opinion among members are either minimized or ignored and relevancy of comments and agendas and opposing points of view are not recognized. A sense of helplessness characterizes the group, as if it is not capable of doing much of anything on its own. The group, however, has not come to an awareness yet of this sense of helplessness.

Awareness of the Great Mother

This phase is characterized by a budding sense of differentiation. Nonetheless there continues to be relatively little awareness of distinctions in the group, and no discomfort or serious disagreement regarding distinctions that are apparent. Differentiation of aspects of the outer world is usually obtained through the use of magical and mythical thinking. For example, the notion may be expressed that the group is special and unique, one that has never existed before. Members seem to be symbolically expressing a concern for relatedness and for being nurtured or mothered. They may initially look to the leader for this mothering, but, if the leader is nondirective or fails to provide a sense of nurturing, the group will be frustrated with this unmet need. The members will then look to the group as a source of mothering, illustrated by increasing use of the terms 'we' or 'the group'. The members remain bound together in an unarticulated way as a method of warding off their unconscious fears of being swallowed by or fused with the group. A sense of fear and impotence may be present, but these feelings are poorly focused and have no direct object. Expressions of fear of abandonment or of being stranded may also be voiced at this time. Images which frequently arise during this phase include references to food and to eating, water and a sense of the group swimming. For the most part, the social system seems to be acting impulsively and instinctually.

Separation of the World Parents

There is a sense that the group is aware, at least symbolically, of the presence of both Mother and Father in the group. This may be reflected in references to issues of relatedness (how members will relate to each other), and power and leadership (reflected in concerns over structure and agenda). Beginning to surface is an expectation that the group will

develop independence and autonomy. However, this hope and expectation remains shaky and shrouded in doubt. The group seems to flip
back and forth between work and emotionality, conscious deliberation
and instinctual response, issues of leadership and issues of relatedness.
The increasing call for or use of rituals, norms, and patterns suggests
that the group is beginning to get boundaries.

Separation of the Good Mother and Bad Mother

This theme reflects the group's awareness that the social system, symbolized as a mother, has a terrible side as well as a good side: that the
group can destroy as well as nurture. The group may be alternately
viewed as something evil – smothering and constraining – and as
something good – representing fullness, abundance, and a source of life
and energy. As a result of this awareness, anxiety and tension in the
group are increased. There is a sense of pain, suffering, and loss in the
group, as well as an awareness of how good it feels to come together. In
its attempt to define its nature, the social system seems to be symbolically weighing its goodness and badness. Swings may be observed,
from being overly self-critical and self-effacing to being self-
congratulatory and having an inflated view of the group. The sense that
'we're all in this together' seems to be breaking down. The major
question that is representative of this theme is the form that relatedness
will take in the group.

Struggle with the Great Mother

The key question reflected in this theme is whether the group will be a
place in which people will relate in a domineering and overpowering
way, or one in which relatedness tends to be nurturing and loving. These
polar positions created ambivalence within the social system and this
theme shows the group's struggles with this ambivalence. Members
demonstrate an awareness that the group has both a good, nurturing side
and a bad, destructive side, and they seem to be intent on establishing
the essential goodness of the group. This activity does not occur without
a sense of fear or regret. This will often manifest itself in open conflict
which centers around issues of relatedness. A pro and con is evident in
this struggle. Frequently, this struggle will focus around or be lead by
one or two persons (see Chapter Three, which discusses the concept of
the focal person). The group is working toward a unity that creates a
strong sense of relatedness, yet there is a sense of an attempt to respect
the individuality of the members.

Fixation with the Bad Mother[1]

One of the possible outcomes of the theme of separation of the Good and
Bad Mother is the possibility of a growing perception that the social

system symbolically represents a Bad Mother. This is manifest in intense feelings of mistrust, fearfulness, and suspicion of the social system. The group is perceived as capable of destroying or severely circumscribing one's individuality. Predominance of this perception is marked by a sense of the group as bleak and bogged down in inertia and fatigue, leading to feelings of pointlessness and meaninglessness. In this theme, there is little attempt to struggle against or fight to overcome this destructive archetypal influence. Rather, the sense of the group is one of resignation and acceptance of the group at drift and where there is no evidence of personal autonomy being asserted.

Resolution of the Great Mother

The resolution of the struggle with the Great Mother is indicated by a sense that the social system is viewed, for the most part, by the members as a source of life and happiness and symbolic of depth, beauty, goodness, and graciousness. The social system is perceived as accepting, supportive, caring, nurturing, and receptive and responsive to individual needs, but not overprotective. That is, confrontation and conflict continues to occur but it is valued for its contribution to growth and development. The social system may often show struggle in its attempt to maintain these perceptions but even in this struggle there is the sense that the group will not accept itself symbolically as Bad Mother. Mother may have her bad days, but she is basically nurturing, supportive and caring.

Separation of the Good and Bad Father

Another cluster of archetypal themes that are manifest in the social system revolves around the central archetype of the Great Father. Like the Great Mother the structure of this archetype is two-sided. On the one hand members may perceive the social system furthering intellectual exploration and development, symbolically reflected in the image of the Good Father. The Good Father is manifest in the social system's desire to take control, make its own decisions, and determine its own destiny. It is perceived by the members as a force that will help the group realize its own nature and empower it with its own authority. On the other hand the social system may be perceived as an overwhelming, aggressive entity that renders the group impotent and deprives it of self-fulfillment, symbolically expressed as the Bad Father. The Bad Father may be manifest by an intense desire on the part of the members that some structure be defined to fulfill their dependency needs. In the theme of the separation of the Good and Bad Father there is evidence that the social system is perceived from these two points of view. The social system vascillates between these two images as members work to further delineate intellectual explorations and the testing of self-determination on the one hand and dependence on existing authority structures on the other hand.

Struggle with the Great Father[2]

The theme of the struggle with the Great Father is characterized by a sense of conflict with and opposition to the Terrible aspect of the Great Father archetype. That is, there is a sense that the group is coming to perceive the designated leadership, the structure, and/or the status quo of the distribution of power in the group as antithetical to its growth. The group seems to be intent on getting rid of those aspects of its existence that are viewed as standing in its way or depriving the group of its own power and authority. The group seems to be developing a means to share and redistribute among the group members the power that once was vested in the designated leader or/and the existing structure of the leadership based on unexamined cultural norms. The social system wants to take control for itself, to assume full responsibility for what happens in the group, to make its own decisions, and to assume its own destiny.

Fixation with the Terrible Father

In this theme the members perceive the social system primarily in terms of an authority figure which seeks to dominate the dynamics of the group. Acceptance of this situation, which defines the fixation theme, is manifest in one of two ways. The group, on the one hand, may remain impotent and totally dependent on the existing authority structure. For example, members may continue to perceive the designated leader as the legitimate and sole source of authority within the group. On the other hand, the social system may come to see itself as the sole source of authority by disregarding the existence of preexisting authority structures and the values and contributions of tradition. There is little or no evidence that the group is consciously or thoughtfully attempting to redefine the structure of authority in order to empower the problem-solving capacity of the social system. Rather the social system appears to be interested in power only for the sake of power.

Resolution of the Great Father

This theme is characterized by a sense that the social system is redefining the existing authority structures. The social system is taking control for itself and assuming responsibility for its own decisions and dynamics. The group seems charged with renewed life and strength in its new-found awareness of its own potential. There seems to be increased emphasis on the importance of dealing with problems rationally and logically. Old rules, norms, conscious tradition, or commentary are seriously questioned as the social system seeks to establish a 'new order', one that is more appropriate to its new level of consciousness. In redefining these issues the social system does not reject out of hand traditions and norms but seeks to incorporate those that further this new order. Adaptation to reality is becoming increasingly more effective with respect to issues involving authority and decision making. A common manifestation of this process of redefining authority structures is the confrontation with the designated leader as the only source of authority in the group. As a result of this confrontation, the designated leader's role becomes more circumscribed.

Journey of the Hero

The most salient characteristic of the journey theme is the emergence of the individual and the decline of the social system's prominence in the dynamics of the group. Individuals appear to be working interdependently toward the pursuit of a shared mission, quest, aim, or purpose. Working on issues of relatedness between individuals is not viewed as being disruptive but, rather, as necessary to the group's progress. Although there is a shared mission, it is understood that individuals will take ownership of and responsibility for their unique contributions to the shared mission. Another aspect of this mature relationship is the continuing integration of the masculine and feminine dimensions within both the individual and the social system.[3] These processes are reflected in a renewed appreciation for seeing, feeling, depth, beauty, inward contemplation, and the acceptance of suffering and pain along with joy and passion as inevitable characteristics of growth.

Description of the coding procedure

In this section, we will summarize the processes and procedures that were used to identify specific archetypal themes as they were manifest in the life cycle of a self-analytic group in graduate education (Dirkx, 1987). An overview of the process will first be presented, followed by more detailed descriptions of each of the major components of the process: development of the coding manual and forms, the unit of observation used in the study, the process of coding, training of the judges, and establishment of reliability and validity of the procedure.

The procedure for identifying archetypal themes manifest in group interaction utilized video and audio-tape technology to record all group sessions. These data were then subjected to a 'coding process' for purposes of classifying periods of interaction. A 'code' is the classification of the observation unit by the judges into one of the twelve archetypal themes described in the previous section or into the 'no evidence' category. Because of the relatively high level of inference required by the coding procedure, three observers or judges were used to independently code all units of observations. The judges' observations were periodically tested for interjudge agreement and any serious discrepancies in codings were reexamined and discussed until the judges agreed on a single coding. The archetypal themes identified for each of the ten group sessions were then analyzed according to the specific questions being pursued in the study (Dirkx, 1987).

In the remainder of this section, the specific steps in this process will be discussed in more detail.

The unit of observation

A 15 minute segment was chosen as the unit of observation. This unit has no analytic significance other than to allow for computations of interjudge agreement, and tabulation of codings. It is an arbitrary unit and, for this reason, it is referred to as a unit of observation or coding rather than a unit of analysis. The time period of 15 minutes was chosen because a shorter period may not allow the archetypal theme to be readily manifest. Conversely, a longer time period could potentially provide judges with too much data to use in making their codings. In addition, if the unit of coding were to be substantially longer than 15 minutes, more than one archetypal theme may be observed. Therefore, a 15 minute unit was chosen to avoid the possibility of multiple codings in longer segments. Each group session consisted of approximately eight to 10 coding units.

The coding manual and form

Judges used an explicit and detailed manual to guide their observations of the study group. The *Manual for coding archetypal themes in small groups* (available from the authors upon request) provided the judges with a theoretical discussion of the conceptual framework upon which the coding procedure was based. The manual also specifies the descriptors which were used to define each of the coding categories. In coding the video tapes, the judges followed the detailed step by step procedure of the coding process outlined in the final section of the manual. To record their observations and codings, the judges used a specially designed recording form. The judges completed a coding form for each 15 minute coding unit. On this form, the judges documented the archetypal themes manifest during the unit of observation and the specifications which supported this coding.

The coding process

Judges made their observations and determinations from the videotape recordings. The audiotape recordings were used as a back-up to the videotape technology. Three judges were employed to code each of the sessions. Prior experience with in-depth coding procedures has shown that relaxation by the judges prior to coding reduces the influence and distraction of extraneous stimuli. For this reason, judges were instructed to relax prior to beginning a session of coding, and not to attempt coding if they felt tired or fatigued.

Each judge was instructed to code the group sessions independently for a 60 minute period of observation. At the end of each coding unit, the judges were told to stop the tape player and complete the coding form for that unit. After the coding form was completed in its entirety, the tape player was again started and the next 15 minute unit was coded. Coding proceeded in this manner for 60 minute intervals. Following each 60 minute period, the codings of each judge were compared. Units of observation for which there was disagreement among one or more of the judges were subjected to review and discussion until judges agreed on a single coding.

During the coding process, emphasis was placed on arriving at an intuitive sense of the group as a whole and what seemed to be going on at the level of the social system. Tentative codings were permissible. The coding of a proceeding unit could be changed if convincing evidence emerged in the next unit which caused the judge to reconsider the coding of the previous unit. Each unit of coding, however, was characterized by a single or dominant archetypal theme.

The date and numerical order of all videotapes were masked and each videotape was randomly assigned a code number ranging from 01 to 10. Each judge was then randomly assigned five tapes to code. The order of selection was preserved as the order in which the tapes were to be coded. This action was taken to guard against any bias that might be introduced as a result of a judge's knowledge of the chronological order of the group sessions.

Training of the observers

The methodology described in this chapter requires the use of judges who have been trained to classify units of observation using the categories of archetypal themes described in the previous section. Individuals with certain prior experiences and background need to be recruited and trained in the methodology. The individuals who are recruited to serve as coders need to have a working familiarity with the concepts and ideas of depth psychology, with small groups in general and the notion of the group-as-a-whole in particular. They should have a demonstrated capacity to perceive group interaction from that perspective. In conjunction with the initial study in which this methodology was used (Dirkx, 1987), we developed a training program for individuals who would serve as observers in a study of the archetypal themes in small group interaction. In the following discussion, we will describe this training program as it was designed and implemented in the initial study.

The purpose of the training program was to ensure that individuals recruited to serve as judges in this methodology accurately and reliably used the archetypal categories in classifying group interaction. The training program consisted of several steps. First, the observers were trained in the theoretical framework employed in the methodology. Judges read and discussed with the trainer articles and text excerpts on the social system of the group (Boyd, 1983, 1984), the notion of the collective unconscious (Hall and Nordby, 1973), and the concept of archetypal themes (Jung, 1971). The judges also reviewed the *Manual for coding archetypal themes in small groups*. This manual provided a listing of the twelve coding categories and the specifications which defined the categories. The observers were then asked to memorize the specifications for each of the twelve categories. The trainer did not discuss with the coders the possibility that the coding categories might be developmentally related to each other. It was specifically pointed out to the judges during training that they were not to view the category scheme in a linear or sequential fashion. They were told that one theme did not necessarily have to follow another in the coding process, and that it was possible that any of the themes could be observed at any time during the course of the group.

Following training in the theoretical framework employed in the methodology and memorization of the category specifications, the coders practiced coding segments of videotape recordings that demonstrated the different archetypal themes. The judges then practiced coding on videotapes from a group similar to the one they would be observing in the study. Practice of coding and discussion of the observations made continued until the judges demonstrated consistency and agreement in their use of the coding categories.

Interjudge agreement

After the theoretical training and sufficient practice to allow the observers to feel comfortable with the process, the procedure was subjected to an interjudge agreement test. A total of seven 15 minute coding units were independently coded by the judges. A weighted proportion of agreement for nominal scales (Cohen, 1968) was used to determine the level of agreement between judges. The proportion of agreement achieved in this test was 0.89. This was considered to be a satisfactory level of agreement and the judges were instructed to begin coding.

Checks of interjudge reliability were also performed for each session coded. The values of interjudge agreement obtained for the coding of archetypal themes are consistent with other category systems that have attempted to study the group in depth using observational category systems (Boyd et al., 1980; Portal-Foster, 1966; Pridham, 1972; Watson, 1963). The coding procedure for archetypal themes demonstrated adequate reliability as measured by the weighted proportion of agreement method.

Validity of the coding categories

The validity of the coding procedure was examined using three procedures: face validity; construct validity; and check for measurement bias. The results of each of these procedures will be briefly discussed.

Face validity

Lists of specifications for each category were derived from Neumann's (1954) descriptions of the archetypal stages. After a draft of the specifications had been prepared, the researchers carefully reviewed the list of specifications for each stage to be sure that each specification corresponded to the description for that stage provided by Neumann. Specifications which had been reworded in the developmental process and which could not be readily identified with Neumann's descriptions were either reformulated or deleted from the list. As a result, the remaining list of specifications for each archetypal theme closely corresponded to the descriptors for the stage provided in Neumann's work.

The coding categories and their specifications were then reviewed by a scholar knowledgeable in Neumann's theory. The definitions of the categories provided by the specifications were judged to faithfully represent Neumann's descriptions of the respective stages.

Construct validity

Neumann's theory suggests that the archetypes manifest in consciousness development appear more or less sequentially, and in a particular order. Therefore, construct validity of the procedure for coding archetypal themes can be examined by comparing the order of the archetypal themes predicted by the theory and the order actually obtained in our initial study.

The finding from the analysis of the sessions corroborated the theory in that the archetypal themes were manifested in the order predicted by the theory. Another pattern also emerged which was consistent with Neumann's work. The coding procedure was able to identify that certain of the initial mythological motifs or archetypal themes emerged, faded away, and then reappeared later in the group. The finding is consistent with Neumann's theory, which asserts that the archetypal contents of each stage continue to maintain influence even after they are no longer prominently manifest. In brief, these analyses support the construct validity that exists in the relationship of the methodology to the theory.

Measurement bias

It was indicated earlier that a conference procedure was used to obtain final codings for units of observation in which two or more of the judges disagreed in their initial, independent codings. Therefore, an analysis was conducted to determine if measurement bias represented a significant threat to the validity of the procedure used. The principal question addressed in this analysis was whether any one of the judges influenced the other two judges in any significant way during conferences over disagreements in codings. The possibility of measurement bias in the coding of archetypal themes was extensively examined in three different analyses. The details and specific results of these analyses are available in the report of the original study (Dirkx, 1987). In summary, the results of these analyses suggest that there was no significant source of measurement bias in the procedure that was used to identify archetypal themes in group interaction.

Thus, following an analysis of content and construct validity, and measurement bias, the coding procedure used to identify archetypal themes was found to be of acceptable validity.

Summary

This chapter presented a methodology for the identification and coding of archetypal themes occurring in small interacting groups. The methodology was structured upon the framework of analytical psychology and in particular the work of Erich Neumann. From extensive observations of small groups certain refinements were made on Neumann's theory of mythological motifs. With the method in hand the argument was advanced that self-analytic small groups could be the setting for the development of individuation. This position was set over against certain views, which have been traditionally suspect, of the contribution groups can make toward the processes of individuation. The development of the methodology provided the means to test the thesis that small groups do express archetypal themes and this in turn gave further credibility to the argument that small groups can be a setting for individuals to work on the processes of individuation. When the group encounters archetypal themes individual members have the opportunity to rework their own relationships with these themes and come to a greater expansion of consciousness. A brief account of an extensive study was reported upon in which such issues as operationalization of the methodology, training of coders, reliability, and validity were addressed. Our study demonstrated that the methodology was thoroughly operational. In addition the examination of construct validity provided further corroboration for the theory of archetypal themes and for our methodology that identified these themes.

Several other dynamics are evident as these processes are taking place. One dynamic which was clearly obvious in our observations was the roles the influential members appear to play in moving the group process in one or another direction. We have long been aware of the significant contributions Redl (1942) had made to our understanding about the influential member's role in the life of a small group. In recognition of this and other investigations of the influential member we had moved to incorporate these dynamics within our larger methodology. The chapter which follows extends our methodology and incorporates the part the influential members play in determining the directions a small group takes.

Notes

1. Our primary focus here is to present general descriptions of each of the twelve themes which constitute the Observational Schedule. It is important, however, to address the various sequences in which these themes may be manifest. Virtually all groups will move through the themes of the Uroborus, awareness of the Great Mother and the separation of the Good and Bad Mother. Following the last theme, the social system may take one of two directions. It may move directly from the separation theme to the theme of the Fixation with the Bad Mother. Alternatively the social system may proceed to the theme of the struggle with the Great Mother. From this theme the social system may manifest either the theme of the resolution of the Great Mother or Fixation with Bad Mother. This pattern is also evident in the patriarchal themes.
2. See note 1 above.
3. This may have reference to the concepts of work and emotionality as discussed by Stock and Thelen (1958).

References

Bion, W. R. (1961). *Experiences in groups.* New York: Ballantine Books.

Boyd, R. D. (1983). A Matrix Model of the small group, Part I, *Small Group Behavior, 14,* 405–18.

Boyd, R. D. (1984). A Matrix Model of the small group, Part II, *Small Group Behavior,* 15, 233–50.

Boyd, R. D., Bressler, D., Dirkx, J. M., Fullmer, R., Levenson, E., Kushel, C. K. and Ullrich, W. (1980). *A report of the Evaluation Study of the Group Dynamics Traffic Safety School, State of Wisconsin.* Madison: Department of Transportation, Wisconsin.

Bradford, L. P. (ed.) (1978). *Group development* (2nd edn). San Diego, CA: University Associates.

Champernowne , H. I. and Lewis, E. (1966). Psychodynamics of therapy in a residential group, *Journal of Analytical Psychology*, *11*, 163–80.

Cohen, J. (1968). Weighted Kappa: Nominal scale agreement with provision for scaled disagreement or partial credit, *Psychological Bulletin*, 70, 213–20.

Dirkx, J. M. (1987). The self-analytic group and the Great Mother: A study of matriarchal consciousness in adult learning, *Dissertation Abstracts International*.

Evertson, C. M. and Green, J. L. (1986). Observation as enquiry and method. In M. C. Wittrock (ed.), *Handbook of Research on Teaching* (3rd edn) (pp. 119–213). New York: MacMillan.

Fordham, M. (1957). *New developments in analytical psychology*. London: Routledge & Kegan Paul.

Gibbard, G. S. and Hartman, J. J. (1973). The significance of utopian fantasies in small groups, *International Journal of Group Psychotherapy*, *23*, 125–47.

Greene, T. A. (1985). Group therapy and analysis. In M. Stein (ed.) *Jungian analysis*. Boston: Shambhala.

Hall, C. S. and Nordby, V. J. (1973). *A primer of Jungian psychology*. New York: The New American Library, Inc.

Hobson, R. F. (1964). Group dynamics and analytical psychology, *Journal of Analytical Psychology*, *9*, 23–49.

Illing, J. A. (1957). C. G. Jung on the present trends in group psychotherapy, *Human Relations*, *10*, 77–83.

Jones, M. J. (1983). The perceptions of Jungian Analysts on the individuation process in group psychotherapy, *Dissertation Abstracts International*.

Jung, C. G. (1968). *The archetypes and the collective unconscious* (2nd edn). Princeton, NJ: Princeton University Press.

Jung, C. G. (1971). The stages of life. In J. Campbell (ed.), *The portable Jung*. New York: Penguin Books.

Lacoursiere, R. B. (1980). *The life cycle of groups*. New York: Human Sciences Press.

Meier, C. A. (1948). Untitled paper given at the International Conference of Medical Psychotherapy.

Neumann, E. (1954). *The origins and history of consciousness*. Princeton, NJ: Princeton University Press.

Portal-Foster, C. W. (1966). An application of work-emotionality theory to adult education, *Adult Education Journal*, *20*, 67–87.

Pridham, K. F. (1972). *Stress resolving moves in an adult instructional small group*. Unpublished doctoral dissertation, University of Wisconsin-Madison.

Progoff, I. (1973). *Jung's psychology and its social meaning*. Garden City, NY: Anchor Press/Doubleday.

Redl, F. (1942). Group emotion and leadership, *Psychiatry*, *5*, 573–96.

Slater, P. E. (1966). *Microcosm: Structural, psychological and religious evolution in groups*. New York: John Wiley and Sons.

Stock, D. and Thelen, H. A. (1958). *Emotional dynamics and group culture*. New York: New York University Press.

Ulanov, A. B. (1971). *The feminine in Jungian psychology and in Christian theology*. Evanston, IL: Northwestern University Press.

Watson, E. R. (1963). *The dynamics of expectations and adaptation to adult learning group cultures*. Unpublished doctoral dissertation, University of Wisconsin-Madison.

Whitmont, E. C. (1964). Group therapy and analytical psychology. *Journal of Analytical Psychology*, *9*, 1–22.

Whitmont, E. C. (1982). *Return of the goddess*. New York: Crossroad.

Chapter three

Understanding group transformation through the focal person concept

John M. Dirkx

It is a common observation that certain individuals in small, face-to-face groups develop considerable influence with the rest of the members. Despite the fact that these individuals are usually not in designated positions of leadership, they become the center of the group's attention at certain, critical periods. It is as if, on these occasions, the entity of the group has developed a special relationship with these individuals. The development of this relationship is even more curious, given the fact that the level of influence that these individuals exert is not always proportional to their contribution to the explicit goals and tasks of the group. This phenomenon, which, for purposes of present discussion, we will initially refer to as the 'influential member', can be observed repeatedly and across many different kinds of small groups.

The purpose of this chapter is to present and discuss a particular form of influential member and the ways in which she/he facilitates group transformation. This form of influential member is referred to as a 'focal person'. The term reflects the essential quality of the phenomenon to which it refers. One member articulates or personifies unconscious concerns which are focal to the group-as-a-whole at that time. The concept is derived from numerous observations of self-analytic groups and from our theoretical understanding of the evolution of consciousness in groups as it is articulated in analytical psychology in general, and by Erich Neumann (1954) in particular. We especially relied on Neumann's notion of the 'Great Individual' to identify the theoretical and empirical properties of this concept. The focal person concept has also been validated in careful and systematic empirical studies of specific hypotheses related to group development and transformation (Dirkx, 1987; Myers, 1986). It is from these prior empirical studies that the present conceptual work is based. Our purpose here is to discuss the theoretical rationale for the focal person concept as a special form of influential member and to demonstrate, through the use of case material from self-analytic groups, its manifestation within periods of archetypal paradox. In the first section of the chapter, the literature on the influential group member is critically reviewed to establish the theoretical gap which we propose the concept of focal person fills in the small group literature. Various forms of influential member that have been proposed within the last 50 years provide support for the basic conceptual properties of the focal person but fail to provide an adequate means for linking the behavior of these individuals to the unconscious, developmental concerns of the group-as-a-whole. The second section provides a brief description of the conceptual basis of the focal person concept, with specific reference to analytical psychology. In the final section, the focal person concept is illustrated empirically with examples of case material drawn from observations of self-analytic groups in graduate education.

The influential group member: a critical review

The literature on the influential group member can be somewhat abstract and theoretical. To ground this discussion somewhat in the concrete realities of a small group, we have provided the following summary of interaction within a self-analytic group. The vignette illustrates the kind of phenomenon to which the present study is directed.

Members of the group were part of the experiential component of a graduate course in the dynamics of instructional groups. This component consisted of ten group sessions of 150 minutes each. The small group was being conducted in a manner similar to that which characterizes the self-analytic or laboratory group tradition. There was no explicit curriculum or agenda other than the members were expected to observe and study their own behaviors and the dynamics of the group as a whole to further their understanding of the dynamics of instructional groups.

It was early in the second session of the group when the group began to discuss the issue whether and when it should take a break. The instructor's syllabus and verbal directions neither specified nor proscribed the scheduling of such an event. Sue, Tim, and Margaret began to discuss whether the group should take a break. Several other members quickly joined the discussion. It became immediately apparent, however, that the group was having some difficulty arriving at a decision on this matter. Some members were questioning whether everyone should take a break at the same time or whether individual members should simply take a break when they needed. The discussion continued for several minutes in a tentative, halting, and ambiguous manner, as if the group was uncertain of the propriety of such a conversation and their role in deciding such an issue. The group seemed unable to make a decision. At this point, Barbara announced firmly but calmly that she did not need the group's permission to 'go to the bathroom' and that she would leave whenever it was necessary for her to do so. The group seemed stunned and a nervous, tense silence fell over the members. For a short time, it appeared that the group was trying to assimilate this blatant show of assertiveness. Then, gradually several members began to challenge Barbara's assertive stance, claiming that such 'individualism' threatened the integrity of the group. Others joined in on the challenge and the discussion became increasingly emotional in tone. Statements such as 'What if everyone decided to do that? Where would that leave the group?' and 'You seem to be putting yourself before the group' characterized the group's response. It soon became apparent that the rest of the group members viewed Barbara's claim as a threat against the integrity of the group. Barbara was clearly the center of the group's attention as the interaction patterns were predominantly between her and the rest of the group members. This period of interaction was animated, emotional, tense, and anxious. As the group continued to explore this issue, however, the conversation became increasingly intellectual, the initial emotionality dissipated, and the conversation drifted to other matters with no real resolution as to the issue of the break.

Several questions may be raised about this and similar periods of group interaction. Why and how does a single individual come to be the primary and almost exclusive attention of the rest of the group? Are there different forms of such individual–group relationships that would suggest different dynamics and functions? Are there particular periods in group interaction in which these individuals emerge? To what extent is this phenomenon related to processes of differentiation and individuation that need to occur within the developing group? What implications does the phenomenon of the influential members hold for leaders and consultants of groups in which they occur?

The literature in small group research provides partial and tentative answers to some of these difficult questions. From a sociological perspective, investigators describe the emergence of the influential member in terms of role differentiation, expectations that some members attribute to others, and the distribution of power within the group. For example, the functional roles of energizer, evaluator-critic, encourager, and group harmonizer (Benne and Sheats, 1948), the socio-emotional and task specialists (Slater, 1955), and the categories of 'task roles' and 'social roles' (Bales, 1958) illustrate this perspective. Others have relied on a more psychodynamic interpretation of this phenomenon (Gibbard et al. 1974). Within this perspective, the emergence of the influential member represents a more covert, latent dynamic, characteristic of the underlying structures or processes of the group-as-a-whole. Examples of this approach include basic assumption leaders (Bion, 1961), role specialists (Dunphy, 1974), emotional leaders (Beck, 1974), and scapegoats (Eagle and Newton, 1981; Toker, 1972).

Thus, both the sociological and psychodynamic traditions have focused our attention on the significance of the influential member to the development and functioning of the group. For the most part, this tradition (particularly, the sociological perspective) has been very helpful in providing group leaders and members with a better understanding of the task or instrumental dimension of group life. That is, the meaning of the influential member to the group-as-a-whole is viewed in terms of its contribution to task or goal attainment, group productivity or more effective decision making. We are concerned here, however, with what one might refer to as the 'symbolic' influential member. More will be said later regarding the symbolic approach to the influential member. At this point it is sufficient to indicate that by the symbolic influential member, we mean the individual within the group who serves to focus the group's attention, either overtly or covertly, on the underlying, unconscious emotions upon which much of the group behavior is based. Several different theoretical formulations of the influential member phenomenon reflect this common theme. A review of these different forms of influential member will provide a better understanding of the theoretical relationship of the focal person to the group-as-a-whole.

Forms of the symbolic influential member

Studies of the influential member attempt to describe particular forms of relationships that form between certain members and the group as an entity. The majority of these studies conceptualize the group in terms of the group-as-a-whole or the social system perspective (Boyd, 1983, 1984; see also Chapter One of this volume). According to this perspective, it is not always helpful or even possible to reduce what goes on in groups to a study of individuals or interpersonal interactions, that is the personality systems. In addition to interacting with other members, the individual can interact and form relationships with the social system. This position is reflected in the observation that, at times, the social system appears to assume a distinct and identifiable stance toward a particular individual in the group. When viewing a group from this point of view, one often has a clear sense that a group attitude exists toward a certain individual. In the case example presented earlier, there is the sense that the social system is in distinct opposition to Barbara. On the other hand, Barbara clearly resisted the social system's need for solidarity and the cultural system's normative code. Thus, the individual–group relationship illustrated in this example and in the phenomenon of the symbolic influential member reflects characteristics that go beyond interactions of individual group members. Rather, Barbara, as an influential member, interacts and develops a relationship with the social system of the group.

The interaction between Barbara and the social system illustrates a general phenomenon that has been of interest to a number of researchers of small group behavior. That is, particular individuals emerge in special and symbolic positions of influence in the group. Within this tradition, a number of different forms of influential member have been identified, each representing partially overlapping but also distinctly different psychological functions in the individual–group relationship. Among the various forms included in the literature are the prophet (Brueggemann, 1978; Heschel, 1962), charismatic individual (Weber, 1946), central person (Redl, 1942), scapegoat (Dunphy, 1974; Gibbard and Hartman, 1974; Mann, 1967) role specialist (Dunphy, 1974), covert role (Gemmill and Kraus, 1988), hero (Gibbard, 1974; Slater, 1966), and focal person (Myers, 1986). The conceptual descriptions of these forms illustrate several properties that, taken together, characterize the essential qualities of the focal person as a particular form of influential member.

The first of these qualities is reflected in the observation that an individual member, through his or her behavior in the group, may crystallize and constellate the latent, unarticulated emotional concerns of the social system. Several forms of influential member illustrate this property, including the charismatic individual (Weber, 1946), central person (Redl, 1942), role specialist (Dunphy, 1974), and covert role (Gemmill and Kraus, 1988). Max Weber (1946) advanced the concept of the charismatic individual late in the nineteenth century, observing that such a person had power over people because they were suffering. In summarizing Weber's notion, Myers (1986) writes:

> Charisma involves an intuitive awareness of what it is that causes the feeling of woundedness among a people. Charisma, therefore, implies a relationship, an almost sacred bond formed between a charismatic person and a community. These gifted individuals embody and are able to articulate the emotions of others. It is particularly in this empathic naming of the origins of pain that their authority and influence in the group is found. Their power exists because of their social relationship with the group. Charismatic persons, said Weber, do not derive authority from ordinances and statutes or from official competence or establishment, but, rather, from a demonstration of the effectiveness of their power in the daily events of their followers' lives.
>
> (pp.54–5)

As will be discussed below, Myers (1986) incorporated this conceptual-ization into his investigations of the focal person's role in the transition periods of group development.

Weber's notion of the charismatic individual describes the individual–group relationship in terms of the source of power that an individual can hold within the group. Redl (1942), on the other hand, represents another kind of influential member in the form of the central person. This concept refers to an individual who crystallizes the un-conscious emotional concerns for the social system and serves to evoke group formative processes within the other group members. According to Redl, the central person is a key figure in the development of a group emotion. The central person provides the means by which members can unconsciously satisfy common undesirable drives and thus avoid feelings of guilt, anxiety, and conflict. Such an individual may intensify aggressive drives and feelings and further constellate the emotion of the group by committing what Redl referred to as the 'initiatory act' (p. 35).

Whereas Redl (1942) was concerned with the role of the influential member in group formative processes, Dunphy (1974) was interested in the different kinds of roles that emerge in a small group and how these roles might be related to phase development. He referred to the influential members who come to play these roles in the group as 'role specialists'. According to Dunphy, 'the role specialists are, above all else, the symbols of the predominant emotional states of the group members' (p. 309). He documented five different role specialists – the instructor, aggressor, scapegoat, seducer, and idol – and argued that each of these specialists represented a particular unconscious emotional concern shared by the group members. For example, he felt that the scapegoat represented anxiety of the group regarding personal weak-nesses, deriving from frustration of dependency needs. The aggressor was felt to represent the group's harsh and repressive superego functions. In Dunphy's view, role specialists serve as symbols of focal conflict in the group. Change in the areas of conflict is indicated by the relative salience attributed to the specialist at different stages in the life of the group. According to Dunphy, the role specialist is an important 'reference point' for group members as they work to elaborate their group culture.

For Dunphy (1974), the scapegoat is one type of role specialist. As a form of influential member, however, it is generally regarded in the group literature as much more than just a group role. Rather, this form of influential member conceptualizes certain structures and dynamics of the social system. According to Gibbard and Hartman (1974), scape-goating symbolizes the social system's reaction to distress and an at-tempt to locate or identify the source of this distress. The perceived source of the distress is experienced as responsible for producing anxiety in the group or is viewed as abandoning, depressing, or potentially destroying the social system. In turn, the social system then seeks to psychologically extrude the source of distress from the group. Often, this 'source' is perceived to be a certain group member or a bad leader, thus the term 'scapegoat'. In this way, the social system seeks to create a 'good group entity' by excluding those elements that are perceived to be bad. Dunphy (1974) and Mann (1967), among others, also share the view that the manifestation of a scapegoat represents facets of the group that members find unacceptable. In the forms of influential member discussed so far, the individual playing the role of the influential member often willingly (if unconsciously) accepts the role. This is not the case, however, with the role of the scapegoat. The scapegoat serves as the recipient of the members' projections of their own anxieties and feelings of dependency.

Another form of influential member that illustrates the property of a representative of the group's underlying, emotional concerns is that of the covert role, advanced by Gemmill and Kraus (1988). In articulating this concept, these investigators attempt to explicate some of the psychological dynamics involved in the emergence of the influential member as a representative of the social system. According to Gemmill and Kraus (1988), covert roles are 'emotional themes based primarily on the latent content of expressed and unexpressed thoughts and feelings and are part of the unconscious of the group' (p. 300). Individuals come to occupy covert roles through their own propensity to express certain emotions that the other members of the group are also feeling but not articulating. Thus, it is through individuals acting within these covert roles that the group's emotional issues are made explicit. The process through which this occurs is referred to by Gemmill and Kraus as the dynamic of 'collective projective identification'. As we will see in the discussion of Neumann's (1954) notion of the 'Great Individual', collective projective identification is the principal psychological mechanism that results in the phenomenon of the influential group member.

Several forms of the symbolic influential member illustrate the second essential quality of the influential member as focal person – that is, the ability of this person to challenge the present order of things, the dominant culture, or tradition. By doing so, these influential members provoke a new awareness within the social system. They call attention to previously taken-for-granted assumptions reflected in the status quo and challenge the validity or usefulness of these assumptions as guidelines for group behavior. Influential group members which have been characterized with this function include the prophet (Brueggemann, 1978; Heschel, 1962) and Myers's (1986) concept of the focal person in the grieving process. The prophet criticizes and rejects the dominant consciousness of the culture, the status quo. In the larger context of

71

society, the prophet acts as a social critic who castigates and judges society. The prophetic voice is filled with anguish, outrage, and passion, crying out against the way things are and how they deviate from society's highest ideals. The prophet arouses and energizes the culture through the promise that things need not be the way they were. Brueggemann (1978) argues that the prophet's mission is to raise the level of awareness of a people who are despairing and are otherwise unable to consider alternative worlds. It is their lot to nourish and evoke a new consciousness, a new perception which is alternative to the dominant culture.

There are striking parallels between the relationship of the prophet to society, and the relationship of the focal person to the small group. These parallels are exemplified in the work of Myers (1986; also see Chapter Four of this volume) who studied the grieving process in small group development. According to Myers, phase movement is characterized by a process similar to grieving. Relying on the work of Bowlby (1975) and Parkes (1987), he identified four phases to this grieving process: (1) Numbness and panic; (2) Pining and protest; (3) Disorganization and despair; and (4) Restabilization and reintegration. In the group that he followed in his case study, Myers found this process to characterize the transitional periods in the phase development of the social system. A central dynamic in this process is the emergence of a focal person. Relying on the traditions of the central person (Redl, 1942) and the prophetic imagination (Brueggemann, 1978) and his experience of this phenomenon in small groups, Myers suggests two fundamental functions to the focal person in the grieving process. First, the focal person is seen as challenging the status quo of the social system. She/he calls into question the present way of seeing and doing things, and urges the social system to consider alternative views. Second, the focal person energizes the social system toward movement and a new direction. Implicit in both of these functions is the notion of a call within the social system to a new awareness, a new 'epistemology', a new consciousness.

Closely related to the property of critiquing and challenging the status quo is a third function that is illustrated in several descriptions of the influential member. This is the voice of transformation, reflected in the prophet (Brueggemann, 1978; Heschel, 1962), the hero as reflected in mythology (Campbell, 1968; Neumann, 1954) and psychoanalytic thought (Gibbard, 1974; Slater, 1966) and also in the focal person in the grieving process (Myers, 1986). As we have seen, the prophet and the focal person in the grieving process call for movement and change in the present form of the social system. These forms of influential members encourage members of the social system to develop a new vision of the present and asks them to commit themselves to work for the realization of this vision. The prophetic voice reflects an audacious imagination inspired by deeply felt forces. Through their outrage, members of society are moved to act and change their present behavior, although often not without considerable anguish, anger, and resentment.

The notion of the hero presents us with an even more dramatic illustration of the voice of transformation. The image of the hero provided to us in mythology (Campbell, 1968; Neumann, 1954) is an active one, standing apart from the masses, fighting evil and terrifying enemies, and leading the people against all odds in a struggle for newness. This is an image of transformation through liberation from the forces that keep us oppressed. Having thrown off the shackles of an old and repressive regime, the hero provides us with guidance for movement in establishing a new direction and a new order (Slater, 1966). In psychoanalytic thought (Gibbard, 1974; Slater, 1966), the hero symbolizes for the rest of the social system the constant and challenging forces of opposition between consciousness and the unconscious and, in so doing, expresses the social system's continuing struggle to achieve liberation from the unconscious. Often, this individual stands alone and directly against the forces of the collectivity. As a result, members of the social system begin to gradually become aware of distinctions and differences, the dawning of consciousness within the social system. Through the actions of the hero, the processes of differentiation and individuation are furthered within the social system.

Thus, we have seen that a fairly extensive research tradition has developed around the phenomenon of the influential member. This research provides support for the symbolic approach to understanding this phenomenon and for the principal attributes that are fundamental to our concept of the focal person. In the preceding section, three major functions of the influential member as a focal person were derived from prior studies of the influential member phenomenon: (1) a representation of the unconscious emotional concerns of the social system which are fundamentally opposing and seemingly contradictory; (2) a critique of the status quo and movement toward a new awareness; and (3) a voice for transformation of the social system. In addition, several qualities or characteristics attributed to different forms of the influential member further define the empirical nature of this concept. Social systems which exhibit the influential member phenomenon develop a polarization between the influential member and the rest of the social system. This is often reflected in a rallying behind the influential member or a concerted, collective action to block or impede the direction suggested by this individual. Some forms of influential member are seen as challenging and energizing the social system. Finally, the research literature suggests that the consequences of the influential member in the social system are not always positive, in the sense that the social system moves toward greater differentiation and integration. At times, these functions can serve considerable negative consequences as well. History is replete with examples of such phenomena.

In what ways, however, does the concept of focal person build on this earlier tradition? Where is the need for yet another conceptual form of influential member? It is to these questions that we now turn.

Relationship of focal person to prior studies of influential member

The previous section established several ways in which the focal person concept is similar to other forms of influential member that have been reported in the literature. In this section, we will investigate the ways in which the focal person concept differs conceptually and phenomenologically from these previous concepts.

One of the most significant differences rests with the theoretical breadth of the focal person concept. While one or more of the functions described in the preceding paragraph can be attributed to any one form of influential member, no other concept seems to adequately account for all these functions within a single theoretical framework. We believe that this is, in part, because many of these different forms do not attempt to conceptually link the behavior of the influential member with specific unconscious concerns that are focal to the social system within a given period of time. The focal person concept, however, conceptualizes not only the behavior of a particular group member but the unconscious emotionality and concerns of the social system as well, reflected in the notion of the archetypal paradox. Each of the three functions identified for the focal person relate to the emergence of the focal person as an influential member within a period of group paradox. The functions serve to explicate, illuminate, and eventually move the social system through this paradox. Thus, while different group members may perform different functions at different times, the behaviors cohere within the focal person concept because the functions are related theoretically to a specific context in the group, that of the archetypal paradox. It is recognition of the archetypal paradox which the social system confronts that helps make sense of the individual behaviors of the influential member as focal person.

Other important conceptual and phenomenological differences, however, also exist. Many of the studies reviewed earlier seek to explain the manifestation of the influential member and the representation of collective unconscious emotions in terms of a personal psychology. In several of these forms of influential group member, the individual is thought to express latent emotions which are experienced by all group members as a result of their individual maturation. Anxieties and fears associated with separation from maternal figures and with relationships with authority figures in the group are two examples of latent emotions manifest in small groups that have been attributed to maturational processes in the individual (Slater, 1966).

Many of the previous formulations of the influential member place considerable emphasis on the volition of an individual. Although there is indication in some of these ideas that the social system 'selects' the particular individual, most of the theoretical elaboration focuses more on the individual member than on the social system. For example, Myers based his conceptualization of focal person primarily on a psychoanalytic view of individual behavior in the group. As such, it relates the function of focal person to a personalistic view of attachment, separation, and loss. His concept of focal person does not explicitly take into account the possibility that such a phenomenon in the social system may reflect deeper, more primordial structures than are evident in personal histories. In addition, his methodology was directed primarily to the study of individual behavior. Individuals were identified as focal persons when their behaviors manifested certain characteristics. Although transactions with the social system were, to some extent, taken into account in this methodology, the social system is not a prominent dimension of his formulation of the focal person and of his methodology for identification of influential group members as focal persons. Other forms of influential member that reflect this personalistic bias include central person, role specialist, and covert role.

The notion of focal person, as it is described here, however, is really a phenomenon attributed to the collectivity which becomes manifest in a particular individual member. Focal person reflects forces which are fundamentally archetypal in nature and are associated with the evolution of consciousness within social systems (Neumann, 1954). The group 'takes possession' of an individual who is then felt to be 'in the grips' of the collectivity. As consciousness develops in the social system, the focal person is gradually released by the social system. During this time, the individual serves to mediate within the social system, becoming less and less powerful over time. Rarely, however, do these other theorists talk about the influential group member symbolically disintegrating in the process of consciousness development. This phenomenon is a fundamental attribute of the concept of focal person.

In several of these earlier formulations there is the sense that the influential group member is serving a kind of defensive function in the group. Characteristic of this stance are the notions of the scapegoat and central person, which are usually viewed as a kind of group psychological defense mechanism against unwanted or undesirable thoughts and feelings. In this sense, they represent a somewhat negative dynamic in the social system's development. Furthermore, the influential member in the form of a scapegoat is viewed as a threat to the group and must be psychologically eliminated from it. The function of the central person, as it is described by Redl (1942), is also primarily defensive in nature. The psychological mechanisms involve the satisfaction of undesirable drives on the part of individual members through the behavior of the central person. Through these mechanisms, members avoid feelings of guilt, anxiety, and conflict. Rather than contributing to separation and differentiation, the central person actually promotes psychological fusion among the group members. This defensive function of the influential member is also illustrated in the concept of scapegoating. In scapegoating, the group protects itself by getting rid of its undesirable content through projection of this content onto a single member and then psychologically or physically ostracizing this member from the group.

The concept of focal person, however, places emphasis on the transformative function of the influential group member. Although the social system's relationship with this individual may initially be decidedly negative in overall emotional tone, as is the case in the example provided earlier, the relationship frequently evolves into one that is more constructive and positive. Indeed, in many cases the focal person may initially be serving a defensive function for the social system. The theoretical emphasis of this concept, however, is not on this defensive function but, rather, on its transformative function. The focal person is viewed within the context of a developing individual–group relationship and the gradual evolution and transformation of consciousness within the social system.

In summary, the literature in small group research clearly supports the idea that certain individuals at certain times in the life of the group become extremely influential. Much of this research is in the sociological or social psychological tradition and is concerned primarily with the manifest, instrumental nature of this role. The psychodynamic literature, however, stresses the importance of the symbolic nature of the influential group member and it is with this form of the influential member with which we are concerned. This tradition stresses the underlying, latent, and largely unconscious emotions, conflicts, and forces that are represented by the emergence of the influential member. In different ways, the influential member is viewed as mediating resolutions to these unconscious conflicts. These characteristics are consistent with our formulation of the influential member as a focal person. There is a need, however, for a framework that conceptualizes this phenomenon as a unitary set of interrelated functions. Such a framework needs to view the influential member as a characteristic of collective behavior rather than individual behavior and as a powerful force in the transformation of the social group. We are proposing that the conceptual framework of focal person, grounded in analytical psychology, represents a more adequate way to view and study the influential member from a symbolic perspective. We now turn to a discussion of this framework.

The conceptual basis for the focal person concept

In this section, the theoretical framework for the concept of the focal person will be discussed in three parts: (1) The symbolic approach as a way of understanding group phenomena in general and the concept of focal person in particular; (2) Archetypal paradox as a way of viewing and interpreting focal concerns of the social system; and (3) The relationship of the focal person concept to Neumann's (1954) concept of the Great Individual.

The symbolic approach to the focal person

The concept of the focal person reflects a symbolic approach to the study and understanding of the influential member phenomenon. By the term 'symbolic approach', we imply a theoretical framework and method for understanding and interpreting human behavior that are provided by the field of analytical psychology (Whitmont, 1969). We have used the lens of analytical psychology and the symbolic approach to develop a fuller theoretical perspective for viewing what the influential member really means to the social system of a small group. It is using this lens that leads us to conclude that, in certain circumstances, the influential member seems to be articulating underlying concerns which are focal to the social system at the time. Thus, it is clear that the focal person concept reflects a symbolic interpretation of small group behavior. Therefore, a few words about what we mean by the symbolic approach seem in order.

In the symbolic approach, overt, manifest behavior and emotions which characterize the emergence of the focal person as an influential member are viewed as representing deeper, largely unconscious concerns with which the group is struggling in its movement toward wholeness and maturity. These concerns comprise what we refer to as the psychic life of the social system. As the social system begins to form and develop, a variety of these unconscious concerns are activated. Understanding and working through these concerns are essential to movement and growth of the social system and of its members. They are not, however, fully knowable through intellectual or conceptual terms alone (Whitmont, 1969). Rather, from the point of view of the symbolic approach, these concerns become manifest through the expression of symbols or images. Symbols express much more than can be put into mere words (Christ, 1989) and are, in a fundamental sense, a means for coming into contact with that which is essentially unknowable (Whitmont, 1969). They are grounded in the unconscious of the group but take their manifest forms by shaping and molding the ideas, behaviors, and emotions present in the conscious dimension of group life. The symbol presents an 'objective, visible meaning behind which an invisible, profounder meaning is hidden' (Jacobi, 1959, p. 77). It is a kind of mediator between opposing and seemingly contradictory forces of consciousness and the unconscious, between the manifest and the hidden. Understanding of the psychic reality of the social system involves the perception and apprehension of the symbols that are expressed through group interaction and of their effect on feeling and intuition (Whitmont, 1969).

Thus, the symbolic approach is concerned with the unconscious, emotional, intuitive, and imaginative realms of group function. It is a way of studying and investigating certain group phenomena. When we view group phenomena from a symbolic perspective, we are trying to understand the deeper, underlying meaning that these phenomena hold for the group, the contradictions implicit in them between the unconscious and conscious forces within the group, between the hidden and the manifest.

The case example provided in the opening section of this chapter provides an illustration of the symbolic approach to understanding group life. At one level, we may view the issue of whether the group should take a break as a routine decision with which most groups must deal in one form or another. We could then examine the process from a decision-making point of view and seek to determine the factors that affected the process. This approach would exemplify an instrumental perspective of the relationship between Barbara and the social system. Yet, as we ponder the significance of this period of interaction, we are struck by the level of significance that the social system seems to be attributing to the issue of a 'break'. The social system's investment in this issue appears to be quite disproportionate to the overall value of the issue to the instrumental life and work of the group. Although the issue was initially raised in a fairly rational and straightforward manner, discussion quickly became animated and emotional in its tone. What started out as a decision about taking a 'break' evolved into an analysis of Barbara's commitment to the group. Conversation and interaction around this issue persisted for approximately 45 minutes before drifting off to other matters, with no explicit resolution of whether the group should take a 'break'. For the investigator using the symbolic approach, attention is drawn to the significance and meaning of this issue for the social system. The 'break' has thus taken on the dimensions of a symbol for the social system. It leads us to deeper questions of meaning, such as trying to understand why the group had so much difficulty in dealing with what, on the surface, appears to be a routine and straightforward issue regarding group procedure and maintenance.

Symbols that arise within group life and characterize the social system are referred to as collective symbols. They are manifestations of universal, fundamentally archetypal forms. Because of their power and the richness of their content, they become assimilated by the larger collective and, therefore, become collective symbols. They express those unconscious factors that are generally more prevalent in the larger group (i.e. the social system) than in individuals (i.e. the personality system). As such their manifestation tends to have a more demonstrable effect on the social system, rather than individuals within the group. The focal person as an influential member represents such a collective symbol. In the case material, Barbara, as a focal person, comes to manifest the symbolic meaning that the issue of a 'break' holds for the social system. Through the 'break', the social system is manifesting deeper, largely unconscious concerns regarding its psychic reality. Barbara comes to serve the role of focal person by raising the issue of the 'break' and the underlying, unconscious concerns associated with this symbol. In effect, she named a deep seated paradox with which the group was beginning to struggle. As a collective symbol, the 'break' expresses opposing and contradictory impulses of the collective unconscious of the social system. The discussion and period of interaction surrounding the issue of the break illustrate what we have come to call an 'archetypal paradox' of the social system. It is within the context of an archetypal paradox that we believe the phenomenon of the focal person is manifest.

The archetypal paradox

The notion of the archetypal paradox is derived from the theoretical framework of analytical psychology, and principally the work of Erich Neumann (1954). The paradoxical perspective is 'concerned with the observation that groups are pervaded by a wide range of emotions, thoughts, and actions that their members experience as contradictory, and that the attempts to unravel these contradictory forces create a circular process that is paralyzing to groups' (Smith and Berg, 1987, p.14). A group paradox reflects a struggle with opposites in an attempt to create meaning and coherence. Such struggles characterize Neumann's (1954) description of the archetypal development of consciousness. These struggles are archetypal in nature and are manifest in universal mythological motifs or symbols which mark the gradual, stage-like emergence of consciousness within social groups (Neumann, 1954; Ulanov, 1971; Whitmont, 1982). Neumann's descriptions of such mythological motifs as the Great Mother, Separation of World Parents, Birth of the Hero, and Slaying of the Mother and the Father vividly depict these struggles and the paradoxes which characterize them. Thus, the term 'archetypal paradox' refers to the fundamental, primordial, and contradictory forces that groups face as they struggle for increasing consciousness.

An illustration of an archetypal paradox that we have studied in the small group is reflected in the symbol of the social system as both a good and bad mother. Many researchers have reported that, in the formative stages of group development, members unconsciously experience the social system as a maternal entity (Bion, 1961; Durkin, 1964; Gibbard and Hartman, 1974; Jaques, 1974; Ruiz, 1972; Scheidlinger, 1974). Furthermore, some investigators have reported that the social system of the group may be perceived as both a good and bad mother. Descriptions of the mother symbol early in the life of a group find their parallels in Neumann's (1954) discussion of the evolution of consciousness (Dirkx, 1987). Neumann's discussion clearly demonstrates how the symbol of the social system as mother evolves from a state of near complete fusion to gradual differentiation into its good and bad aspects. Neumann equates this process with the dawning of consciousness within the social system.

What is of relevance here, however, is the paradoxical nature of the social system reflected in this dual image of the mother, and the role that certain individuals play in its resolution. Members perceive the social system as a mother that is both good and bad. For example, individuals often act as if the group is an accepting, supportive place, only to find out that the group can, at times, seem very unaccepting and un-supportive. This creates a sense of the group as a bad mother, which then invites enquiry into why it is so, manifesting, in the process, aspects of the good mother. It is, as Smith and Berg (1987) suggest, a vicious circle. It is only when members begin to see that the good and bad aspects are intrinsic to the nature of the social system that they are then able to move beyond this debilitating paradox.

Key to the resolution of the paradox, then, is the emergence of an individual who, on behalf of the rest of the social system, is capable and willing to 'do battle with the mother dragon' (Neumann, 1954). For the group to successfully resolve the archetypal paradox, an individual – the focal person – must be present in the group who serves to crystallize for the social system its own feelings toward the powerful archetype that is at the core of the paradox. The focal person serves as a repository of the members' unconscious concerns regarding the archetype. In the case of the group as both a good mother and a bad mother, the group comes to discern the qualities of the Good and Bad Mother archetypes through the actions of the focal person. The focal person acts to symbolically challenge the relationship that the group has to the Great Mother or to energize the group to attend to and deal with this powerful archetype.

Again, much of this 'activity' is going on at the symbolic level within the social system. At the overt level, group interactions with this individual often manifest characteristics of the paradox at issue in the social system. For example, the particular individual who is serving as the focal person for the group will express ambivalence toward the group as mother, reflecting an ambivalence toward the mother that characterizes the social system itself. This ambivalence is illustrated perhaps most clearly in the sense that the focal person expresses, usually symbolically, both attraction to and avoidance of the mother image. In so doing, the focal person reflects the group's unconscious concerns surrounding this archetype. As a result of the focal person behavior, the group is able to mobilize itself in a particular direction relative to the archetypal paradox. If the focal person is not present, these feelings will remain diffuse, poorly articulated, and the group will not be able to successfully differentiate the good and bad aspects of its matriarchal dimension. Movement in the social system to resolve the associated archetypal paradox is unlikely and the social system will be characterized primarily by the qualities which characterize the image of the bad mother. In other words, a predominantly negative form of matriarchal consciousness will continue to dominate life in the social system.

The focal person concept is closely related theoretically to another idea derived from analytical psychology, that of the Great Individual. We close this section with a brief discussion of how these two ideas are related and a brief synopsis of the process of collective projective identification, the psychological mechanisms through which this phenomenon comes about.

The Great Individual and the focal person concept

We have chosen to label the individual who comes to represent the primary, unconscious concerns of the social system as 'focal person'. The term identifies the essential quality of the concept – namely, certain individuals play a focal role in articulating the social system's concerns. Theoretically, the concept is grounded specifically in Neumann's (1954) work on the development of consciousness and, specifically, in his notion of the 'Great Individual'. Neumann was concerned primarily with articulating the phylogenetic and ontogenetic basis for consciousness and did not specifically address the problem of consciousness in face-to-face groups. The dynamics and characteristics that he attributes to the Great Individual are quite applicable to certain forms of symbolic influential members in small groups as well. For this reason, we have chosen to refer to this phenomenon in the small group as 'focal person' to clearly indicate that we are referring to an aspect of small group life, rather than larger, cultural, or social groupings. To better understand the specific nature and characteristics of the focal person concept, however, we will briefly review Neumann's characterization of the Great Individual and the related notion of the 'hero'.

In his essay, 'The group and the Great Individual', Neumann (1954) argues that the collective unconscious of the group manifests itself by taking possession of an individual in the group. The group experiences its unconscious psychic wholeness in the person of the Great Individual. This person serves as both the group self and the unconscious self of each member. The individual becomes the archetypal representative of the group's totality. The function of the Great Individual is to convey to the group, either unconsciously or through conscious participation in his/her role, the contents of the collective unconscious. In this sense, the individual is the forerunner of consciousness in the group. The role of the individual in the consciousness of groups and its accompanying emotional arousal are also addressed by Harding (1965) who argues that the pattern of the group presupposes the existence of a leader. This individual voices the unconscious or partly unconscious wishes of the crowd, which can lead to redemptive as well as destructive consequences. In the process of consciousness development, the Great Individual gradually develops a mediatory function, yielding more and more of its manna to the group members. In this sense, the Great Individual is thus disintegrated and 'dismembered' in the process of consciousness development. Neumann cites as an example of the Great Individual the temporary leader of a group who has no relationship to the permanent leadership but who contributes something unique and valuable for the group within a specific situation and for the moment only.

Neumann's (1954) second and third forms of the 'Great Individual', as they relate to the individual–group relationship, embody the principal characteristics of the focal person concept. The Great Individual is a representative of the emotionality attached to unconscious issues and conflicts of the larger culture. Through his or her actions, this individual challenges the social system's present definitions of the status quo and calls for the development of a new awareness and level of consciousness. Finally, the Great Individual acts as a voice for transformation. The image of the hero, of which Neumann and others in the field of analytical psychology were concerned, is also a form of the Great Individual. The hero is viewed as assisting the social system in wrestling consciousness from the seductive pull of the collective unconscious (Neumann, 1954; Samuels, 1985). The hero emerges in opposition to the collective, regressive pull of the social system, embodying for the rest of the group the desire for ego consciousness. The struggle represented in the image of the hero's drive for ego consciousness in the midst of an overwhelming unconsciousness is a central attribute of the concept of the focal person.

The focal person phenomenon emerges in the small group through the psychological process of collective projective identification. A thorough discussion of the process is beyond the scope of this chapter. A brief discussion of its more salient aspects may help us better understand the relationship of the focal person to the social system of the group. For purposes of our discussion of the influential member, it is sufficient to say that this concept refers to a process in which the social system projects unconscious content onto a particular individual who has a 'hook' on which the social system can 'hang' the projection (Ogden, 1982). Having done so, the social system then continues to partially identify with the projected content, thereby creating the complex of feelings and emotions that usually accompany the emergence of a symbolic influential member. Given a certain level of congruency between an individual's propensity for an emotional concern and the social system's concerns, this individual will be unconsciously selected by the group to express at an individual level what the social system cannot or will not explicitly express at a collective level. In particular, the notion of congruency between the unconscious emotional concerns of the individual and the group is an important quality of the individual–group relationship reflected in the concept of the focal person.

The focal person concept: case examples

We are now in a position to elaborate on the specific characteristics of the focal person concept. Broadly speaking, the three fundamental characteristics or functions of the focal person concept are: (1) Representation of the unconscious concerns of the social system; (2) Critique of the present order, way of seeing things, or framing of problems; and (3) Voice for change and transformation of the social order. Each of these broad, conceptual categories will be defined further through empirical specifications. These specifications make reference to phenomena which, given the appropriate frame of reference, one can readily observe in an interactive small group. We will utilize case material from self-analytic groups in graduate education to empirically illustrate each of these categories and their related specifications and to serve as the basis for further discussion.

Representation of the unconscious concerns of the social system

A fundamental characteristic of the focal person concept is the ability of the individual as a focal person to crystallize and call forth the unconscious emotional concerns of the social system. The following excerpt of case material is designed to illustrate this quality of the focal person.

83

It was the second meeting of the group which consisted of eight women and two men, all returning adult students and most of them employed in education or business. During the first 15 minutes, discussion was not particularly focused and many topics were brought up and then dropped. At first, members appeared to be looking frequently at the designated leader while they talked. The designated leader, however, did not respond to their visual contacts and was silent during this period. Gradually, however, members began to look more at each other as they talked and appeared less concerned about the leader. Some members expressed dissatisfaction with the quality of the videotape from the first session. In a friendly and caring way, Betty asked Mike about his lack of expression in the group so far. Mike acknowledged his behavior but indicated it was not unusual for him. He then asked about the purpose of this group. His question lead to a more focused period of discussion about the progress of the group so far. Loretta suggested that the group needed more structure in order to progress. Several of the members joined in at this point and the discussion revolved around the question of whether to have structure or not, and how much. Some suggestions were made as to how they might introduce some structure. Betty responded to this by talking about how this group was different from the business groups with which she worked, where one is expected to act in certain ways. She then said, 'You know, the nice thing about this group is that if you all decided you wanted to do something this week, like read a paper or something, I'd feel totally free to say, "You go ahead. I'm not going to do that this week." I'd feel totally free to say that. I feel that I would have permission to say that.' The group appeared stunned for a moment, as attention seemed to turn directly to her. One of the members half-jokingly said, 'Who gave you permission?' and the rest of the group laughed nervously. Betty reaffirmed her feeling of freedom in the group to not go along with the group's plans. Interaction at this point was punctuated by a series of short silent pauses after Betty's comments and the group appeared to be increasingly focusing on Betty. Interaction was still friendly on the surface but there was a sense of tension in the comments and questions that members directed toward Betty. Some members asked her about who she felt responsible for and that actions of one member surely affect the others as well. Others said that they didn't feel Betty was trying to 'break up the group or anything like that'. Betty then indicated that this sometimes happens with business groups and she sometimes urges, but doesn't force the 'deviant' member to go along with the group. Mary asked Betty if she would want them to urge her to go along with the group. Nora wondered what Betty would think if they told her that her not going along would affect their level of learning in the group, to which Betty responded, 'I'd like to believe that I would be able to say, "That's your problem." ' 'Again, this comment was followed by a brief period of silence in which the group appeared stunned. Nora explained that in community and political action groups it was very important for the members to know that others were committed to the group and that they could trust each other not to put themselves above the group. Clara expressed some concern about Betty's earlier comment about this group being so different from other groups. Betty responded by saying that, if she pulled out of a group exercise, her behavior would make the group more honest, not more unique. Clara then said that she found Betty's comments acceptable but she wondered how they were going to manage or keep going without structure. Several members mentioned the idea of commitment to the group and indicated their own commitment to being in the group. The group leader then offered a metaphorical interpretation of the group's behavior, 'You have to learn to love the mother before you can love the father.' His comment was followed by a brief pause and then loud laughter in the group, as several members expressed complete surprise and confusion over the interpretation. Attention seemed for several minutes to be directed at what the leader might have meant by this metaphor but then began to talk about the term 'Instructional' in the title of the course. This was a topic of discussion for several minutes as several members suggested ways to interpret 'Instructional' for their group. Clara suggested that she would like to talk about mothers more. Betty at first responded by taking the discussion back to the issue of the course title and then seemed to come back to Clara's suggestion by asking people if they had read the book, *My mother, myself*. The group's attention again seemed to be riveted on Betty as she spoke briefly about her relationship with her own mother. Gradually, other members began to talk about their own lives and relationships with their parents and interaction became less focused on Betty and more evenly distributed throughout the group.

This brief summary of a relatively short period of group interaction exemplifies one of the major characteristics of the focal person, that of acting as a representative of the unconcerns of the social system. The particular individual assuming that role in this segment is Betty. Several qualities of this interaction reflect the specifications of this category. First, there is little doubt that Betty gradually became the focus of the group's attention. Discussion and interaction during the first 15 minutes was relatively diffuse and unfocused. Gradually, however, a group theme began to emerge around the issue of structure in the group. Betty's reaction to the implicit suggestions in this discussion was to say, in effect, that she probably would not go along with any group plans for assignments or exercises. Both verbal and nonverbal patterns of interaction leave little doubt that Betty quickly became the center and focus of the group's concern and attention. For the next 15 minutes, most of the members were either talking directly with Betty or about her position.

Within this period of interaction, there is also an increase in the level of emotionality in the group. As the group increasingly focused on Betty's comments and the meaning of what she was saying, the group became more tense and anxious. This is reflected in the strained pauses that followed Betty's comments, the nervous laughter which frequently punctuated interaction, and the overall sense of strain that the group seemed to be feeling.

What, then, do these two qualities suggest about the underlying, here-and-now concerns of the social system? From a manifest point of view, the group appears to be talking about the kind and level of structure that may be adopted in the group. At a symbolic level, the discussion reflects the unconscious concerns of the social system. There can be little doubt as to the meaning of the group's reaction. Clearly, Betty's behavior was interpreted as a threat to the integrity of the group and its formative processes. Members were quite concerned about the effects of such actions on the rest of the group. The interaction raises to the observable level the fundamental paradox with which the group is struggling. At one level, we can speak of this paradox as one of the individual versus the group. Group work, the interaction suggests, requires commitment and trust from all the members but, if we commit to the group, we might lose our individual freedom to be ourselves. If we act, as Betty is suggesting, as individuals, then the integrity of the group will be in jeopardy. From an archetypal point of view, however, Betty's behavior may be interpreted as activating the members' unconscious concerns regarding the social system as the Great Mother. Similar to the group's behavior, the archetype of the Great Mother represents a struggle with an overwhelming entity that is perceived at once as both containing and constraining, as protecting and destroying, as nurturing and enslaving (Neumann, 1954). In myths which manifest the archetype, individuals fear the awesome, smothering power of the Great Mother, but also fear separating from her and leaving her to be on their own. They both desire and loathe the containment that the Great Mother provides.

Thus, in the case material, Betty's behavior and the group's reaction to it strongly suggest that the matriarchal archetype was activated within the collective unconscious of the social system. Betty, as a focal person, is symbolically calling the group's attention to this archetypal paradox and their need to address its opposing and contradictory forces (i.e. the aspects of the social system as both a good and bad mother). That her call is tapping into a concern of the social system is affirmed by the group's reaction to her statements of individuality and personal freedom, and also the direction and content of the interaction that followed. As group interaction became less focused on Betty and more evenly distributed, members began to share fairly personal stories of their own lives and relationships with their parents. Again, at the symbolic level, we may interpret this behavior as a willingness on the part of the social system to work on the paradox that is at the heart of the Great Mother archetype. The members are, at once, becoming more individuated from the group, while affirming the social system as a good mother, one that is receptive and supportive, one that nurtures, cares for its members, and fosters relatedness and connectedness (Ulanov, 1971). It should come as no surprise to learn that the good mother–bad mother issue is far from resolved in this interaction. This group continued to struggle with the opposing sides of this paradox for many sessions.

In summary, when a focal person emerges as the representative of the social system's unconscious concerns, periods of group interaction are characterized by a single individual (usually, but at times it may involve more than one person) increasingly becoming the exclusive focus of the group's attention. Discussion and interaction seem to revolve around this individual. Virtually all other members are directing their comments and attention to this one person who, in turn, is usually talking to and interacting with the group, rather than with any one particular individual. This individual appears to consume the group's time and energy for the duration of this interaction, as illustrated in the case example. In the next selection of case material, we focus on the second fundamental characteristic of the focal person, that of critiquing the present order and challenging the group to develop a new awareness.

Critique of the current social order

Another way in which the focal person helps the group move through the paradoxical situation is to offer a direct challenge to the group through a critique of the way things are. The focal person calls into question present assumptions regarding how the social situation is defined (Myers, 1986). This function is, in a sense, a call to reframe the paradoxical situation in which the group finds itself (Smith and Berg, 1987). The following selection from the first 30 minutes of session illustrates the development of focal person activity within the context of the good mother–bad mother paradox.

The group started this session by several members relating personal experiences since the group had last met. The topics in this discussion included experiences in a local election, a funeral that one of the members had attended, and a visit from a grandmother. Sylvia, a member who had provided considerable negative characterizations of her mother in earlier sessions, took a few minutes at this time to relate to the group her mother's visit. Nell asked what was next and Candy suggested that this was the last chance for their own agenda. A couple of suggestions about what to do were raised, such as reflecting on what the group had done right and what they had done wrong and planning for reunion, but none of these were taken seriously. Interaction during this time was punctuated by periods of giggling and several members talking at once. Candy then asked if individuals felt things were resolved, indicating that she did not have a sense of resolution about several things. As she talked, Candy became very excited and animated, demonstrating considerable energy over the issues she was raising. Some of the issues were concerned with conflicts that she felt were unresolved. She wondered how safe people felt about bringing up conflicts and the level of safety and security that others felt in the group. She asked the group why they had not confronted their conflicts. Indicating that she felt anxious as she talked, she voiced resentment about dealing with 'Mother outside of the group'. Some one suggested that perhaps there are not any safe groups. Candy clearly had the attention of the group during this time when Betty entered the discussion. Interaction then seemed to occur primarily between Betty and Candy. Betty also began to criticize the group for not effectively dealing with the conflicts which seemed to largely involve her. She said that she could not trust the group to 'work things out', and felt threatened when she wanted to disagree. She referred to this state of affairs as a 'real sickness'. The group then began to talk about the conflict that occurred in the group, but the discussion seemed to become somewhat more abstract and intellectual. It was at this time that the leader intervened and the group's attention then turned to a consideration of his interpretation.

This vignette clearly demonstrates the critiquing function of the focal person. Similar to the preceding case material, this period of interaction is characterized by a focusing of the group's attention on a single individual. In this case, however, two individuals emerged to alternately serve in the capacity of focal person (Candy and Betty). The interactions were highly charged emotionally and the focal persons were addressing what seemed to be a contradictory and irreconcilable problem, that of raising conflicts but not being able to openly confront them or work them through satisfactorily. There is also a sense of polarization between the focal persons and the rest of the group around these related issues. Candy and Betty are challenging and 'pushing' the group in some manner. In this short vignette, it is not possible to develop a firm sense of the social system. Candy and Betty dominated most of this period while the rest of the members sat and listened attentively, with some members making occasional comments. While they were quiet, there is little question that all the members were deeply invested in the interaction and were actively, if nonverbally, participating. This level of involvement reflects the kind of rallying or sense of infatuation that, at times, focal persons are able to elicit from the social system. At other times, however, the social system may push back, instead of falling in behind the focal person, as was the case in the preceding vignette.

When the focal person is in the role of critic, he/she may be viewed by the group as either a source of irritation and agitation, or as a source of hope for the future. In the former sense, the group will attempt to get the individual to return to the fold, or will reject him/her as a member. In the latter, the group will rally behind the individual in the hopes of being lead out of their present predicament. This is clearly the situation in the case material at hand. Both Candy and Betty are challenging current definitions of the status quo. They are calling for new assumptions that may guide them or allow the group to redefine their situation. The next section focuses on the role of the focal person as a voice of transformation.

A voice of transformation

The role of the focal person as a voice of transformation is closely related to the characteristic of critique of the present social order. The differences may well be ones of degree, rather than kind, in that, in the process of challenging the social system and encouraging the development of new awareness, the focal person is also laying the ground for the overthrow of the present way of doing things and the establishment of a new order or a new epistemology (Myers, 1986). While the focal person as critic may well point out what is wrong with the status quo, the focal person as voice of transformation also is prepared to lead the group in the establishment of a new way of being. This function is illustrated in the following case material, taken from the seventh session of another self-analytic group in graduate education. The group was composed of six men and six women.

> In the third session of the group, Jake, one of the male members who had an administrative role in a local school district, had severely criticized Emma. This confrontation went unchallenged by the social system or any single member and Jake continued to exert considerable power over the other members. As a result, the group

developed an oppressive climate in which Jake dominated the group in a quiet but seductive manner. It was clear that considerable tension existed between the social system and this male member and the group appeared stuck, being unable to resolve or work through the conflict implicit in the situation. In session six, Ruth raised the question of who should be the leader in the group. She was obviously calling into question the legitimacy of the *ipso facto* leadership that had been assumed by Jake and suggesting that the whole issue of leadership be redefined and examined. Her call, however, went unanswered and she mustered very little support from the rest of the social system. In session seven, Ruth sat quietly for much of the session, until someone asked her to share what was going on with her. Her response was careful and measured but her voice was full of quiet rage. She said that last week she had taken a risk for the group and had urged the group to stand up to Jake and his reification of the current regime and power structure. She indicated that she felt abandoned and, in a sense, hung out to dry. The response of the social system was as if they had not heard what she had said. Ruth said no more for the remainder of the session and, for that matter, closed down emotionally for the duration of the group.

In this segment, Ruth and the social system display all the principal characteristics of the focal person that we have articulated in this chapter. In session six, when Ruth comes forward to openly challenge Jake's leadership in the group, she articulates the tension and anxiety that has been almost palpable in the group up to then. The conflict between Jake and the rest of the group is clearly observable. Like the emperor who had no clothes, however, no one wanted to give voice to this underlying conflict, until, in the sixth session, Ruth decides to take the risk. In challenging Jake, Ruth also challenges the present status quo and calls for a new form of leadership, a new way of doing things. She is attempting to energize the group in a new direction, to reframe the problem that they are facing, and to help them out of their entrenchment. Her voice is one of outrage, anguish, and anger. She is asking the group to join her in a struggle for a new order. Ruth is much like the hero in analytical psychology and mythology, who stands very much alone in the face of the collectivity, staring into the mouth of the dragon. She is a spokesperson for increased consciousness and further differentiation. Like the hero, however, she is 'devoured' by the social system. She returns, in her silence, to the matrix of the social system's collective unconscious.

This segment represents the emergence of a focal person who articulates the unconscious concerns of the social system. In return, the social system rewards her by further alienating and psychologically isolating her in the group. Thus, the consequences of focal person behavior are not always positive, either for the individual and/or the social system. The case example illustrates the immense struggle that is sometimes faced by the focal person and the social system as they attempt to deal with the challenge the focal person presents. Typically, the social system is increasingly faced with the decision to either move forward in the direction called for by the focal person or retreat further into a deeper entrenchment. Considerable tension and anxiety will surround this situation as the focal person increasingly challenges the social system to adopt a new way of seeing – a new level of awareness and consciousness. At some point, the social system will then either decide to move forward or to stay where it is and, thereby, retreat. Clearly, the latter alternative is the route taken by the social system in the case example.

In summary, a principal quality of the focal person concept is the fact that it is not a property of any one individual or individuals but, rather, an aspect of the transaction between the social and personality systems of the group (Boyd, 1983, 1984). An individual acts and the social system responds and in that transaction lies the phenomenon of the focal person. The three case examples demonstrate that the focal person concept is characterized by three principal functions. One function is to represent the unconscious concerns of the social system. These concerns are emotional in nature and involve archetypal material. They are manifest in feelings, thoughts, and actions which seem opposing, contradictory, and irreconcilable. In these case studies, we have concentrated on archetypal paradoxes which evolve out of the archetype of the Great Mother, but additional archetypal paradoxes involving the Father, the Hero, and the Captive and the Treasure (Neumann, 1954) are also possible. These paradoxes reflect a sense of entrenchment that comes to pervade the social system around issues of group development and transformation. They are inevitable markers in the path of the evolving social system. The second function that the focal person serves is to critique the status quo and to challenge the members to a new way of seeing. This function involves a 'reframing' of the situation that has lead to or produced the paradox (Smith and Berg, 1987), so that, out of the apparent opposition springs the possibility for new life and energy. The critique sets the stage for the third function of the focal person, that of the voice of transformation. This is an energizing function, in which the focal person seeks to move the social system to a new order or a new way of doing things, in other words a new society.

Summary and conclusion

The focus of this chapter has been on developing a more adequate conceptual understanding of the individual who comes to occupy special and symbolic positions of influence in small, face-to-face groups. That is, certain individuals at certain times in the group's development, sometimes overtly but usually covertly, serve to focus attention on the underlying, unconscious concerns of the social system of the group. We refer to this general phenomenon as the 'influential member'. Within the last 40 years, scholars of small group behavior have identified a number of different forms. As we demonstrated in a critical review of this literature, these various concepts have underscored the importance of viewing group phenomena from a symbolic perspective. In addition, this research has identified several different functions that the influential member may serve in the process of group development. None of these prior concepts, however, provides an adequate conceptual basis for linking the phenomenon of the influential member with the dynamics of the social system. We are left with several different versions of the influential member, some of which appear to be the consequences of conservative and defensive functions of the social system, while others suggest a more active role in group development and transformation. A more comprehensive and theoretically inclusive concept is needed which can conceptually unify these various functions and which can help us better understand how and why these individuals assume the significance that they do to the social system of the group.

The focal person concept was proposed as a way of filling this theoretical gap in the group literature. Based on the theoretical framework of analytical psychology, the focal person concept aims to help understand and interpret the behavior of certain influential members within a framework of group transformation. The notion of archetypal paradox was advanced as the group context in which the focal person emerges. Within the period of the archetypal paradox, the focal person serves to crystallize and to name the sense of the entrenchment that members feel and the unconscious concerns that are at the core of the archetypal paradox, to challenge and to critique the present order of things, and/or to energize the group toward transformation of the social order. Through these three key functions, the focal person facilitates a re-framing of the group's situation and movement through the paradox. The emergence of a focal person, however, does not always result in positive, transformative consequences for the social system. As was clearly evident in the last case example, the social system may be viciously resistant to the voice of the focal person, who often, in situations like this, succumbs to a psychological fate not unlike that of the hero in Greek mythology.

The work presented in this chapter offers a somewhat different and conceptually more comprehensive perspective for viewing and understanding the particular individual–group relationship reflected in the focal person phenomenon. From our own observational studies, the focal person concept has been shown to be a useful way of conceptualizing certain manifestations of influential members. This research (Dirkx, 1987; Myers, 1986) demonstrates that focal person phenomena are clearly associated with periods of group paradox and transformation. Additional observational research, however, will be necessary to corroborate the conceptual relationships inherent in this perspective. The extent to which this association is exclusive remains to be determined. That is, are there other periods in the social system that are not explicitly paradoxical or transformative in which focal persons are present? Additional studies are needed to address this question.

There are several other questions that remain to be clarified by future studies as well. For example, why do particular individuals seem to occupy the role of focal person? Is there something in the psychological nature of these individuals that social systems find more 'suitable' for this role than others in the group? We can find a partial theoretical answer in the notion of collective projective identification. Empirical studies of this phenomenon, however, are needed to help us better understand the nature of the individual–group relationship that constitutes focal person activity within periods of group paradox. Previous research has introduced such possibilities as an implicit congruence between the ambivalence of the focal person toward the archetypal material constituting the paradox and the ambivalence of the social system towards this material (Dirkx, 1987). More work, however, is needed to bring these ideas beyond the speculative stage.

Another important line of research in the focal person concept is to comprehensively describe the nature of the archetypal paradoxes in which this phenomenon plays a part. In this chapter, we discussed the focal person within the archetypal paradox of the group as both a good mother and a bad mother, the archetype fundamental to the matriarchal stage of consciousness. Based on Neumann's (1954) work, we would anticipate similar group behavior around the different phases of archetypal development, including that of the Great Father, the Hero, and the Captive and the Treasure.

The work presented here provides a sound, theoretical grounding for interpreting the behavior of influential group members. As the preceding discussion demonstrates, however, considerable work remains to corroborate and refine this concept. The research so far, however, provides some implications for those who facilitate small face-to-face groups over time in various settings. Identifying the phenomenon of the influential member as focal person also identifies latent, unconscious concerns of the social system. Often, groups get stuck and bogged down with little understanding of the real reason why they are stuck. Looking to and understanding the voice of the focal person as a symbolic voice of the social system may help facilitators be in a better position to assist the group through its 'stuckness' and toward transformation.

Related to the perspective of the focal person as a symbolic representation of the unconscious concerns of the social system is the notion that focal person activity is an indication of underlying transformative processes in the group. An influential member acting as a focal person is a suggestion that the transformative impulses of the social system are making themselves heard and seen. The focal person can draw attention to the archetypal paradox, which, in turn, can help facilitators better understand the specific direction that the transformation will take.

In this regard, the group paradox is not unlike psychological crises, which are inevitable but crucial periods of transformation in the lives of individuals (Erikson, 1950). Future research and application of the focal person concept will help us better understand and facilitate groups through these predictable periods of opposing and conflicting forces and feelings of entrenchment. It provides researchers, group facilitators, and group members with one perspective for making sense of the difficult and usually painful process of group transformation.

The painful process of group transformation is characteristic of personal transformations. It is difficult generally for social systems and individuals to give up what they now know and believe they can handle and move onto something new, and perhaps something they may not be able to handle as well. This is even the case when the present situation is unsatisfactory and even painful. We had often observed this in the life of a small group. Myers (1986) undertook the leadership in developing a methodology for the study of this phenomenon. It paralleled the characteristics of grief work in cases of bereavement and therefore it seemed reasonable to stay with the term. Not only do individuals give evidence of experiencing grief in making major changes in their lives but the social system in its own ways appeared to manifest a form of grief work. The methodology which was developed allowed us to study the social system in transition through what we came to call social grieving. The following chapter presents the methodology for the study of social grieving.

References

Bales, R. F. (1958). Task roles and social roles in problem-solving groups. In E. E. Maccoby, T. M. Newcomb, and E. L. Hartley (eds), *Readings in social psychology*. New York: Holt, Rinehart & Winston.

Beck, A. P. (1974). Phases in the development of structure in therapy and encounter groups. In D. A. Wexler and L. N. Rice (eds), *Innovations in client-centered therapy*. New York: John Wiley & Sons.

Benne, K. D. and Sheats, P. (1948). Functional roles of group members, *Journal of Social Issues, 4*, 41–9.

Bion, W. R. (1961). *Experience in groups*. New York: Ballantine Books.

Bowlby, J. (1975). Processes of mourning. In A. C. Carr and
B. Schoenberg (eds), *Grief: Selected readings*. New York: Health
Sciences.

Boyd, R. D. (1983). A matrix model of the small group, *Small Group
Behavior, 14*, 405–18.

Boyd, R. D. (1984). A matrix model of the small group: Part 2, *Small
Group Behavior, 15*, 233–50.

Brueggemann, W. (1978). *The prophetic imagination*. Philadelphia:
Fortress Press.

Campbell, J. (1968). *The hero with a thousand faces* (2nd edn). Princeton,
NJ: Princeton University Press.

Campbell, J. (1972). *Myths to live by*. New York: Viking Press.

Christ, C. P. (1989). Symbols of goddess and god in feminist theology.
In C. Colson (ed.), *The book of goddess past and present: An
introduction to her religion*. New York: Crossroad.

Dirkx, J. M. (1987). *The self-analytical group and the great mother:
A study of matriarchal consciousness in adult learning*. Unpublished
doctoral dissertation, University of Wisconsin-Madison.

Dunphy, D. C. (1974). Phases, roles, and myths in self-analytic groups.
In G. S. Gibbard, J. J. Hartman, and R. D. Mann (eds), *Analysis of
groups*. (pp. 300–14). San Francisco: Jossey Bass.

Durkin, H. (1964). *The group in depth*. New York: International
Universities Press.

Eagle, J. and Newton, P. M. (1981). Scapegoating in small groups: An
organizational approach, *Human Relations, 34*, 283–301.

Erikson, E. H. (1950). *Childhood and society*. New York:
W. W. Norton.

Gemmill G. and Kraus, G. (1988). Dynamics of covert role analysis: Small
Groups, *Small Group Behavior, 19*, 299–311.

Gibbard, G. S. (1974). Individuation, fusion, and role specialization.
In G. S. Gibbard, J. J. Hartman, and R. D. Mann (eds) *Analysis of groups*,
San Francisco: Jossey-Bass.

Gibbard, G. S. and Hartman, J. J. (1974). The significance of utopian
fantasies in small groups, *International Journal of Group Psychotherapy*,
23, 125–47.

Gibbard, G. S., Hartman, J. J., and Mann R. D. (eds) (1974). *Analysis of
groups*. San Francisco: Jossey-Bass.

Harding, M. E. (1965). *The 'I' and the 'Not-I': A study in the development of
consciousness*. Princeton, NJ: Princeton University Press.

Heschel, A. J. (1962). *The prophets*, 2 vols, New York: Harper & Row.

Jacobi, J. (1959). *Complex/archetype/symbol in the psychology of C. J. Jung*.
Princeton, NJ: Princeton University Press.

Jaques, E. (1974). Social systems as a defense against persecutory and
depressive anxiety. In G. S. Gibbard, J. J. Hartman, and R. D. Mann (eds)
Analysis of groups. San Francisco: Jossey-Bass.

Mann, R. D. (1967). *Interpersonal styles and group development*. New York:
John Wiley & Sons.

Myers, J. G. (1986). *Grief work as a critical condition for small group phase development*. Unpublished doctoral dissertation, University of Wisconsin-Madison.

Neumann, E. (1954). *The origins and history of consciousness*. Princeton, NJ: Princeton University Press.

Ogden, T. H. (1982). *Projective identification and psychotherapeutic technique*. New York: Jason Aronson.

Parkes, C. M. (1987). *Bereavement, studies of grief in adult life*. Madison, CT: International University Press.

Redl, F. (1942). Group emotion and leadership, *Psychiatry*, 5, 573–96.

Ruiz, P. (1972). On the perception of the 'mother-group' in T-groups, *International Journal of Group Psychotherapy*, 22, 488–91.

Samuels, A. (1985). *Jung and the post-Jungians*. New York: Routledge & Kegan Paul.

Scheidlinger, S. (1974). On the concept of the 'mother group'. *International Journal of Group Psychotherapy*, 24, 417–28.

Slater, P. E. (1955). Role differentiation in small groups, *American Sociological Review*, 20, 300–10.

Slater, P. E. (1966). *Microcosm: Structural, psychological and religious evolution in groups*. New York: John Wiley & Sons.

Smith, K. K. and Berg, D. H. (1987) *Paradoxes of group life: Understanding conflict, paralysis, and movement in group dynamics*. San Francisco: Jossey-Bass.

Toker, E. (1972). The scapegoat as an essential group phenomenon, *International Journal of Group Psychotherapy*, 22, 320–31.

Ulanov, A. B. (1971). *The feminine in Jungian psychology and in Christian theology*. Evanston, IL: Northwestern University Press.

Weber, M. (1946). The sociology of charismatic authority. In H. H. Gerth and C. W. Mills (eds) *From Max Weber: Essays in Sociology*. New York: Oxford University Press.

Whitmont, E. C. (1969). *The symbolic quest: Basic concepts of analytical psychology*. Princeton, NJ: Princeton University Press.

Whitmont, E. C. (1982). *Return of the goddess*. New York: Crossroad.

Chapter four

Grief work
A social dynamic in group transitions

J. Gordon Myers and Robert D. Boyd

In previous chapters we have discussed the archetypal themes which describe the sequential phases of group development. This chapter presents a way of looking at the transitions occurring between phases in group development. *change transformation*

We explain this in-between period as one of social grieving. Traditionally, grieving has been associated with the death of a loved one. Here grieving, conceptualized within the Jungian framework of death and rebirth, is made explicit in its application to transitions within the social systems of small groups.

The chapter will include five sections: (1) the rationale for studying grieving as a phenomenon occurring within the social system from the perspective of analytical psychology; (2) the theoretical basis for the framework presented in this chapter; (3) a description of the categories used to identify the manifestation of social grieving within a group transition; (4) a report on an empirical study designed to test the feasibility and validity of the methodology; (5) a presentation and discussion of the findings from the study.

Social grieving from the perspective of analytical psychology

Following the publication of the Matrix Model (Boyd, 1983, 1984), our initial work was primarily focused on determining its structural validity. Much of this work involved conducting empirical studies to test the existence of phase development in the identity and reality-adaptive realms. The problem was not investigating the basic idea of phase development, as this phenomenon is a widely recognized and accepted fact. The focus of our research studies investigated the existence of sequential sets of developmental phases which described the identity and reality-adaptive realms of a small group. It was not until later, after empirical evidence accumulated to corroborate the existence of these realms, that the question of transitional phenomena between phases arose. The question can be put in the following way: How does the transition occur from one group phase to the next?

The above account of our research would give the impression that our work progresses in an orderly manner where leaps of insights and intuition are not admitted. This is far from being the case and the present study is such an example. It was during that period when Boyd was working on archetypal phases in the small group that Myers observed that some group phenomena had similar configurations to processes of grieving that individuals experience with the death of a loved one. Our efforts were then divided between the two lines of research. The notion was formulated, after extensive discussions and reflections on group observations, that a group's transition from one developmental phase to the next was accomplished through grief work. It was at this point that the study was formally undertaken to determine if the transition processes between phases could be characterized as grief work.

The notion that a small group is an entity was discussed fully in Chapter One and will not be gone into again at this point. The significance of this idea, however, is critical to the type of phenomena that is under study and the manner in which observational categories are specified. We view grieving as an existential quality of human existence. Not only do individuals grieve, but also a small group, a social collectivity, and a society can be observed grieving on occasions of significant loss. We have taken this observation further, as a means to explain the developmental transitions in small groups. This explanation was then set as the conjecture to be tested empirically.

Placing grieving, or what we have come to speak of as social grieving, in the context of group development can be explained most adequately in the premises of analytical psychology. The movement of a group from one phase to the next sequential phase has the basic qualities of a transformation. The small group, as a social entity, moves from one state of being to another state which is based on some resolution of the former, and in turn it then has to deal with more complex issues. For example, the crisis of Autonomy vs. Shame/Doubt arises with the group's resolution of the crisis of Trust vs. Mistrust and the group issues and problems that then become the agendas of the group reflect the content of both stages. To stay with the example, when a group after much anguish has come to a resolution of the crisis of Trust vs. Mistrust, there is little enthusiasm initially to take on something new. There is a comfortable feeling in the group to stay where it is. In Jung's terms there has been a 'rebirth' from a 'death' but that transformation must invariably lead to the next life problem. Life does not stand still for an individual nor for a small group. That emotion of loss or moving out of a given state of being is a basic quality of a transformation. It is this quality of transformations, to a large extent, that identifies them as involving social grieving processes.

We took as our premiss that the transition between group phases was a transformation, the type Jung (1969) labelled as the 'expansion of consciousness'. Having established that as the conceptual basis for our study, we were then in a position to examine the merits of the notion of grieving as the manifest expression of transformations as experienced by the social system of a small group.

The theoretical basis for the framework

The intention of this chapter is not to pursue the work that has been done to establish the existence of the social system or that this social system may change, progress, or regress in patterned ways over time. We start this study from that point where the social system and phase development in groups are taken as given. Starting from that point our focus is to examine the social processes which enable the social system to successfully move from one phase of development to the next. Here it is asserted that the key to whether or not successful phase movement occurs depends in part upon the ability of the social system to facilitate its own grief work.

Grieving

A developmental crisis within the social system of a group specifically means that the social system's present stage of development is no longer adequate to the life of the group; the way the group has until now come to identify itself seems no longer to have relevance. A de-mythologizing of the status quo is underway, and an almost involuntary disruption of order is taking place. Faced with the existential necessity to change from within, the social system attempts to conserve what has been while coming to terms with the entrance of what will be. In struggling to come to grips with this developmental moment, the group's social system confronts loss. This phenomenon clearly parallels the processes of grieving that individuals experience as a result of the loss of a loved one. The psychological processes of adjusting to loss as described by Parkes (1972) and others provided an analogous account of the turmoil which we had observed in small groups during transitional periods. This insight lead us to propose the notion that social systems struggle through the stages of grief work in leaving one developmental phase in order to achieve the next.

Experiences of grief are evoked when the social system's ability to continue the established pattern of meaning is threatened and discontinuity is becoming more apparent than continuity. Grieving results from the exchange being made between the social system's prior and predictable way of interpreting reality and its not-yet, unpredictable future way. Grieving results from the classic conflict between conservation and innovation.

Grief, then, writes Peter Marris (1974, p. 28), is the

> expression of a profound conflict between contradictory impulses – to consolidate all that is still valuable and important in the past, and preserve it from loss; and at the same time, to re-establish a meaningful pattern of relationships, in which the loss is accepted. Each impulse checks the other, reasserting itself by painful stabs of actuality or remorse, and recalling the bereaved to face the conflict itself.

In the small group setting, grieving becomes the vehicle, the social system's best hope for ensuring continuity when the familiar patterns of operation are irretrievably broken. Potentially grief becomes a transporting process through which the group's social system may eventually arrive at its next stage of development.

The social system, therefore, is challenged to work through the loss, the disintegration of its former level of maturity. Grieving enables the social system to abstract from its past what was fundamentally of value, reconstitute that prized tradition, and reintegrate it into the present in a way that brings new meaning based on a new interpretation of its own identity as a System (Marris, 1974; Myers, 1986).

Grieving – a psychoanalytic perspective, 1900–1960

Principally because of the ground breaking work of Sigmund Freud, Melanie Klein, Erich Lindemann, and Edith Jacobson, the processes of grieving can now be studied as a sequence of subjective states which follow upon the experience of loss. Prior to Freud in particular, grieving was approached by studying depressive illness and melancholia in adults (Bowlby, 1975).

The psychical task of grieving outlined by Freud prior to 1920 focuses primarily upon detachment from what is no longer. This detachment, he asserts, sets in motion 'grave departures from the normal attitude to life' (1917, pp. 243–44). According to Freud (1917), these departures represent major characteristics commonly found in bereaved persons: profoundly painful dejection, cessation of interest in the outside world, loss of a capacity to love, and inhibition of activity.

In the late 1930s and early 1940s, Melanie Klein (1936) advanced a process perspective to the conversation by seeing grieving as a movement, accompanied by fear and guilt, from disorganization to reorganization. For her, the bereaved's task is to reestablish and re-integrate certain critical links with one's inner and outer world.

Edith Jacobson (1946), building on Melanie Klein, offers 'yearning for the past' as a further characteristic of grieving and suggests that the quality and texture of attachment to the lost relationship strongly con-dition mourning. In addition, she distinguishes between normal and pathological grieving based on the presence or absence of aggression.

Finally, Erich Lindemann's (1944) research and writing was especially significant for two reasons. First, his systematic study called attention to the array of responses to loss both in content and in process. He postulated that characteristics of mourning vary in intensity of appearance as well as in the timing of the procedure itself. Second, Lindemann's careful testing of experience provided the psychoanalytic community with confirmation of prior conjectures.

Until the 1950s, the study of depression made an occasional refer-ence to grief work. Currently, however, it is not uncommon to consider depression as an integral part of a much larger affective process called grieving or mourning (Bowlby, 1980). Healthy grieving processes are now viewed as instrumental in affecting a withdrawal of emotional concern from a lost relationship (Marris, 1974). The foregoing historical views regarding the task of grieving, its process, characteristics, and idiosyncratic tendencies need to be brought forward into contemporary psychoanalytic thought which introduces a developmental perspective on grieving.

The developmental perspective on grieving

John Bowlby, a British psychiatrist, writing some 40 years after Freud's contributions on mourning and 15 years after Lindemann's research, finds grief to be 'a peculiar amalgam of anxiety, anger, and despair following the experience of what is feared to be an irretrievable loss' (1961, p. 16). He observed that letting go of the old, the what-has-been, in order to make room for the new, the what-will-be, is a painful if not dangerous task for human beings.

The loss of a love-object, Bowlby asserts, unleashes a sequence of behaviors which is varied and yet predictable. This behavioral sequence embodies initial feelings of anxiety and anger, followed by pain and despair, and eventually resolved into hope. This movement may oscil-late violently at times; yet, according to Bowlby, a plainly observable movement can be discerned from protest through despair to some new equilibrium of feeling and behavior.

In Bowlby's studies (1961), grieving has an observable movement or predictable sequence of adaptive processes which fall into three distinct phases: (1) the urge to recover the lost object; (2) disorganization and disintegration; and (3) reorganization.

During phase one, the mourning person's response systems are strenuously centered upon the lost object while making oftentimes anger-filled efforts to recover it. Moreover, these efforts may continue, even though their fruitlessness is painfully evident to others and sometimes even to the grieving person. Blameful anger, directed toward the lost object, toward others, and even toward oneself, is unleashed during this initial phase. It is as if once the villain is found and punished, in a miraculous way the loss shall be recovered. Pining for the past becomes a form of denial, a resistance to acknowledging a union now broken. For Bowlby, then, 'repeated disappointment, weeping, anger, accusation and ingratitude are all features of the first phase of mourning, and are to be understood as expressions of the urge to recover the lost object' (1961, pp. 18–19).

When the momentum and movement of grieving continues with integrity, these response systems gradually surrender their attention to, and volatile search for, the lost object. The resulting surrender issues in phase two, which is characterized by the disorganization of personality accompanied by pain and despair (1961). The accumulated disappointments of phase one have taken their toll as hope of reunion fades and the past slips away. The attempts at fabricating what no longer exists give way to despair as the person's behavior becomes disorganized. Bowlby cites Lindemann's graphic description:

> There is restlessness, inability to sit still, moving about in an aimless fashion, continually searching for something to do. . . . (A)ctivities do not proceed in the automatic, self-sustaining fashion which characterizes normal work . . . There is . . . a painful lack of capacity to initiate and maintain organized patterns of behavior.
>
> (1961, p. 19)

Bowlby's basic concept of depression is critical to an understanding of his concept of grieving. For Bowlby, disorientation, at times verging on feelings of disintegration, is critical in dealing with loss; it signals depression, distinct from depressive illness, as the essence of the subjective state of phase two. He suggests that depression in grieving is relevant to other situations as well. 'In addition to our behavior being organized toward the maintenance of certain libidinal relationships, much of it is concerned with the reaching of work or recreational goals' (1961, p. 20).

When these interchanges between self and world, so necessary to goal-oriented achievement, are terminated, depression occurs. The termination may be due as much to what may have been gained as to what may have been lost when the goal having been successfully reached is now relegated to the past. 'No matter what the causes', asserts Bowlby, 'until such time as new patterns of inter-change have become organized towards a new object or goal we experience restlessness or apathy, with concurrent anxiety and depression' (1961, p. 20).

Bowlby's insight is that the depressive phase of grieving results from the disorganization of behavior patterns which in turn originate in any significant loss in the internal world of feelings or the external world of objects and goals. As an inescapable aspect of life, depression in grieving is normal.

Moreover, the behavioral processes which accompany depression are not only normal but also play an adaptive role. Human development – new linkages established with objects and goals – requires that inappropriate present linkages be broken down. Bowlby summarizes his view by drawing an analogy with a child at play:

> Just as a child playing with Meccano must destroy his construction before he can use the pieces again . . . so must the individual each time he is bereaved or relinquishes a major goal accept the destruction of a part of his personality before he can organize it afresh toward a new object or goal. Although unwelcome, such phases are a necessary part of being alive.
>
> (1961, p. 21)

As a footnote to the point and most germane to this study, Bowlby draws attention to learning:

> 'The painfulness of new ideas and our habitual resistance to them can also be seen in this context. The more far-reaching a new idea is the more disorganization of existing theoretical systems has to be tolerated before a new better synthesis of old and new can be achieved.
>
> (1961, p. 21)

Accordingly, phase two of the grieving process is disorganization of personality, accompanied by feelings of pain and despair and behaviors which portray withdrawal and chaos. In short, it is the phase characterized by depression.

Phase three, much less dramatic and thereby more difficult to describe, is called 'reorganization as adaptive processes'. This is the transitional phase to recovery 'during which reorganization takes place partly in connection with the image of the lost object and partly in connection with a new object or objects' (Bowlby, 1961, p. 21). To the degree that the relationship with the lost object has been restructured, the person experiences the final phase of grieving; in so far as a new object(s) has been discovered, the person enters into a new object relationship.

By restructuring, Bowlby means that over time the person in mourning is able to distinguish between those patterns of thinking, feeling, and behaving which are clearly no longer appropriate and those which can remain with integrity. The widow cited by Lindemann as saying; 'I used to put the kettle on and make tea for him. Or when I'd come home and find him not there, I'd think he had just gone out' (1944, p. 145), clearly articulates the patterns which must be allowed to fade. On the other hand, mourners who over time are able to abstract or bring forward those values and ways of being in-the-world which originated or developed in and through the relationship now lost have successfully identified the patterns which can persevere with integrity. By remaining bonded in this way, without seriously distorting reality, the lost love relationship is able to flourish anew (Bowlby, 1961).

John Bowlby's contribution stands firmly on the shoulders of those students of psychology before him who concerned themselves with understanding grief. Bowlby builds on their effort by carefully nuancing the phases of grieving, distinguishing depression in mourning from depressive illness, as well as by expanding the human context of what occasions grieving. In turn his work has been carried forward under the guidance of a British social psychiatrist, Colin Murray Parkes, whose enquiries into grieving have been conducted at the Tavistock Institute of Human Relations, London.

In the foreword to Colin Murray Parkes's book, *Bereavement: Studies of grief in adult life*, John Bowlby cites Parkes for giving 'attention equally to the promotion of scientific understanding [regarding grieving] and to the development of professional skills based upon it' (1987, p. 8). Parkes set out to investigate the typical shape of grief. Standing with Bowlby, he attempts to move the study of grieving out of the realm of physical and mental illness and into the life fabric of healthy human existence.

The study which proved most useful to our efforts at conceptualizing grieving was the study Parkes conducted with 22 widows in Boston. Each widow participated in a standardized interview at least five times in the 13 months following the death of her husband. By means of this longitudinal strategy, information was then systematically gathered regarding the process of grieving and its phase development over time (Parkes, 1975).

Parkes sees the movement of grief from one phase to the next as rarely distinct; also, he points out that characteristics common to a former phase may persist into a later phase. In general, though, Parkes's findings confirm Bowlby's in terms of the phasic process of grief. However, he identifies four phases of grieving to Bowlby's three (1972).

The additional phase comes at the beginning of grieving and is characterized by a state of numbness which gives way at times to outbursts of extreme behavior or 'panic attacks'. One of the widows studied said: 'I felt numb and solid for a week. . . . Everything goes hard inside you . . . like a heavy weight.' Several times during her first month of grieving, another woman ran out of her home panic stricken and took refuge with friends next door. She described herself during this period as so fragile that 'if somebody gave me a good tap I'd shatter into a thousand pieces. . . . I felt desperate' (Parkes, 1970, p. 65).

Parkes summarized his findings for phase one:

> Episodes of panic or distress alternate with longer periods of numbness or restless 'busyness'. Feelings are seldom admitted fully to consciousness but when they do 'break through' they are experienced as overwhelming or as harming . . . the very fact of the loss is commonly avoided in one way or another.
>
> (1970, p. 65)

This identification of an initial phase of grief seemed so sound to John Bowlby that he later revised his classifications to bring them into harmony with Parkes's conclusions (Bowlby, 1980).

According to Parkes, phase two of grieving is like phase one in that it is situated along a continuum of feeling; however, in phase two the movement is from 'yearning' at the one end to 'protest' at the other end.

Yearning and protest both represent consequences of the emerging conflict of phase two: searching for the lost object (holding onto the past) versus letting-go of inappropriate behavior (being open to the full reality of the present). For Parkes, this characteristic searching is exemplified in its four components. The first component is 'pining and preoccupation with thoughts of the deceased person'. This represents the key sign that grieving is taking place; it stands as the central and pathognomic feature of grief. Second, those in mourning focus their attention toward places and objects which are associated with the lost person. Third, there emerges a 'mind set' for what has been lost so that the grieving person attends to those stimuli which suggest the continued presence of the lost object while ignoring those stimuli which contradict that presence. The fourth component is weeping, accompanied by a growing degree of restlessness. Tearfulness is interpreted by Parkes as both an attempt to reunite with the lost object and to reach out for help. The accompanying restlessness develops into frustration and anger and becomes a demonstration of protest in this phase (Parkes, 1970).

Protest, which falls at the far end of the continuum for phase two, is described as general irritability or bitterness. Anger directed toward self, usually present as guilt; anger toward others for rather slight offenses; even anger toward the deceased – 'Why did he do this to me?' – all appear during this phase. Parkes claims that protest is commonly associated with the general feeling that the world has become an 'insecure and potentially dangerous place'. Exaggerated protest or irrational anger flows from the 'sense of insecurity and frustration [resulting] from the loss of a major source of support, [and] the wish to bring under control the impersonal destructive events of the bereavement.' (1972, p. 71).

Over time, as pining and protest diminish and each pattern of inappropriate behavior is confronted with reality and thereby recognized as useless, a period of uncertainty, drifting, and apathy follows. Parkes agrees with Bowlby in calling this third phase disorganization and despair. The characteristic emotion is depression which Parkes treats in like manner to Bowlby (Parkes, 1972).

Phase four involves gaining a new identity, which means 'learning new solutions and finding new ways to predict and control happenings within the life-space. It also means seeking a fresh place in the hierarchy, [which involves] reassessing one's powers and possessions, and finding out how one is viewed by the rest of the world' (1972, pp. 104–5). Thus the old ways of thinking, feeling, and behaving, those prior assumptions now judged as inappropriate and unnecessary, are surrendered, the individual is free to 'take stock and to make a new start'. As certain assumptions from the past are judged ineffective in the present, the person's old identity or prior way of seeing self and the world dissolves and is gradually replaced by a different identity.

For Parkes, then, phase four emanates from a back and forth movement which on the one hand involves directly attacking the problem through painful reality testing, while on the other postpones one's search for identity and meaning. The former enhances perception and thought regarding one's past, present, and future, while the latter provides a harbor for rest and safety.

What is it that allows a person to journey successfully through the pain of the first three phases to the successful resolution of grief and the hope-filled arrival at phase four? Parkes (1972) answers this question by proposing that mitigation, or more specifically mitigating elements or defense mechanisms, trigger intermittent remissions from the pain of grief.

These elements or positive, enabling forces housed within phases one through three are used to bracket the full reality of loss, to suspend belief if only for a moment. A more common term for mitigation is defense; for Parkes, some elements of defense are essential 'in helping [the person] to regulate the quantity of novel, unorganized, or in other respects disabling information an individual is handling at a given time' (1970, p. 74). In a sense, such mitigating factors as denial, loss of feeling, dreaming, selective forgetting, continuing to feel the presence of the lost person, and withdrawal all serve as problem-solving devices. They buy time; more especially they enable appropriate distancing from potential danger and enhance a person's tolerance for biting sorrow. In this way they form a strategy for survival and for growth.

With Parkes's contribution, the portrait of the grieving person has come into sharper focus. His work has expanded our understanding. The physical and emotional reactions, the development of a maturing identity, the search for meaning, the attempts to avoid reality, and the gradual building up of a new sense of an ego–self relationship are principal elements of grieving.

Concluding comment

Considering the attention given to the subject of grief work by Freud over 60 years ago, coupled with the classical research study by Lindemann some 40 years ago, it still remains a puzzle that the psychoanalytic community has not focused more interest upon grief as a major mental health hazard and perhaps more significantly a universal basis for personal growth and development. With the contributions of John Bowlby and Colin Murray Parkes, much of that oversight has been addressed.

It should also be noted that a significant amount of empirical research has been conducted on the theory of grieving and its critical role in personal and social change. These studies have proceeded in two directions: (1) to extend the concept of loss beyond separation from concrete attachments (for example, the death of a loved one) to include situations that fundamentally involve the anticipated or actual invalidation of central assumptions and interpretations about the way the world in which the individual lives really works (Carr, 1975; Marris, 1974; Myers, 1986; Weinstein and Platt, 1973); and (2) to extend the understanding of grief reactions beyond the proximate time of loss to several years beyond the loss. A variety of studies have found evidence of loss and grief reactions among individuals in such disparate situations as urban relocation and immigration (Fried, 1963; Marris, 1974).

These and other studies have not been reported in detail here because the primary intent was to conceptualize grieving as it applies to the phase development of a small group's social system. The works of Bowlby and Parkes were seen as contributing most significantly to that end. The major task was to discern from their work a sequence of portraits, which portray a group's social system in transit from one phase of its development to the next. This has been accomplished and is discussed in the next section of this chapter. Further documentation of Bowlby's and of Parkes's work through the detailed discussion of other related empirical investigations has not been attempted in this chapter. It is noted that further studies do exist and a rich source of these is found in *The place of attachment in human behavior* by Parkes and Stevenson-Hinde (1982), *Holding on or letting go* by Osherson (1980), and *Loss and change* by Marris (1974).

The methodology to identify social grieving in small groups

The works of Bowlby and Parkes provided a firm theoretical structure as well as extensive descriptive materials. These materials, as rich as they were, did not address the phenomenon of grieving that we believe occurs in social systems. At this point, the task before us was to develop a set of descriptors which would identify the stages of grieving in a small group's social system. Such a set of descriptors would have to be consistent with Bowlby's and Parkes's works if they were to serve as the theoretical framework and the descriptors would have to be empirically grounded in the sense that such descriptive observations could be made on the dynamics within small groups. These demands necessitated an integration of the research conducted on individuals with research conducted on social systems of small groups. These tasks then defined the project that was undertaken.

Our first task was to develop a set of descriptors for each stage of grieving as they could be observed in a small group's social system. A coding manual was developed as a product of this work.

Formulating descriptors – establishing content validity

Two investigators assembled and reviewed resource material which described behaviors of bereavement. Based on these resource materials, the investigators then identified specifiers which described grief work. These specifiers or descriptors were phrased in terms that would reflect behaviors occurring in small groups. The investigators were careful to maintain a direct link between the specifiers and the resource materials on bereavement. As a further check on content validity, another knowledgeable person was asked to serve as a judge on the content validity. This third judge, using the same resource materials, reviewed the specifiers, and indicated where modifications were needed. In this way, the descriptors were modified three times until there was total agreement between the three judges.

The four phases of social grieving

Phase one

- -
Numbness   and   Panic

The initial phase of the process of social grieving is characterized by an oscillating movement from a feeling of numbness which gives way at times to panic. In viewing the social system of the group during this phase, an observer may note a period of bluntness, an absence of feeling, as if the group were anesthetized. Activity appears to be automatic; the social system seems dazed and distant as if what is going on simply is not registering, not getting through. The group seems to be waiting endlessly for something to happen. This emotionally blank period, however, oscillates with outbursts of panic-laden activity. In a highly scattered way, the group communicates a sense of dashing about, attempting in vain to fill up its life with operations. Whether the group is in a place of dullness or compulsively moving about in a panic-stricken way, the unreality is apparent – the group appears suspended in time.

This phase of grieving is illustrated in the following description of a small group's interactions. Certain topics had been proposed as possible group agendas during the first hour of the group. None of them appeared to capture the interest of the members. Although they continued to talk about the merits of pursuing these topics the group was unable to decide on any one with any sense of commitment. A member, appearing to be joking, described their indecision as the tyranny of democracy. The awkward laughter that followed his comment gave further evidence that the group was waiting for the designated leader to take over the direction of the group – a role he had stated at the outset he was not going to take. The members were unable to accept this role and continued to believe that their helplessness would have him give up this 'experimental project' and become what a leader should be. Although he apparently heard their appeal there was no indication in his behavior that he was going to assume direction for the group. Following this incident the energy seemed to have gone out of the group. Although the members were obviously disappointed and angry at the leader they did not openly express these feelings, rather they became restless. This period was followed by some members proposing activities which were clearly of the nature of busy work. The task before the social system was to recognize and give up its culture of dependency – a task it was finding difficult to accept.

The six descriptions which follow provide anchoring terms that portray the group during this first phase of grieving:

- a restless almost hyperactive busyness
- avoidance of feelings
- a loss of the traditional pattern of relating (e.g. How do you behave toward an authority figure who acts as if he does not have authority?)
- a loss of energy
- a feeling that the system has shut down due to a severe blow
- a shocked sense of sudden calamity (e.g. If we give up our culture of dependency, we will surely have chaos.)

Phase two

Pining   and   Protest

The second phase of the process of social grieving within the group as a whole is similar to the first in that a rhythmical movement is also present. During the second phase, however, the oscillation is between a painful pining or yearning for that which has been lost and protest that the loss should have occurred. The anger seen during this phase expresses itself as irritability and bitterness and is not as acute as the aggression which emerges during the next phase.

In viewing the social system at this point, an observer may note an apparent preoccupation with what has been in the group's social realm and an attempt to search for and cling to a lost object. The social system seems to have lost its home and wishes painfully to return to it. Finding itself in a strange environment, the social system repeatedly circles back over earlier experiences of its life, as if this scanning will keep alive the hope of finding the safe place of an earlier time.

Frustration emerges as the social system remains unsuccessful in its search. Often blame results as the impression is given that it is someone's fault; someone is responsible for this loss. During this phase, the theme of protest is most clearly exhibited by the group appearing to be furious with both the leader and with itself.

An example of this phase of grieving occurring within the social system of a group is given in the following account. The group had established the Good Mother as the predominant theme of the social system. It had spent two full sessions enjoying the warmth and general sustenance that is provided by this theme. There has arisen, however, a movement toward the claiming of autonomy for the group. The social system appears to be torn between returning to the sense of security experienced with the Good Mother theme and moving on to the challenges perceived in the next developmental stage. There is a yearning to go back and at the same time a protest that attempts to deny the reality that returning to what has been is impractical. Some members expressed the feeling of sadness – of having left something behind that is very dear to them. This characterized the social system, as did the criticism made of Professor B's metaphors which the members saw as negative comments on the group's achievements. They blamed themselves for listening to his metaphors and they blamed him for his destructive interventions.

The six descriptions which follow capture the essential nature of grieving in the second phase:

- an unfulfilled searching which leads to frustration and then anger
- a yearning for the past

- a hollow emptiness
- a need to blame
- a painful wishing to have something restored
- endless legitimizing of prior group experiences.

Phase three

- -

Disorganization   and   Despair

The third phase of the process of social grieving is characterized by an oscillating movement from disorganization to despair. The group's social system appears disoriented in its mode of operation. Earlier attempts at sustained activities have proved disappointing; present attempts at initiating systematic patterns of industry have collapsed; activities no longer build one from another. Despairing that anything worthwhile can come from the present endeavors, the social system appears on the verge of collapse. A climate of apathy and depression abounds.

In this phase we observe the group as a social system expressing grieving as in the following case study. The group appeared unable to return to the theme of the Good Mother yet equally unable to move to the next theme of the Separation of the Great Parents. From another perspective, the group from the vantage point of the social system had felt good about the establishment of Trust in the group but now to move onto Autonomy vs. Shame/Doubt appeared as yet an impossible task. In the face of this inertia the group vacillated between the expression of disorganization on the one hand and despair on the other.

Certain key phrases may serve to identify a general portrait of the social system within the third phase of grieving;

- painful disappointment
- boredom
- a mood of despair
- a feeling of collapse
- unexpressed anger
- depression.

Phase four

- -

Restabilization   and   Reintegration

Phase four of social grieving emerges from the psychological struggles toward reintegration resulting in the reformulation of meaning and social identity coming out of phases one through three. The rhythmical movement of phase four is between a hope-filled sense of recovery based on a reconstruction of meaning and a reorganization of task procedures and ways of being together as a social system. If the group has been able to tolerate the extreme buffeting of emotion, the seemingly endless searching and reexamining, the prolonged frustration which at times has broken out into feelings of anger and depression, then gradually it also becomes able to recognize and to accept the loss of its prior existential structure. In this phase previous patterns and social modes that had governed and directed behavior have been recognized and accepted as now being inappropriate for present actions and the resolution of immediate issues and agendas. An integration of what has been with what now must be ushers in a new formulation of meaning. A new social system, restructured from its past, comes into being as it defines the issues of its new crisis.

Such a development is described in the following account. There had been a sense that the group had not been getting anywhere during its last three sessions. Some members who appeared to be voicing the quality of the group's life talked about it as being analogous to the play *Waiting for Godot*. In the initial period of the following session the discussion went back to their reference to the play. In the discussion which followed there began to appear, slowly at first, but steadily growing, a firmer conviction both in the way the members were beginning to express their ideas and to what was being shared. The discussion was dealing with power, who had it and who could exercise it in the life of a small group. It dealt with commitment to oneself and to others as a way to express autonomy. This was the manifest content and the latent content was a clear reintegration of the social structure as a social force. As a group, they could direct their lives and the leader had power over the group only to the extent that the social system would allow and they were the social system. The reintegration of the social system empowered the membership. Their struggles through the phases of grieving had given to the social system a new mode of operating and to each member a personal transformation.

The six descriptions which follow accurately portray the social system of a group during this fourth phase of grieving:

- a deepened investment
- a mood of hope-filled optimism
- a sense of togetherness
- a renewed sense of meaning and purpose
- action under the guidance of a new awareness
- action on the basis of a new identity.

A concluding note

Special attention must be given to the rhythmical movement among the four phases of grieving. This movement, called oscillation, is observed not only within the various phases but between the phases as well. To say that four phases of grieving may be observed is not to say that all four appear one at a time and always in a sequential order in their initial expression. Overlapping does occur between phases, and one phase may loop back over a prior phase before moving to the next phase. The phases do have an ascending period which marks their sequential pattern. Our observations have thus suggested the conjecture that for a small group's social system to successfully move from one stage of development to the next all four phases must be negotiated.

An empirical study

Our aim from the outset had been to test our work empirically. There were two interrelated questions to which we sought answers. First, did social grieving occur in small groups as we had proposed in our schema? The answer to this question depended upon demonstrating that knowledgeable observers could identify the categories of grieving as they occurred in a small group. Second, were the group transitions or phases of group development associated with the phase sequence of social grieving? Whether we would pursue this second question would be determined by the findings of our first enquiry. With these questions before us, our next step was to design an empirical study to obtain answers to the questions which have been posed.

The group selected was a self-study group. Several such groups have been conducted in our Group Dynamics Laboratory at the University of Wisconsin-Madison, and the one chosen for this project was composed of nine women and three men. The group met for ten weekly sessions each two and a half hours in length. The leader took a non-directive role which is described in some detail in a later chapter. His interventions did not address the processes of social grieving and none of the literature describing the course would have alerted the members to these processes and the nature of the study that was being conducted. All of the sessions were videotaped and these were to be used later as the data base for the study.

The video tapes were to be analyzed for two types of data. First, it was necessary to determine whether there were times in the life of the group when group transitions or group phase developments occurred. Determining the presence of group transitions was a critical step if we were to test the conjecture that social grieving was associated with periods of group phase development. Second, the video tapes would then be analyzed to determine whether the phases of social grieving were in evidence. The achievement of these tasks depended upon coders who had to be adequately trained to meet the requirements for the study. There were two sets of coders – one set determined the existence of phases of group development; the other set determined the phases of social grieving.

The methodology for coding phases of group development has been used in many studies that have been conducted in the Group Dynamics Laboratory. The methodology follows the general format of delineating the characteristics of the various phases and then the coder employs these specifications to differentiate and identify the particular phase the group is in at a given time. The reader is referred to studies by Boyd *et al.* (1980), White (1976), and Davie (1971). The coders were tested on their knowledge of the methodology and on inter-coder reliability. The coders, after a training period, demonstrated that they had met the standards which were set for this methodology.

Once it was demonstrated that the two coders who were to analyze the video tapes for phases of group development had achieved an acceptable level of competency they were given the task of coding the entire ten sessions of the study. Tests of reliability were conducted systematically throughout their work of coding the sessions. Their coding of the sessions identified occurrences of group phase development. Having established the existence of transition periods, the conditions were present to test for phases of social grieving. The question could now be posed: Were the four phases of social grieving associated with the transitions which had been observed in the phase development of the group?

To answer that question it was necessary to apply the coding procedure to the video tapes of the sessions to determine the existence of social grieving. The first task then became the training of coders in the social grieving methodology. Two graduate students were chosen who were unaware of the nature of the study and who, during the course of the study, were only aware of their role in the study. As was the case with the coders of phase development, every effort was made to avoid indicating that there was a progressive sequence to the phases. Specific series of steps were taken in the training of coders (Myers, 1986). At the end of the training period they were tested against the standards set as the accepted level of performance. As part of that procedure, an inter-coder reliability check was conducted. The results of the reliability test showed an 80 percent level of agreement between the two coders. These tests of the coders performance demonstrated that they were applying the methodology accurately and that they were highly consistent in their codings. Following the training period, inter-coders agreement studies were conducted during the coding of the video tapes. There was an 89 percent level of agreement between the two coders in identifying which of the four phases of social grieving was present within the 21 coded segments of 50 minute duration. The paired agreement was at the 69 percent level on the codings which identified the most prominent phase of social grieving. These results gave us a sufficient level of confidence in the coding data to move forward with the interpretation of the findings. This discussion rested not only upon the acceptable level of inter-coder agreement but also on the many steps that the coders were required to take in coding in order to determine the most prominent phase in a particular segment of time. In addition, the sheer volume of data they had to deal with must be taken into account in considering the level of inter-coder agreements.

Specific steps were taken in the coding of the group sessions and it is necessary to have an understanding of these procedures in order to follow the discussion of the findings presented in the next section. Each session of two and one half hours was divided into three coding periods of 50 minutes each. The coders' task was first to identify the type or types of social grieving in evidence, that is being expressed in the group, during a given period. The coders then employed a set of criteria to determine which of those expressed types of social grieving, if there were more than one present in the period, was the most prominent: that is to say, the phase of social grieving that the group was observed to be primarily focused upon and working through. Thus one or two designations was given to each coding, either the phase was most prominent or it was less prominent. Therefore in any one coding period a coder may observe and record: (1) no evidence of social grieving, (2) one type of social grieving as most prominent, (3) more than one type present and with one being more prominent than the others, (4) types of social grieving present but none observed to be prominent.

An analysis and discussion of the findings

The findings from phase development analysis told the story of a group striving to mature; it also provided the evidence by which to demarcate the beginning (sessions two, three, and four), the middle (sessions five through eight), and end (session nine) of a significant experience of change within the group. With this evidence in place, the coding and then the analyzing of the group's transitional, or in-between, state could begin in order to determine evidence of social grieving.

As discussed earlier, the presence of social grieving during a group's transitional period was tested by a coding procedure which resulted in judgements concerning the presence of grieving within the group's developmental periods. The findings demonstrate that grief work was present when the group was in a transitional period moving from one phase of group development to another phase of group development. This evidence is based upon the extensive observational notes of the coders and their recorded judgements but in the discussion which follows these observations will be presented in a case study narrative form to help the reader better gain a sense of the transitional dynamics within the group's experience. The four phases of social grieving will be identified in the narrative by a Roman numeral(s) in parentheses.

Since the group's first meeting was an orientation session, our case study begins with the group's second meeting. The group appeared disoriented and drifting while trying to establish a purpose or reason for being together. The group's apparent uncertainty as to direction was accompanied by anger expressed indirectly through humor and sarcasm (III). Early on in the meeting, Brian, a group member, spoke of the group's style of communication as 'disjointed ramblings'. When group members ignored Brian's criticism, he called for 'more risk taking and trust' within the group. Members continued to resist Brian's remarks by offering testimonials to the value and importance of their own dis-organization as well as blaming Brian, himself (II). Rather than explore the issue of risk-taking and trust, the group continued to search its past, talk was about what had been in the group's life (II) as if by this way it hoped to find answers which would relieve the growing pressure to get on track. This led to further frustration, irritability, and disorientation (II & III). Eventually, a recovery period began to surface during the second 50 minute period of the meeting. The group slowly began to reassess its situation which, during the final period, led to a new sense of purpose and a deepened investment in the group's life. Group members began responding directly and openly to Brian's challenge. The conversation focused on trust not in the abstract but in the concrete communication and conduct of the group. By the close of meeting three, the group had moved to an increased cohesiveness and a renewed sense of meaning (IV). In addition, the group, as seen through the lens of phase develop-ment, was favorably resolving its developmental crisis of Trust vs. Mistrust. Therefore, according to two teams of coders operating in-dependently, phase four of grieving, Recovery and Reorganization, coincided with the group's phase development resolution. The climate within the group had changed dramatically. The earlier back and forth arguments in which Brian had served as a focal person for the group had been resolved and in the process a growth in trust had been achieved. Meeting four found the group once again in transition, this time working to resolve the question of power and authority. Brian challenged the group to risk more, but this time 'to stand on its own', to 'quit waiting around to be led'. As in the group's earlier transition, social grieving once again was evident. Characterized by a preoccupation with the past meeting (II), the group was primarily trying to make sense of its life by returning to an earlier time when its experience as a group was more certain and less precarious. Members reviewed their progress to such an extent as to memorialize the past (II). This constant searching into what had been only escalated their uncertainty as to what was. Brian con-tinued to press his opinion. Several group members appeared angry, agitated, threatened by Brian, describing his behaviors as attempts to 'control' and 'manipulate' the group. The group was drifting from topic to topic with no apparent direction to its discussion. The fourth meeting ended in disappointment (III); the group appeared disillusioned at the prospect of anything worthwhile occurring as a result of their life together as a group (III).

The issue of leadership replaced the topic of trust during the fifth meeting. Brian challenged the group to 'greater self-reliance'. For him, the group was being too tentative and safety conscious. The climate was characterized by disillusionment. The group's reason for existence, and its prior feeling of consolation arrived at during meeting three, was collapsing into apathy.

During the initial period of meeting six, Brian continued his critical challenging of the group, but this time with more vision. 'We are all teachers and learners and leaders together', he pleaded. The group responded by once again becoming preoccupied with the past, searching in their experience for some form of lost meaning; blaming and fault-finding continued (II). In addition, throughout the remainder of meeting six, the group appeared exhausted from its 'desert wandering'; a state of inertia settled in. They became disoriented and conversation nearly came to a halt. During the middle portion of meeting six, the group appeared in shock, acting as if a major calamity had occurred. As the inertia continued, so did the apathy, disillusionment and disjunctive activity. A biting bitterness set into the group's emotion. Brian accused the group of 'following Professor B like sheep'. One member accused him of 'manipulation', another member as 'phony', while still another as a 'clouded intellectual'. Most denied Brian's accusations and asserted their freedom to follow or ignore Professor B's leadership.

Meeting seven resembled six in several ways. The group continued to remain in despair throughout (III). But in meeting seven, though, the group was struggling with the question of power and leadership. The group was burning up energy as it continued to deny that Professor B's style of leadership had any influence upon it. Instead, the group un-leashed its pent-up anger onto one of its own members. This scape-goating activity only further distracted and disoriented the group (III). The despair deepened (III).

Toward the close of meeting seven, Helen, a group member, offered a metaphor to help the group imagine an alternative way of being together as a group. She related a story of her watching a volleyball team practice and compared that to the group's life. The team members had been avoiding the shots, afraid of taking them or, more importantly, afraid of setting up shots and relying on the team to follow through. In a relaxed manner, Helen suggested that the group had been taking easy shots by not confronting the most pressing issue they faced and by not setting up passes and depending on other group members to help them out or support them. Speaking in a quiet, almost relieved way, she suggested that the group members did not have to continue to bicker and avoid issues if they would only take risks and support one another.

The group responded to Helen's metaphor and explanation with a new openness. One member invited the group to look 'beyond Professor B's style of leadership to the group's perception of and reaction to' that style. During the final segment of meeting seven, a sense of new energy and hope began to emerge (IV). (It should be noted that just at this time, as the coders for group development saw the group beginning to face the reality of its problem with authority, so too, the coders of social grieving saw the group adopting new courses of action with increased cohesiveness.)

In meeting eight, development continued and centered around the issue of authority and leadership. The question the group members explored, dropped, and returned to time and again involved the meaning and expression of power in the here and now of their existence as a group. This 'approach-avoidance' group phenomenon was evident throughout meeting eight as the group initially demonstrated a strong recovery and later once again became disorganized.

Toward the end of meeting eight, the group's momentum was building to a successful completion of its journey through the four phases of grieving, and the group was about to enter phase four more fully. A third group member, Jeff, acting as a focal person, encouraged the group to 'decide how power and authority within the group would be shared'. The group responded to Jeff by coming together more tightly with a deepened sense of investment (IV).

The anticipated breakthrough became a reality in meeting nine; the group favorably resolved the Autonomy Phase of its development. During this final meeting, the group was acting on the basis of a new identity, an increased cohesiveness, and a deepened investment in its own life (IV) was evident. The group was once again attacking problems, generating solutions, and adopting courses of action with a renewed sense of meaning and purpose. (Here again it should be noted that there was total agreement between the coders concerning the developmental achievement of the group and its successful negotiation of the four phases of grief work.)

Implications for theory and practice

Theoretical implications

The theory of small group development is advanced by linking social grieving to identity phase development within a group's social system.

Though grieving has been identified earlier as important for personal development and for societal change, this particular four-pronged portrait of bereavement had not been tested in the small group setting, nor had it been explicitly explored within the Matrix Model which provided this study's conceptual setting concerning the constitution of a small group.

A careful search of the literature has not detected any investigation which explores the in-between period of a group's transitional state nor finds grief work as instrumental or even associated with small group phase development. For instance, the classic study conducted by Bennis and Shepard (1956) identified the fact that groups move through phases of development, but posited no explanation as to the social system's dynamics which makes this movement possible. This study, therefore, stands as a contribution and not a replication of prior investigations.

The fundamental insight which is evident in the association of social grieving and small group phase development is the dynamic equation of death and rebirth. During the group's developmental movement it struggles with the question of its social identity and corporate mode of making meaning. Prior assumptions no longer seem relevant. Former beliefs which provided assurances concerning the group's identity and capacity to act in a coordinated manner have decayed. The death of part of the group's reason for existence must be grieved if new life is to come forward. This perspective moves the theory of group development more closely toward the truth that death and life are intricately and mysteriously related. In short, this investigation identifies an essential link between small group phase development and social grieving.

The knowledge of grief work serves the theory of small group development by taking what previously had appeared to be a random explosion of disparate feelings and behaviors and identifying these as an integrated and comprehensive process of communal grieving. Group members, acting as a social system, are seen as expressing their sorrow; contradictory impulses characterized by attempts to either escape into the past or leap into the future are eventually acknowledged as unworkable solutions to the present distress. In viewing the group as a social system through the lens of grief work, one witnesses the group discerning what from its past is to be let go of and what is to be held on to as it moves toward a new and viable construction of identity and meaning. This kind of knowledge which generates this mode of interpretation presents a new dimension to the theory of small group development.

Practical implications

The theoretical implications discussed above carry the potential for practical action. The knowledge generated in this study expands and alters our awareness of the personal and collective thoughts, feelings, and behaviors occurring during a time of change in the small group setting.

The knowledge which emerges forms a working model, a kind of communal anthropology, which demonstrates a new way of looking at the dynamics of group life during a transitional period. Social grieving as formulated, tested, and analyzed in this study is intended to offer a new point of view, rather than a ready-made set of programmatic answers. Yet, programmatic understandings can be developed which can guide a leader's interventions and instruct members in the evolving dynamics of small groups. Rather than make specific recommendations here, however, the following discussion describes where and in what way an understanding of loss, seen through the lens of social grieving, might well inform the choice of action.

This study makes the point that during an identity transition within the social system of a group, the coherence of social structure based upon fundamental assumptions and beliefs about the personal and collective management of reality begins to disintegrate under the pressure of anomalies and contradictions the social system cannot assimilate. As this decay and disintegration continues, relationships within the group become increasingly confused, irregular, and difficult to predict. The group's ability to make decisions, solve problems, and plan its future is seriously jeopardized.

Grief work, carried out in the group setting when the capacity to make meaning or to attach previously composed meaning to present events is critically blocked or seriously impaired, is not by itself the solution. It does not satisfactorily resolve from the outset the group's problems which circle around the absence of meaning, purpose, and identity. As a way of seeing, however, social grieving asserts confidently that the group's present crisis can be resolved, that the anomalies presently active are not intractable. New forms of meaning, purpose, and identity can be worked out as predicted in phase four of the grieving process. There is hope.

Phase four of social grieving represents a reinterpretation of both past and future so as to restore a thread of continuity, a sense of abiding human purpose. Like the development of knowledge itself, grieving incorporates past experience, but sets it in a radically different framework of explanation which promises and provides a better sense of the group's conflictual situation.

In addition to providing hope in an otherwise despairing situation, grief work also makes a strategic contribution. The length and intensity of a transitional period is dependent upon the way the group's present crisis is articulated and contained within a supportive structure. The central thrust of this study is that grief work insists upon an identification of the nature of the crisis and also provides a meaningful structure to a transitional situation whose outcome is still clouded by risk and ambivalence.

Social grieving becomes the organizing principle of individual behavior and group activity as group members, acting collectively, come to terms with the immediate demands of their developmental challenge. Group members can take meaning from their struggles if they have the knowledge that grief work is an evolving dynamic in the developmental life of a group. Interpreting the chaos of the developmental moment as grieving dramatizes the transition by making of it a meaningful sequence of actions; the working out of this sequence becomes a form of group discernment or negotiation in which individual members acting as a social system can formulate a new communal identity and reason for existence.

Several other practical implications flow from this study's fundamental assumption concerning the implicit bond between death and rebirth. First, a dynamic understanding of grieving may better prepare group members, designated leaders, and trained facilitators to withstand the strain of change inherent within the group's patterns of growth and development. Beyond coping, the clarity which results from accurately assessing the nature of the stresses and confusing reactions evoked during this critical period may well give meaning to the pain of growth within the group and also encourage members, designated leaders, and trained facilitators to manage change differently.

This 'dynamic understanding of grieving' is knowledge which spills over into effective action. It provides group participants, whatever their roles may be, with an ability to see into and to identify accurately the dynamics of social change occurring within the group's transformative journey. Knowledge used in this way enables 'seeing' and 'solving' to become one inseparable event.

A concluding statement

The notion of social grieving arose from two lines of enquiry. Group phase development had been an area of research in the empirical study of the Matrix Model theory. A number of studies had given validity to the conjecture that small groups progress through a series of stages or phases of identity development. These findings encouraged our efforts and further investigations were undertaken to determine whether we were correct in positing a more daring conjecture, namely that small groups had stages of consciousness development analogous to those that individuals experience. But there was always the question: What processes were associated with these transitions? Myers proposed, at this time, from his readings of Bowlby and Parkes, that he believed grieving was an essential dynamic in those learning which involved fundamental changes in what and how we know. In subsequent discussions with Boyd, together they related the phenomenon of grieving to the transformative notion of death and rebirth. This conceptualization of grieving led them to the explanation that group transitions were always associated with grief work. It was at this point that the concept of social grieving took form.

Myers, with the assistance of Boyd, undertook a study to test the notion that grief work was associated with transitions in phase development. A category schema was developed specifying four phases of social grieving which drew heavily upon the works of Bowlby and Parkes. Once the schema was in place it was then possible to design an empirical study to test the conjecture that the sequential phases of social grieving were associated with the phase transitions in small groups. This project was then undertaken.

The findings demonstrated that the schema of the four phases of social grieving can be successfully employed to code the grief work of a small group. The results provided evidence which corroborated the conjecture that had been advanced. Although the evidence is supportive, it is clearly recognized that more extensive testing of the conjecture is needed before it can be accepted as a well-grounded explanation.

The next logical step in our research program would have been to design a study to test the notion that grief work is involved in the personal transformations of individual group members. Case material appeared to support this notion. Sometimes opportunities for research arise, however, that must be taken when they become available. Jean Rannells Saul (Rannells 1986) was given the opportunity to study a group of women who were members of a university course which had as its topic the examination of female deity images as a way to better understand their self-definition as women. It was our view that such explorations must involve aspects of individuation. This systematic study of individuation suggested six episodic themes of individuation. The chapter which follows explains these themes and relates them to the behaviors of individual members of a small group.

Saul's work provided an operational methodology by which to identify the processes of individuation as they occur in the life of a small group. As this research was moving forward Boyd and Myers (1988) were writing a paper which did consider grief work which individuals engage in during periods of personal transformations. It now remains for their work to be related to episodic themes set forth in Saul's research.

References

Bennis, W. G. and Shepard, H. A. (1956). A Theory of group development, *Human Relations*, *9*, 415–17.

Bowlby, J. (1961). Processes of mourning, *International Journal of Psycho-Analysis*, *42*, 16–21.

Bowlby, J. (1975). Processes of mourning. In A. C. Carr and B. Schoenberg (eds), *Grief: Selected readings*. New York: Health Sciences Publishing Corp.

Bowlby, J. (1980). *Loss, sadness and depression*. New York: Basic Books, Inc.

Boyd, R. D. (1983). A matrix model of the small group: Part 1, *Small Group Behavior*, *14*(4), 405–18.

Boyd, R. D. (1984). A matrix model of the small group: Part 2, *Small Group Behavior*, *15*(2), 233–50.

Boyd, R. D. and Myers, J. G. (1988). Transformative education, *International Journal of Lifelong Education*, *1*, 261–84.

Boyd, R. D., Bressler, D., Dirkx, J. M., Fullmer, R., Levenson, E., Kushel, C. K. and Ullrich, W. (1980). *A report on the Evaluation Study of the Group Dynamics Traffic Safety School, State of Wisconsin*. Madison: Department of Transportation, Wisconsin.

Carr, A. H. (1975). Bereavement as a relative experience. In B. Schoenberg *et al.* (eds), *Bereavement: Its psychosocial aspects*. New York: Columbia University Press.

Davie, L. E. (1971). *Eriksonian ego crises theory applied to small group phase development*. Unpublished doctoral dissertation, University of Wisconsin-Madison.

Freud, S. (1961). Mourning and melancholia, *Standard Edition*, Vol. 14, pp. 243–58. (Original work published 1917.)

Fried, M. (1963). Grieving for a lost home. In L. Duhl (ed.), *The urban condition*. New York: Basic Books.

Jacobson, E. (1946). The effect of disappointment on ego and superego formation in normal and depressive development, *Psychoanalytical Review*, *33*, 129–47.

Jung, C. G. (1969). *Collected works of C. G. Jung*. Volume 9, Part I, Princeton: Princeton University Press.

Klein, M. (1936). Weaning. In Rickman (ed.), *On the bringing up of children* (p. 41). London: Kegan Paul.

Lindemann, E. (1944). Symptomatology and management of acute grief, *American Journal of Psychiatry*, *101*, 141–48.

Marris, P. (1974). *Loss and change*. London: Routledge and Kegan Paul.

Myers, J. G. (1986). *Grief work as a critical condition for small group phase development*. Unpublished doctoral dissertation, University of Wisconsin-Madison.

Osherson, S. D. (1980). *Holding on or letting go: Men and career change at mid-life*. New York: The Free Press.

Parkes, C. M. (1970). The first year of bereavement, *Psychiatry*, *33*, 65–74.

Parkes, C. M. (1972). *Bereavement: Studies of grief in adult life*. London: Tavistock Publications.

Parkes, C. M. (1975). Unexpected and untimely bereavement: A statistical study of young Boston widows. In B. Schoenberg *et al.* (eds), *Bereavement: Its psychological aspects*. New York: Columbia University Press.

Parkes, C. M. and Stevenson-Hinde, J. (eds) (1982). *The place of attachment in human behavior*. New York: Basic Books.

Rannells, J. S. (1986). The individuation of women through the study of deity images: Learning from a Jungian perspective. Unpublished doctoral dissertation, University of Wisconsin-Madison.

Weinstein, P. and Platt, G. (1973). *Psychoanalytic sociology*. Baltimore: Johns Hopkins University Press.

White, S. W. (1976). *The relationship of small group members' ego-identity concerns and their employment of mechanisms of coping and defense*. Unpublished doctoral dissertation, University of Wisconsin-Madison.

Chapter five

A conceptualization of individuation in learning situations

Jean Rannells Saul

Individuation is thought 'of as an ongoing and lifelong process of becoming conscious of ourselves through self-knowledge' (Jung, 1966, p. 178). This chapter presents a thematic point of view of individuation in which the individual's daily life experiences can be understood as observable events in the process of individuation. Such a thematic point of view of individuation is useful to those persons interested in understanding and facilitating individuation, particularly in learning situations.

This chapter examines this conceptualization of individuation, the thematic point of view, from three perspectives. First, the traditional view of individuation is discussed as it points toward the thematic view. Second, the development and conceptualization of seven aspects of individuation which comprise the thematic point of view are presented. A discussion of an empirical investigation of the conceptualization is included. Third, examples from a small instructional group are used to illustrate individuation from this conceptualization.

The traditional point of view of individuation

Jung (1966) states, '(T)he aim of individuation is nothing less than to divest the self of the false wrappings of the persona on the one hand, and the suggestive power of primordial images on the other' (p. 174). In this manner the conscious and the unconscious 'complement one another to form a totality, which is the self' (p. 177). The process of knowing, of recognizing, the voices and stirrings of the unconscious is 'becoming one's own self . . . coming to selfhood . . . (coming to) self-realization' (p. 173).

While individuation is an individual matter, a process of differentiation, the individual's existence presupposes a collective relationship. Individuation leads 'to more intense and broader collective relationships and not to isolation' (Jung, 1966, p. 155). This would indicate that at least one aspect of individuation occurs as the individual is actively involved with other persons.

Jacobi (1965/1967) describes individuation as a series of journeys into and from the underworld; '(E)very act of conscious realization is a plunging into the darkness of the underworld and a reemergence from it' (p. 70). In this regard, Jacobi's depiction elaborates on Jung's use of the death–rebirth metaphor in relation to individuation. There are several forms of rebirth that Jung (1959) delineates; however, the form most appropriate for this discussion is that of *renovatio*. Rebirth in this form occurs when the personality is renewed but not changed in its essential parts so that 'only its functions, or parts of the personality, are subjected to healing, strengthening, or improvement' (Jung, 1959 p. 114).

Jacobi (1965/1967) states that 'rebirth can only proceed step by step, affecting the individual first in one part and then in another, until it finally encompasses his [sic] whole life' (p. 61). She suggests, 'The course (individuation) follows is rather "stadial" consisting of progress and regress, flux and stagnation in alternating sequence. Only when we glance back over a long stretch of the way can we notice the development' (p. 34).

The spiral-like nature of individuation is reported also by Whitmont (1984). Certain motifs and problems within a person's life experience reemerge periodically; this provides the opportunity to deal with the issue at a different level of meaning and significance. The individual appears to move through small steps of expanded consciousness which in various combinations can lead to the death–rebirth transformations of individuation. These small steps are observable in the realm of the everyday.

Jung (1959, 1966) used incidents from two sources as evidence for his conceptualization of individuation through the death–rebirth process. The first source consisted of the dreams of his analysands and the contents of their paintings, which Jung believed contained streams of outpouring from the unconscious. The second source was the mythology that had been created and collected about human experience of various cultures. The myths contained the symbols of the archetypal elements which exert an influence within the psyche. It was these symbols and images within the mythology that were evident in the dreams and artwork which Jung became aware of and interpreted. Ulanov (1971) quotes Jung, 'Myth is a primordial language natural to these psychic processes, and no intellectual formulation comes anywhere near the richness and expressiveness of mythical imagery.'

Individuation is fostered as the individual becomes conscious of the relationships between the archetypes and their symbols and the events and decisions of the individual's daily life. The archetypes that appear through the myth offer the potential of broadening the field of consciousness and thus the maturing of the personality: '(O)ur task consists simply and solely in keeping the conscious mind constantly on the alert, so that as many of the unconscious portions of the personality as possible can be made conscious, experienced, and integrated' (Jacobi, 1965/1967, p. 98). Whitmont (1984) adds, 'The individual once touched by the power of the archetype, must be moved to change, to integrate the dreams and legends of the autonomous complex into life' (p. 30).

In summary, four statements from the traditional theory of Jungian individuation are foundational for the work reported here. First, inter-actions with other persons can precipitate an encounter which advances individuation. Second, realization of the self occurs as the individual pays attention to the dialog between the inner voices and the outer circumstances. Third, psychic death–rebirth experiences can be identified in an individual's ongoing reflective activity. Fourth, progress toward individuation comes not steadily but cycling round issues as the individual's reflections invite.

Individuation in learning groups

Certainly in educational settings, individuals encounter many opportunities for expanded consciousness through the intellectual and emotional challenges to the student's current understanding of self. Such a challenge comes to the student first through the discourse of the group. One member says something which stirs a reflective response. A second member makes a comment and another reflection is stirred. Thus, within the contents of the dialog the student finds material for the personal reflection that will offer the opportunity to further her/his individuation. That is, a verbal or nonverbal component of the discourse stimulates reflection within the individual. It is this reflection which is of interest as we investigate within the educational setting the potential for progress toward individuation. An example will make this relationship clearer.

The group of women and men had been discussing leadership and what that meant to the group. Questions such as these had been asked: 'How does one fit into a group? How can you be independent in a group and still be a group member?' One group member suggested that the group was like a family because families encourage its members to be both independent and dependent. Sally spoke next. She was in tears as she talked about the demands of her family. When her family has a gathering, everyone is expected to be present. Her family has no com-prehension that someone might already have other plans. If one member does not attend, then that member is accused of not being committed to the family. Sally said, 'Families don't want you to be independent. If you are not there, you are not committed.' She felt deeply the hurt of this pressure. She continued by connecting these comments with her feelings about the group. 'If I am independent in the group, you will say I am not committed.'

Sally's tears indicate that the discussion and reflection were a critical struggle for her. She appears not only to be considering the independence issue in the group, but more importantly the class discussion connected with similar feelings she had not acknowledged from her out-of-class (family) life. The pain and hurt become real to her again because of this interaction. She is able to see her thoughts and actions in the group in a similar context to her thoughts and actions in her family. 'How do you find a balance between independence and dependence in the group (in my family)?', she asked.

Certainly, Sally has encountered a personal dilemma and is struggling to make it conscious in order to come to a resolution. The classroom dialog represents the outer circumstances that have stimulated Sally to pay attention to inner voices which speak of a sense of self in relation to family. Again Sally can experience independence and dependence in relationships as she works through the class discourse. Whether this reflection can lead to a psychic death–rebirth experience depends upon the manner in which Sally responds. How can this encounter be characterized within the framework of individuation?

The thematic point of view of individuation

As an educator interested in providing educational experiences through which adult students have the opportunity to progress in individuation, I wanted a conceptualization of individuation that would allow me to observe and document a person's progress toward individuation within educational settings. On the one hand, individuation is a complex, lifelong process, and is never fully achieved. On the other hand, the educational setting is bounded by time limitations; groups usually agree to gather for a particular time period each week and for a certain number of weeks. How, therefore, could individuation be conceptualized to identify the individual's potential growth over a short period of time? How could a person's experience in the group be demarcated so that progress toward individuation might be examined? In other words, this conceptualization must (a) value the uniqueness of the individual's personal response to the group discourse, (b) view that response as a possible contribution to the individual's lifelong journey toward individuation, and (c) be consistent with the theory of individuation.

First, the spiral-like quality of individuation was helpful in this regard. Since certain motifs and problems within a person's life experience reemerge periodically, the individual has the opportunity to deal with them at several times during his/her lifetime (Whitmont, 1969).

Thus, issues that would emerge for consideration by the individual during the duration of a group would be similar to those encountered during her/his lifetime.

In the example above, the issue Sally was dealing with might be considered broadly as independence. In an earlier group session she explained that several years earlier, she moved half-way across the country to be away from her family; she was the only one of her siblings to move more than a short distance from her parents. Yet just recently she moved back to the state to be closer to them. While we do not know the specific details about motives and resolution, we do understand that this issue of independence has emerged several times for Sally. The group discussion offers her another opportunity to reflect upon independence.

Second, the discourse of a group, as well as the reflective thought of an individual, is not constant; topics change, speakers alternate, attention wanders, and moods vary. In this way, group dialog appears to be a series of single events connected together. Within each event is the potential for reflection and increased understanding of self. Sally's reflection on family and independence is one such instance. I felt it ought to be possible, therefore, to identify single events within the group's life which might exemplify progress toward individuation. Individuation over the life span of an individual is the aggregate of many such instances. Some instances are simple, others are complex involving much energy and reflection; some can be demarcated easily and clearly, others are a 'chain reaction' and only with difficulty, if at all, can such instances be separately identified from the flow of events.

Third, a group member can be totally involved in the dialog of the group, yet becomes aware of a desire to attend to a very personal experience that is called to mind by the discussion. How is it that the individual makes a connection with the inner personal experience and the content of the external situation? In Sally's experience, the ideas of family and independence from the group discussion called her inner attention vividly to feelings and hurts from earlier experiences.

It seemed to me that the individual formed a link between an aspect of personal experience and an aspect of this symbol that emerged from the discourse of the educational situation. A bond was created between the individual's experience and the symbol. The bond is a manifestation of the content used in the dialog between the conscious and the unconscious. Sally created a bond between the symbol called family and a particular personal experience with family.

Fourth, within the literature that describes the process of individuation, I was able to define six distinct elements of the individuation process. Each 'episode of individuation' represents a unit of the individuation process, one aspect of one event in an individual's life experience. Each episode, like each event, is integral to the whole process, yet each is a single, developed instance of the continuing process. Each of the episodes represents a new awareness of an aspect of one's self; each differs from the others in the intent or direction of the new awareness. With individuation conceptualized in this way I was able to demarcate an event of an individual's life and to classify it, if appropriate, as a particular aspect of the individuation process.

The six types of episodes of individuation are described briefly below. They are defined completely, with illustrative examples and literature references, in a following section of this chapter.

(1) Discovery of Newness represents the discovery of talents, attitudes, feelings, and interests that exist within one's self.
(2) Empowerment means an increased sense of power and autonomy, a new affirmation of self-worth and confidence.
(3) Turmoil is the manifestation of an inner state of confusion, chaos, and pain, the severity of which depends upon the situation.
(4) Self-responsibility results from the decision making that shows one is taking a new responsibility for and interest in one's self and one's future.
(5) Integration comes with the experience of a togetherness (where there was none before) within oneself and/or with parts of one's world.
(6) Interiority represents the deepened relation to one's inner self.

An empirical investigation of the conceptualization

To test this conceptualization in a learning situation, I selected a setting in which symbols were very obvious and members were encouraged to reflect upon their experience. If an individual were unable to create a bond with a symbol and unable to exhibit episodes of individuation in such a situation, I would seriously doubt the reliability of the formulation of bond and the episodes of individuation.

The topic of the learning setting was 'Women and Mythology'; both feminist and contemporary interpretations of Greek and Sumerian mythologies were discussed and related to the lives of the group members. Twenty-six women and no men participated in the group. Each woman was asked to examine the literature about a particular deity and to write a personal response regarding that deity. Women also kept a personal journal and prepared a creative project to exemplify an archetype of personal interest. I conducted an in-depth interview with each woman near the end of the course. I was a participant observer in the group.

The research included an examination of the construct validity of the notions of bond and the six episodes of individuation. A Jungian analyst and two other professionals knowledgeable in Jungian principles reviewed the descriptions of the notions to ascertain their adherence to the Jungian theoretical construct of individuation. Two women unfamiliar with Jungian theory were trained to code interview narratives and papers for the presence of bond and episodes of individuation. The findings indicated that bond and each of the episodes did occur at least once and each of the 26 women interviewed exhibited evidence of at least one episode of individuation. All but one woman created a bond with one of the deity symbols.

These brief excerpts from one of the case studies that were prepared during the analysis will illustrate the notions of bond and the episodes of individuation called Empowerment and Integration.

Ann says, 'Artemis is the one I can relate to. She was a single woman and never had any children but she still had a very nurturing role to play for women and men. She was in the forest and I love being in the forest.' Here is an obvious attraction (bond) to this deity image for Ann. The links she makes from her personal experience are these: Ann is single, so is the deity. For medical reasons, Ann will never bear children, neither did Artemis. Yet honored as a midwife, Artemis exemplifies definite nurturing activities; Ann was a nanny for three children and enjoys the closeness she still feels with them.

(Rannells, 1986/1987, p. 108)

Evidence of Empowerment is seen in a journal entry written early in the semester; 'I feel the stirrings of inner reasons to study mythology. I feel enlivened by the goddesses. They give me energy! There is an ancient tradition of women's power that validates my right to have social and economic goals.' In this instance the key words are *enlivened* and *energy* which speak of the new affirmation she feels as a woman of worth with the support of other, powerful affirming women. Ann experienced no such power before and actually felt that to be a woman with social and economic goals was not supported by the culture in which she grew up.

(Rannells, 1986/1987, p. 112)

During the interview Ann said, 'There isn't just one model of a woman and every woman must try to be that. There are as many models as there are women. I'll just be this one. I thought I had to suppress parts of myself because they did not fit the model as I had learned it from society.' This represents individuation in the form of Integration, integrating into her conscious being a wide variety of interests and activities.

(Rannells, 1986/1987, p. 113)

131

I have included the report of this investigation in order to supply evidence of the validity of the concepts of bond and the episodes of individuation. A further examination of the concepts was conducted with a learning group which was constituted differently. A group of eight women and two men met for ten weeks as the experiential portion of a university semester-long course on small groups. The professor participated in the group by being with them each session; his verbal participation was slight and limited to interpretative comments offered in the form of metaphors. The sessions were videotaped and the students were encouraged to review the tape before the next group session.

The occurrence of individuation in this small group was examined through a study of selected video tapes. Only the actual discourse of the group sessions was analyzed. In this learning group, archetypal symbols were not obvious; and although group members were encouraged to be thoughtful in their comments, the ongoing group dialog did not represent the same type of reflectivity as written papers would. Thus this situation presented a different investigation of the research question, 'How is progress in individuation manifest within the context of a small group?'

Bond and episodes of individuation

In what follows is a more complete definition of the notions of bond and the six episodes of individuation. An example of each notion from the group sessions is given.

Bond

The notion of bond refers to a coming together of an aspect of an archetypal symbol and an aspect of an individual's personal experience. A bond has two primary qualities. First, there is an attraction to the archetype through the symbol. This is primarily unconscious, a welling up, a stirring from inside one's self. Second, an aspect of one's personal experience is associated with – brought into consciousness – by the symbol. It is as though the personal experience is called forth by the archetypal image.

In this instructional group, 'family' had become a symbol with which each member could identify in her/his own way. The group seemed to have been drawn to the metaphor 'the group is like a family' but each offered a different response. Alice wondered about her own parenting tendencies – would she be a smothering mother? Mary, although she was not a parent, could see in her sisters the tendency to carry on in the same manner they were parented. Mark said his family had no overt conflict in it so that he sees conflict as, 'Now we are getting somewhere; something is happening.' Ann said her family had a lot of conflict and she was not happy with it. She also indicated that she had misunderstood Mark's anticipation of conflict; she thought perhaps his family was a lot like hers and so conflict was all he knew.

The concept of bond is observed in the references to the symbol named 'family' in the incident reported above. The statement 'the group is like a family' called forth one image, and yet, at the same time, many different images from the group members. Each was able to interact with the symbol from her/his own experience. Each seemed to find a meaningful link between her/his previous experience and the current group context with the symbol of family.

Discovery of newness

This type of episode of individuation represents a new awareness of talents, attitudes, values, feelings, interests, and other potentials that exist within the individual. The value of the new capacity as positive or negative is not the issue; what is important is the individual's conscious awareness of the new capacity (vonFranz, 1964; Washbourn, 1977; Whitmont, 1969). Discovery of Newness is expressed as a sudden realization or recognition, as a perception or an idea that one has become aware of, or as a learning or an understanding.

For example, Mark watched the video tapes of a particular group session in which he made some strong statements about the leadership abilities of Ann, another group member. Ann's behavior and words appeared to be the stimulus for his assertions. However, as he viewed the tape, Mark realized that it was his own personality characteristics to which he was responding. Ann's behavior reminded him of parts of himself that he did not like and to which he wanted to respond too strongly.

Although the actual stimulus to the comments was known only in reflection, Mark was in possession of new information about himself. What he does with the information is a new decision point and beyond the significance of this discussion. The interaction in the group discussion prompted an inner dialog in which Mark came to a new understanding of his behavior and attitudes. Accordingly, this incident was coded Discovery of Newness because of Mark's discovery of the new information about himself.

Turmoil

This episode of individuation, Turmoil, is evident when the individual is in an inner state of confusion, chaos, pain, suffering, or woundedness. Turmoil involves indecision – wavering between two possible courses of action or states of mind. The feeling level is not mild. The sense of Turmoil can be expressed as one of two states: (a) as being stirred up, dragged down into a very confused state (Ulanov, 1971) or (b) as being embroiled, mentally or spiritually troubled (Jacobi, 1965/1967; Perera, 1981).

The initial example given above of Sally's response in the discussion of independence/dependence is an example of Turmoil. Sally was in a state of inner confusion and woundedness. The group discussion connected with these feelings she had not acknowledged from her out-of-class (family) life. The pain and hurt became real to her again because of the group discussion. While several options for action and further reflection exist now for Sally, these are not the concern of this aspect of individuation. Identifying the condition of Turmoil is sufficient.

Empowerment

The episode of individuation called Empowerment is a new affirmation of one's self-worth, a new understanding of one's power. It represents a resounding 'I AM . . .' spoken deep in one's being. Within this 'word' is the intent 'I am . . . and I can do . . .' although action may not be the result or even contemplated in the affirmation. It is felt as an experience arising from within (Ulanov, 1971). It is expressed as emotional strength, zest, and vitality (Edinger, 1972; Ulanov, 1971).

Sally made comments which reflected intense feelings and opinions during one session. Thinking about it throughout the week, she wondered whether she really did believe that intensely. Watching the video tape of the session reaffirmed her position; she still believed strongly in what she did and said. The next week she recounted the process of doubting and then checking her perceptions via the videotape. Her affirmation to the group reflects the empowerment; she said, 'I stood up and I stuck to what I believe.' That was a very powerful affirmation of her self and her action.

Self-responsibility

This episode of individuation involves making new decisions about the directions of one's life. Taking new responsibility for one's future is a process of increasing and accentuating one's independence as a person. It recognizes one's right and responsibility to be accountable for one's actions and life direction (Ulanov, 1971; Whitmont, 1969).

Mark indicated that he often felt inferior to another person and in such situations adjusted his thinking to be aligned with theirs. He is not comfortable with this tendency because it violates his own sense of self and that of the other. Being more specific, Mark admitted that when the professor made a comment, Mark would stop thinking about the on-going conversation with the students and try to determine his response to the professor. This he felt was unfair to the group members and their commitment to the ongoing conversation. If each member is to be valued then each must be listened to intently and 'heard' equally. He wanted to change this tendency of his. He invited Sally (in particular and others if they wished) to 'hold him accountable' when she felt he was not attending to her comments as an equal member.

Self-responsibility can be coded here because Mark identified a life pattern with which he was displeased. He determined how to change the actions by naming his intention to the group and by asking for help from them.

Integration

An occurrence represents the episode of individuation called Integration when the individual experiences a togetherness where there was none before. It is a conscious realization of wholeness through a process of hidden qualities being made known. The self is experienced as whole. The experience of integration comes as a conscious realization of one's unique reality, as a feeling of at-one-with and together-with others, or as an experience of oneness with the nonhuman aspect of the world (Jacobi, 1965/1967; Perera, 1981; Ulanov, 1971).

Jo recalled the discussion the previous week which she had had with Ann. They had even talked several times outside of the group. Jo realized that the discussions had been good for her because she was successful in expressing her feelings – something she had not always been able to do. She risked making a comment in this situation; she had not withdrawn. Jo told the group that she was able to do this because during the discussion she tried to remember 'I like you AND I feel this way'. In other situations she had been able to attend to only one set of feelings – either liking someone or her feelings of difference; this lead her to withdraw, deciding not to make another comment for fear of being hurt. Two parts of her self were in conflict and she valued each one. In this situation, however, by connecting and affirming both feelings she was able to express her own feelings of conflict and her friendship with Ann. These aspects of her self were integrated. Jo felt a new wholeness expressed as confidence; she said she did not feel 'half as scared' of speaking as she usually does.

Interiority

This episode of individuation, Interiority, represents the experience of deepening one's relationship to one's inmost being. Interiority can entail a new receptivity to and/or active seeking of an inner voice which alerts one's attention to new meanings and values (Edinger, 1972; Jacobi, 1965/1967; Ulanov, 1971; Washbourn, 1977).

At one point in the class time, the professor's presence in the group was an urgent issue with Sally; she wanted the professor to leave the room. Sally felt his presence was an inhibitor to the group's growth. She returned to the question several times during the session even as she had to call the attention of the group back to it since they were on to a different topic. At the following session Sally spoke of her actions. Tearfully she explained that it was very scary for her to trust herself and to say what she wanted to say at the last session about the professor's presence. 'Yet', she continued, 'something told me to trust this and go with it. And I did.' Her comment indicates she was in touch with and listening to an inner voice, trusting her intuition, in a way that she usually does not. Clearly, Sally was aware in a new way of an interior sense of her self and the importance of listening to this voice.

Summary

In this chapter I have examined the idea of Jungian individuation from three perspectives. First, I discussed the elements of the traditional view of individuation that served as the foundation for the development of this formulation. The ideas of myth and symbol as they exemplify archetypal themes acting in daily life were shown to contribute to further realization of individuation. Second, I discussed the development of a conceptualization of a thematic point of view of individuation which consists of the notions of bond and six episodes of individuation. Third, this thematic point of view was illustrated with examples from a small instructional group.

I have taken the position that participation in educational groups can enhance the individual's progress in individuation. The group member engages in discussion and builds relationships which offer content for personal reflection. With such dialog and reflection, symbols and images are called forth and are linked with the individual's collected personal experiences. The notion of bond and the episodes of individuation enable us to recognize elements of the psychic work that engages the group member. Bond identifies the symbol which links an aspect of the group dialog with an aspect of the group member's personal experience. Since a symbol is part of the world of meaning, it attempts to 'express something for which no verbal concept yet exists' (Jacobi, 1959, p. 89). The symbol and the individual's response help us understand potential areas for reflection within which the individual might discover a deeper understanding of self. Identifying an individual's reflection as one of the six episodes of individuation enables us to understand the group member's new self-understanding as she or he is becoming aware of it.

In this manner the individual's outer journey, consisting of the group encounters, is linked with the inner journey, as unconscious contents of the psyche are made conscious. Members of the group in their discourse give evidence of the reflection and struggle and inner dialog that is necessary as one works to identify and integrate various aspects of one's personality. It is this work that constitutes progress toward individuation.

Inner dialogs frequently involve encounters with such psychic elements or figures as the shadow, anima, and the animus. Our observations have provided extensive data on the roles taken by the anima and animus to influence the behaviors of group members without their awareness that this is occurring: that is to say, their behaviors are being influenced in an unconscious manner. These unconscious elements may influence behavior in a constructive manner but they too often can distort and block the realization of any of the episodic themes and thus prevent personal transformations. To establish a more systematic program of study it became necessary to develop a methodology that could identify the influences the anima and animus were having on individual behavior. The following chapter presents that methodology and briefly reports on certain empirical investigations which were conducted.

References

Edinger, E. F. (1972). *Ego and archetype: Individuation and the religious function of the psyche*. New York: C. P. Putnam's Sons.

Jacobi, J. (1959). *Complex/archetype/symbol* (R. Manheim, Trans.). Bollingen Series LVII, Princeton: Princeton University Press.

Jacobi, J. (1965/1967). *The way of individuation* (R. F. C. Hull, Trans.). New York: Harcourt, Brace, & World. (Original work published 1965.)

Jung, C. G. (1959). *The collected works of C. G. Jung* (Vol. 9, part 1). Bolingen Series XX, Princeton: Princeton University Press.

Jung, C. G. (1966). *The collected works of C. G. Jung* (Vol. 7). Bollingen Series XX (second edn), Princeton: Princeton University Press.

Perera, S. B. (1981). *Descent to the goddess: A way of initiation for women*. Toronto: Inner City Books.

Rannells, J. S. (1986/1987). *The individuation of women through the study of deity images: Learning from a Jungian perspective*. Doctoral dissertation, University of Wisconsin-Madison. *Dissertation Abstracts international*. 17, 9A.

Ulanov, A. B. (1971). *The feminine in Jungian thought and in Christian theology*. Evanston: Northwestern University Press.

vonFranz, M. L. (1964). The process of individuation. In C. G. Jung (ed.), *Man and his symbols* (pp. 157–254). New York: Dell Publishing Co.

Washbourn, P. (1977). *Becoming woman: The quest for wholeness in female experience*. San Francisco: Harper & Row.

Whitmont, E. (1969). *The symbolic quest: basic concepts of analytical psychology*. London: Barrie and Rockliff.

Whitmont, E. (1984). *The return of the goddess*. New York: Crossroads.

Chapter six

The anima and animus in the transactions of small groups

Robert D. Boyd and Mary Ellen Kondrat

Overview

Clinical case studies have documented the many ways in which the anima and animus have furthered and impeded the processes of individuation. Few writers have described how these archetypal figures play out their influences in the dynamics of small groups. Yet even a cursory examination of group dynamics from the perspective of analytical psychology will reveal projections involving inputs from an individual member's anima or animus. Our observations of small groups continually returned us to the necessity for a systematic empirical examination of the roles the anima and animus play in the interpersonal and intrapersonal behaviors in small groups. In this chapter, we report on our attempts to conduct an enquiry directed to those ends.

We had two primary goals in view. First, operational specifications for the concepts of the anima and animus had to be formulated from the existing literature. As will be discussed later, this necessitated that we make a choice among the different conceptual perspectives now current in analytical psychology. Second, an empirical study had to be designed, organized, and conducted. The chapter reflects this organizational sequence. We first present a discussion of the conceptual framework and a description of the paradigms specifying the elementary and transformative characters of the anima and animus. We then discuss the nature of the various forms of anima/animus and set forth descriptors of their elementary and transformative characters. Following this we present a description of an empirical investigation we conducted and a brief discussion of the methodology that was used in the study. In the final major section, we present observations illustrating various ways in which members' behaviors reflect the actions of their anima or animus within the dynamics of the group. The chapter concludes with a statement summarizing the key contributions of our work and briefly identifying certain issues that remain to be clarified.

Conceptual framework

Many contributions have been made to our understandings of the anima and animus since Carl Jung's (1966 a, b, 1968 a, b) initial development of these constructs. Such contributions generally focus on particular aspects of the phenomena and advance either a developmental or an archetypal point of view, depending upon the particular orientation of the author (Samuels, 1985). Both the developmental and archetypal perspectives afford valid insights, although it is generally recognized that either perspective alone provides only an incomplete account of the dynamic. Consequently, the conceptual framework which undergirds the present study is an integrated structure, drawing upon both points of view. Thus, it can be noted as we move forward in the development of our paradigm that we have drawn upon the works of various authors who have been identified with one or another of the these perspectives in the literature.

When these different points of view are taken as a whole, four different but interconnected levels of analysis emerge to enrich our understanding. These four levels are the topological, the structural, the dynamic, and the developmental. The topological view presents the anima and animus as discrete and identifiable entities within the human psyche, occupying a psychological space between the primary archetypal images and the ego. In our discussion of the topological view, we will incorporate much of the pioneering work of Erich Neumann. The structural view, identifying the biological, experiential, and archetypal elements of the anima and animus, is the classic conceptualization. It has been extensively described by many authors representing the different generations of analytical psychologists. The dynamic view examines the manifestations of the animus and anima as forces in human behavior. Projection, acting out, and specific kinds of creativity are examples of the activities in which the anima and animus may engage in transactions with other individuals or in interactions with selected aspects of the social environment. Finally, there is the developmental view. The designation 'developmental' is used here in a very specific manner. We do not propose that the anima or animus as entities have their own course of development. They can be represented as having different stages of development but these are potential stages and are not a life course schema that unfolds epigenetically. These potential stages are realized only through the struggles of the ego to relate on the one side to the exterior world and concurrently on the other side to psychic relationships. The works of Neumann, vonFranz, and others have contributed greatly to the paradigm we present in this chapter. The remaining discussion in this section is organized around these four ways of understanding the anima and animus.

Topological view

In the demarcation of the anima and animus from other elements of the psyche, it is necessary to identify the nature of the relationship between these two constructs and other psychic constituents. Neumann (1955) has given one of the most explicit conceptualizations of the relationship between the syzygy and other constituents of the psyche. His schema shows the intermediary region the anima and animus occupy between the Great Parents and the ego. The masculine and feminine principles revealed in the archetypal images of the Great Parents are experienced as omnipotent, threatening as well as life giving to the emerging ego. Although the ego must confront these archetypal forces if it is to act as the conscious agent in furthering individuation, it cannot do this alone. Some ally must be there to support the weak ego in its encounters with the Great Parents. The anima and animus perform that intermediary function. Although they are themselves aspects of the archetypal psyche, they are experienced as familiar and immediate because they share with the ego its existential world. They are the imaginary and intimate friends of childhood who share secrets and fantasies (Bion 1963; Jung, 1967) away from the searching eyes of Parents.

The syzygy – the constituent elements of the anima and animus – is located in that region of the psyche where the personal and collective unconscious merge and overlap. The anima and animus are within both the collective unconscious and the personal unconscious. They are creatures of two worlds. The importance that their topology has to human behavior and development will become evident as we examine the other three approaches to understanding the anima and animus.

Except for minor extensions in the specifications of the anima and animus, we have adhered to the conceptual formulations initially set out by Jung (1966 a, b, 1967, 1968 a, b) and amplified by Neumann (1954 a, b, 1955, 1959) and others who followed Jung's lead. A serious difference arose when our observations of the behaviors of individuals in small groups revealed what appeared to be the projections of an anima and an animus in the behaviors of both men and women. Men as well as women on occasions acted as if dominated by an opinionated and pseudo-logical animus. Women as well as men had moody periods, times when the anima-like behaviors control the conscious life of the individual. These observations were not compatible with the accepted theory. The conventional response to the presentation of such observations is to identify them as the presence of the shadow. In consistent observations of the behaviors of men and women in small groups, the explanation that the shadow was the central actor became increasingly difficult to support. The available evidence continued to point us in another direction. There was an undeniable power being exercised in these transactions as if an archetypal source of psychic energy was involved, an energy which was more powerful and of a different kind than could be explained by the construct of the shadow.

It was at this time in our enquiry that Hillman's (1973, 1974) articles came to our attention. His work provided the explanations that clearly accounted for the transactions we had observed. In addition, his analysis was not a counter position to Jung's basic formulations but a clarification of certain conflictual developments in the formulation. The immediate import of Hillman's papers to our enquiry is that they provide the basis upon which to explain the existence of the anima and animus in both men and women, and thus they afford a more consistent account for the kind of transactions we have routinely observed in small groups. Certain of Hillman's arguments are reviewed here in order to make explicit the conceptual formulations adopted in our work.

Jung (1966 a) stated that the masculine element for the male, and the feminine element for the female, were reflected in the shadow of each respectively. This notion excluded the possibility of the anima as part of the female's psyche. The shadow defined in this manner is conceptually ambiguous, as it is both the repository of the personal repressed content and the psychic structure containing anima elements for the woman and animus elements in the case of the man. Hillman (1973) proposes that a more precise notion of the shadow could be achieved by keeping it reserved for the morally repressed content.

Whether the anima and animus exist in both the male and female psyches is a question that involves much more than our discussion above on the shadow. The question that must be examined directly is: Must both men and women struggle to experience and express soul and spirit to realize their being? Obviously, the answer must be 'yes' for the soul and spirit constitute our nature of being who we are. The soul and spirit are not the sole nature of one or the other gender but the innate qualities of our human nature. Leaving Hillman's treatment aside for the moment, an explicit exploration of the issue is presented in Neumann's (1956) discussion of Psyche's development in *Amor and psyche*. His interpretation of the myth as an account of feminine development supports Hillman's (1973, p. 115) contention that women are not exonerated from working at anima cultivation simply because they are born female. The story of Psyche's struggles document the trials a woman must encounter and resolve to realize her soul. One of the many insights Neumann makes clear, in his interpretation of the myth, is Psyche's realization of her anima element which is shown in her opening of the box containing the potion of divine beauty. Neumann points out that this rash act was taken to make herself even more attractive for Eros. Indeed all her trials were undertaken to reunite her to

Eros. That the animus was also being encountered was illustrated clearly in the tasks that Aphrodite had set for her. It was Psyche's daughter-like relationships with the 'earth' forces which helped her to live with the masculine forces that she encountered. Those daughter-like relationships that Psyche so naturally undertook and from which she benefited were the expression of the anima. The interplay between the anima and animus which was evident throughout the myth of Psyche is also addressed in Hillman's article. He states: 'Animus development with which the anima does not keep pace will lead a woman away from psychological understanding' (1973, p. 117). In psychological development, the anima, in women, is required to counterbalance the animus. What has been described here concerning the existence and roles of the anima in women has its unique counterpart in men.

The development of identity through the resolution of psychological crises (Erikson, 1950) is one of the primary tasks faced by every person. The anima and animus play central roles in the individual's identity development. Their role in identity development can be readily perceived when we recall that they are composed of archetypal elements, experienced as biological entities and structured from personal experience. For a woman to experience an animus, for example, and to have no comparable contrasexual entity with which to contrast it, would create a difficult if not an insurmountable problem for her in delineating her identity as a woman. The shadow could not perform this function for her as it is composed of repressed material and for the most part of negative content. On the basis of logic alone, the resolution of identity crises requires the encounter of opposites. Let us take the case of the male; every boy, youth, and man must relate not only to the feminine elements and forces in his unconscious, a position repeatedly posited by Jung (1966 a, b) and other analytical psychologists (Harding, 1965; Whitmont, 1982) but to the internalized experiences with males, the personal experiences of his own biology, and the images that these have evolved in him in both his conscious and unconscious, and finally to the masculine archetypes. An observer who is willing to look carefully and in depth at the transactions occurring in a self-study group will see the evidence of this phenomenon. In specific terms, men, as members of such a group, discuss events concerning their relationships with others in dealing with masculinity, they reveal personal dilemmas involving psychological and biological experiencing of masculinity, and they present personal encounters with patriarchal forces that are described in a manner that differentiates them from actual experiences of known persons. To follow the case of the man, there would be no development of identity without reference to and encounter with the archetypes of the Great Parents and the respository and transformative functions of the animus and the contrasexual image of the anima, with her contributions to the man's psychological development. In brief, the ego, in the male, is faced with the task of resolving the crises of masculine identity which is culturally and physiologically forced upon the ego of the male. The animus, serving as a gender archetype, is involved as a party to the resolution to this identity crisis. The anima is also party to this crisis. The contrasexual images evoked by the anima in the male's psychological life serve to further his masculine identity by providing such counter feminine images to the images of masculinity. A similar pattern of identity development holds for women.

Denying the man an animus and woman an anima would create a void in the relationships that men and women must have between the ego and the Masculine and Feminine archetypes. These relationships are essential in establishing identity because they connect the ego to these two psychic forces of life. This latter notion was examined by Hillman (1973) who concluded: 'By denying woman anima and giving her animus instead, an entire archetypal pattern has been determined for women's psychology. The per definitionem absence of anima in women is a deprivation of a cosmic principle' (1973, p. 117). An analogous statement can be made in regard to the denial of the animus in men. If, indeed, the anima and animus are archetypally based, theoretical consistency would require that they be posited in the psyche of both men and women.

Hillman (1973) raises other criticisms of the more conventional Jungian position which excludes the existence of the anima in women and the animus in men. For example, he points out that women have reported dreams in which feminine archetypes play a significant role, and men have described dreams in which male archetypes appear. These elements are not manifestations of the shadow for they play the role of psychopomp in the dream-life of individuals. They indicate ways toward transformations and not denied or repressed forms of being.

The final point that is to be made on this issue here takes us back to the contributions Neumann has made on this subject. Neumann's (1955) schema which gives a diagramatic presentation of the planes of consciousness illustrates the ego encountering the anima and animus. There is no indication as to whether the ego is that of a woman or a man, and in point of fact it would not matter, because the schema clearly shows that the Masculine and Feminine archetypes are equally the basis upon which consciousness is structured. It is interesting to consider how Neumann could construct this schema and obviously see the anima and animus as integral to the processes of consciousness development and yet not perceive what Hillman so clearly understood from a very similar perspective some eighteen years later. In recent years, Samuels (1985) in his review of post-Jungian theory posits the existence of the anima and animus in both men and women.

From our observations of men and women in small groups and upon an analysis of the conceptual issues presented above, the position has been adopted in this study that both the anima and animus exist and play a central role in the psychological life of men and women. Evidence which is presented later in this paper corroborates this conceptualization.

Structural view

Jung's (1968 a) observation that the anima and animus are each composed of archetypal, biological, and experiential elements remains the accepted formulation. This general agreement suggests that a brief overview will suffice for our purpose.

First, and most critical to the theory, is the archetypal element. The archetypes, including here the archetypal masculine and feminine, function as both 'psychic aptitudes' and as 'psychic forces'. As 'aptitudes', the archetypes serve as *a priori* categories or anticipatory structures by means of which the individual actively goes to 'meet' and shape experience and perception. As 'psychic forces', the archetypes energize our responses to our perceptions, experiences, and memories. In particular, the masculine and feminine archetypes inform and condition both the manner in which we know the other as the same or as a different sex-other, as well as the manner in which we apprehend our own self as a gendered individual. The archetypal element is present even when we have no conscious awareness of the origin of these forces, affects, or perceptions.

A second source for the animus/anima comes from one's own biologically based sexual and contrasexual peculiarities and dispositions. The chemical and physiological changes, interactions, and transformations unique to each gender are important influences in the evolution of a gendered identity. Meanings and understandings constructed on the basis of human morphology contribute to the nature and configuration of the animus and anima.

A third factor is the experiential. As the term indicates, it is derived from experiences with the Other, as it accumulates over a lifetime of interactions with primary significant persons, especially, but by no means exclusively, with the same and oppositely gendered parent. Personal experiences structure the way the feminine and masculine are perceived and give a unique and singular character to an individual's anima and animus.

Dynamic view

The archetypal components of the anima and animus are in the lineage of the Great Mother and Father respectively. Thus, the anima and animus are in their own way dynamic expressions of the feminine and masculine principles respectively. This relationship explains their general modes of operation and most of their agendas. To gain an understanding of the ways the anima and animus operate, it is first necessary to take a closer look at the feminine and masculine principles, specifically as archetypes of the human psyche.

The feminine and masculine archetypes are each composed of two characters, the elementary and the transformative. The general nature of the elementary character in the feminine archetype is experienced as a force directed toward conservation whereas the transformative character is experienced as a movement toward amplification. In the masculine archetype the elementary character is experienced as a force directed toward separation and the transformative character is revealed in experiences of diversification. To introduce the stage development notion of the anima and animus at this time is to get ahead of ourselves; however, there is an important point to be made which does involve the basic qualities of the elementary and transformative characters and the four stages of the anima and animus. Not to deal with it at this time may result in some confusion in the discussion on the four stages considered in the next section. The concern here is to make clear the pervasive and enduring nature of the basic forces of the elementary and transformative characters. As the anima and animus move from one stage to the next stage of development and the basic natures of the elementary and transformative characters are expressed in different modalities, their primary qualities of conservation in the case of the elementary character and of amplification of the transformative character remain unchanged. This is to say that at every stage, the elementary character of the feminine pursues conservation and the transformative character promotes amplification. The aims of separation and diversification are evident in the elementary and transformative characters respectively in every stage of the animus's development. The modalities that express these primary natures of the feminine and masculine characters in the four stages of the anima and animus are dealt with in a later section.

There is a 'good' and 'bad' aspect to the elementary and to the transformative character. One way to identify the positive and negative aspects of the elementary and transformative characters is to view them in terms of the flow of energy. For example, in the case of the anima's elementary character the 'good' aspect, manifest in 'her' giving, is evident when the ego experiences a release of energy as if it were coming from a reservoir deep within the body. At such times, the ego may experience a feeling-tone of being a receiver of or being joined by some supportive or nurturing force. The negative or 'bad' aspect, where there is a sense of withholding, has been described in general terms by

Neumann (1955, p. 26) as psychic gravitation where consciousness is pulled back into the unconscious. In incidents involving the negative elementary character of the anima the individual experiences, for example, such feelings as deprivation and niggardliness. Neumann (1955, p. 31) points out that neither the 'good' nor 'bad' aspects of either the elementary or transformative character is experienced as wholly positive or negative. His observation recognizes not only the ambivalent nature of the feminine and masculine archetypes but the sensitivities of human consciousness in its potential capacity to perceive in various ways these conflicting forces. This realization of ambivalence is illustrated in the lingering feeling of ensnarement that can accompany a sense of having been joined by a nurturing and supportive force within our being. A sense of everything going well with our world – but.

Although the elementary and transformative characters may initially appear to represent opposite forces they are not antithetical. The combining relationship that can exist between these two characters was illustrated by Neumann (1955, p. 29) in the act of feeding when the elementary character is presented as preservation and the transformative character accents growth. It is generally possible, however, to discern the dominant character. For example, the combining and dominant relationships between the elementary and transformative characters as they are played out by the anima and animus are critical in affecting locomotion and stagnation in a small group. Ann's behavior expresses her joy in being in the group. At the same time, she is encouraging and infusing a sense of excitement within the group about the project it is about to undertake. The one behavior is of the elementary character – the joining and being one with the other. The other behavior is transformative – the anima that inspires.

Neumann (1955, p. 31) emphasizes the notion that the elementary and transformative characters of the feminine archetype are experienced differently by women and men. This notion is extended here to include the masculine archetype as well. In this broader formulation, the specific qualities expressed by each of the characters and as represented by the anima and animus are experienced differently by men and women because of the unique bio-psychosocial factors as well as the critical cultural forces that operate in their lives.

Projection puts the anima or animus into human relationships. The ego may call up these entities making them active players in the events of the day. But they can also 'crash the party' on their own initiative. A powerful anima or animus may take possession of the situation and dictate its terms to the ego. In less dramatic modes, they can promote images and feeling-tones. In such cases, they may draw up imaginary figures or represent alternative modes of perception and behavior and even propose different value systems. They may act as guides and serve as channels of communication between the ego and the unconscious. In active imagination and in dreams they can act out scripts and carry on dialogs which inform and instruct the ego. They can also lead the ego into destructive byways. Literature is replete with stories of men lead by their negative animas into their own self-destruction. The animus that has taken possession of a woman's life leads her to the denial of her own life and the sacrifice of others who chose to love her. The dynamic view of the anima and animus is critical to an understanding of these elements in the daily life of men and women.

Developmental view

In normal maturation an individual encounters a number of animas and animuses within his/her personality. Specifically, as individuals progress through maturational periods different types of animas and animuses come into being and assume the central relationships previously occupied by earlier types. In adolescence and young adulthood in the course of normal development, the anima is a young maiden and in her positive character a fascinating earth creature who invites us to join her in celebrating the exploration of life. In our later years the anima comes to us as a mature woman, gentle and wise – a wisdom in knowing that is based upon the ebb and flow of what has been. The negative anima, on the other hand, is evident in such behaviors as relentless ownership. Its possessive nature is expressed as not-to-be-questioned prerogative which is insisted upon at the expense of personal growth and creativity. These animas are different psychological entities at different stages of a person's life. It must be clearly understood that we are not proposing that the anima or animus has developmental stages apart from the life of an individual. What we are proposing is that in the course of human development, individuals encounter animas and animuses which serve as contemporary partners and which address stage-specific issues. And it is in this sense only that we speak of stages in respect to the anima and animus.

Our observations concur with previous formulations that there are four groupings or four developmental stages into which we can categorize the different types of animas and animuses. Each of these four groupings are divided into the elementary and transformative characters of the anima or animus. These two characters are again divided into a positive or a negative character. Thus, in the case of both the animus and the anima there are eight categories. This scheme is described in detail in the section which follows.

The developmental view contributes to our conceptualization of the anima and animus by relating their various character types to the broad stages of human development and to the unique conflicts in an individual's life course.

The stages of anima and animus

Three topics are addressed in this section. First, we examine the task of observing the anima/animus phenomenon in a small group. Certain considerations which come to play a role in these observations are discussed and the positions we have taken are advanced. Second, the basis of our descriptive schema is identified. Third, the specifications or descriptors for the four stages of the anima and animus are presented in summary form.

Observing the anima and animus in small groups

An individual reflecting upon his or her experience refers to it in terms of personal 'I'. The 'I' is the name given to personal content that is acknowledged, conscious, and owned. It is personal content which exists at the surface of an individual's psychic life. It can be readily acknowledged and claimed, or it can be simply accepted, but it cannot be denied. There are aspects of these contents which are experienced as a feeling, a mood, an undefinable emotionality, something that at the same time is part of the 'I' and yet foreign to it. These 'visitations' are frequently the manifestation of the anima or animus. The dynamic relationship between 'I' and the animus or anima most frequently occurs outside of the individual's awareness.

This dynamic has both an intra- and extra-psychic manifestation. Thus, the character attributes of the animus and anima at each of their respective stages may be experienced in two ways. They are experienced either as arising from within oneself or as being confronted in another person or object. In the former, there is some intimation of ownership of the attribute. While acknowledging ownership, the individual may have no sense of conscious planning or conception. If the individual is pushed to give a reason for the particular feeling, urge, or affect, a logical explanation may be provided, but there would be a hollow ring to it, and the explanation may even appear forced. One of the naive and yet accurate explanations concerning the origin of the phenomenon as experienced may be found in the most frequently given response: 'This is simply how I feel.'

Projection is the other way the animus or anima is experienced. The individual sees a person acting in a manner that takes on much affect and meaning for the one observing, and, accordingly, the other is experienced in a highly personal and emotional manner. For the individual, the other person exists, not as a unique individual, but as a living symbol of a particular character. In this relationship, there is no ownership of the character; however, the relationship reveals a fascination exhibited by the individual toward the other – a fascination which may express either positive or negative qualities.

These two ways of experiencing the anima or animus may be illustrated by examining the manner in which an individual experiences the positive, elementary character of giving, which is an attribute of anima's initial stage of development. When this quality is experienced as arising from within oneself, there is a sense that one has the capacity to bestow that which is being requested, without reserve, simply and unproblematically. The concern here is not with the substance or content of the giving but with the disposition of giving. In the case of projection, the other person is experienced as a giver. This personification of the other as giver may be restricted to the context of the individual's relationship with the other. That is to say, the other as giver may be narrowly perceived as existing only in that dimension. It is in this sense that the relationship between the individual and the other may be said to exist symbolically.

Though the individual actor may be only dimly aware of an existing mood and even less aware of the source of fascination involved in projection, his or her behavior may be observed and identified by knowledgeable observers. This is so because the inner reality may involve an outer manifestation. For example, when a group member takes on or adopts an agenda of the group as his or her own, it is because that agenda is the individual's agenda, and its meaning has personal, psychological significance. The assumption of symbolic and structural parallels between inner, psychic phenomena and their outer expression is key to the practice of analytical psychology; it is equally essential to the empirical study of archetypal phenomena.

According to analytical psychology, unconscious contents and processes are represented to consciousness in archetypally based symbols which are formally and structurally isomorphic to an inner, unconscious world of meaning. The symbol gathers up and expresses unconscious contents to consciousness. Such contents are understood to be weighted with affect and rich in layers of pre-verbal meaning. Because 'symbol' retains elements which are pre-conceptual or extra-conceptual, it forms a bridge between the inarticulate unconscious and the conscious world of concept and idea. In this view, specific, symbolic images, and all that attaches them by way of affect and impulse, manifest the structural underlay of unconscious behaviors.

The Jungian understanding that the constitutive and organizing principle of the unconscious is archetypally structured is the theoretical basis for the approach to group observation utilized in studying the manifestations of animus and anima in group interaction. This understanding is coupled with another fundamental, methodological premiss: that the unconscious yields up the fullest measure of its meaning and content to the observer who interrogates it in categories consistent with the logic and structure governing unconscious mental activities generally. The use of Jungian, archetypal symbols as orienting categories to guide observation is based upon these two assumptions. It is the language of this theoretical system which is used both to 'question' the phenomena and to interpret their 'answer'.

Procedural steps in the development of descriptors

As noted elsewhere, a number of analytical psychologists have made contributions to the conceptualization of the constructs 'anima' and 'animus'. Among these, the work of Erich Neumann is recognized as presenting one of the most extensive and systematic statements on the subject. These conceptualizations serve as the basis for the formulation of behavioral-affective specifiers in terms of which presence or absence of anima/animus content could be observed and coded in group transactions. The task of specifying descriptors to guide the observer in identifying the various manifestations of the anima and animus in group dynamics involved a careful review of Neumann's works (1954 a, b, 1955, 1956, 1959) of the primary material from Jung (1966 a, b, 1968 a, b, 1982), and of the related contributions from vonFranz (1964), Harding (1965), Hillman (1973, 1974), and Ulanov (1971). The present authors utilized these writings to formulate the descriptors of the anima and animus set forth in the *Manual for coding observations of individual behavior showing presence of the anima and animus* (Boyd et al. 1984).

In the development of the manual, every attribute of the four stages of the animus and anima identified by one authority was carefully checked to determine whether it was consistent with other authorities and with the basic propositions of analytical psychology. The manual sets forth descriptions of the stages, each in their elementary and transformative characters as viewed from three formats. One format identifies specific characteristics or attributes for each of the four stages. Another format presents figures and episodes from mythology which convey the essence or primary qualities of the animus/anima in their various stages. Finally, a conceptual treatment of the nature and dynamics of each stage is presented.

The following summary, drawn from the coding manual, gives a brief sketch of the positive and negative polarities of the four stages of animus and anima development, each in its elementary and transformative characters. The summary is provided to assist in the recognition of some of the ways these psychological processes manifest in human behavior.

The reader is encouraged to place him or herself in an actively receptive mode and to use the following sketches as a 'prime' in recalling instances of group experience which conform to the descriptors given. A more extensive and detailed set of specifiers for each of the 32 coded categories is available in the manual mentioned above. The qualities and characteristics outlined here are personifications and the reader should approach them metaphorically, not literally. They are offered as a device to prompt the observer's memory and impression for symbolic and affective Gestalts.

It is an important additional footnote to recall that in our framework, anima and animus are archetypal configurations which belong to both men and women, albeit with differing emphases and meanings in each case. Thus, for example, when we speak here of the fundamental characteristic of the animus as 'separation' and that of the anima as 'relatedness' we are not limiting these characteristics to one gender or another.

Anima's four stages

The stages of the development of the anima may be summarized by the following words and phrases: stage one, the purely instinctual – giving and accepting vs. withholding and rejecting; stage two, the romantic and aesthetic – joining and inspiring vs. ensnaring and vilifying; stage three, bringing forth life as on a physical or spiritual level – fructifying and creating vs. diminishment and devouring; stage four, experiencing integration and wisdom vs. disintegration and inanity. A primary quality is constant through all of these stages, for the anima never loses or changes its basic principle of relatedness (in the positive sense of increasing, enlarging, expanding and in the negative sense of narrowing, contracting, enclosing).

Anima: stage I

The positive aspect of the elementary character of the anima at this stage is very much the child of the Great Mother. In this stage the anima expresses the uncritical and uncomplicated acceptance of the role of daughter. She so identifies with the positive aspect of the Great Mother's givingness and bounty that she is ignorant of both Aphrodite's preoccupation with primordial fecundity and the Mother's great wrath. Indeed, the child anima is unable to cope with these realities and can only retreat before them. Her alliance with the nurturing aspect of the Maternal, as well as her ignorance of the Mother's bivalent maternity, allows the child anima to exist in an unconscious, pristine world. Her proximity to the all-encompassing Maternity of the unconscious is the source of her apparent unconcern about the dangers of a world apart from her own. She seems unaware that such worlds exist and that they constitute a threat. Her innocence of the world manifests in her giving, which is like the earth's bestowing of fruit and seeds – a giving without asking, openly extended. In her presence, one experiences a simple celebration of life.

As with all archetypal phenomena, there is a negative aspect to the elementary character of the anima at this stage. Living in an innocent, safe, and uncomplicated world, she resents any intrusions which might disturb that world. This anima is a girl-child who clings to Mother and is apprehensive of strangers. Her demeanor appears to others to be suspicious, unsharing, niggardly, apprehensive. She holds back or retreats from others when 'giving' would be the expectable part of the transaction.

At each stage, the anima is characterized by a transformative as well as an elementary character. The distinction between a transformative and an elementary character to the animus/anima is derived from Neumann's (1954b) treatment of the symbolism of the masculine and feminine. The transformative character at any stage is defined in terms of its contribution toward or its negation of an expansion of consciousness.

At the first stage, anima's positive, transformative character may be described in terms of an acceptance of another which makes possible the building of relationships. As a girl-child, she welcomes your participation and input. There is a sense here that the Other is being welcomed into anima's own world, rather than a mutuality of participation. Such activity is the prolegomenon to partnership, rather than partnership *per se*. Of course, in the Jungian formulation, outer events are matched by and symbolize concomitant inner development, so that what is also being illustrated here is the earliest relationship of anima to ego. In its positive manifestation, this relationship leads to a gradual enlargement of consciousness.

The negative half of this transformative character is best captured by the term 'rejecting'. The outer psychological dynamic here involves a turning away from transactions which, in furthering relationship, would expand consciousness. The parallel inner dynamic involves a shunning of the invitation to initiate a relationship with some aspect of the unconscious self. The individual may describe the experience as prompted by a fear of being rejected by others or as a response to an anxiety from some unexplained feeling of loneliness. Relatedness is both desired and rebuffed; its absence is keenly felt. Both the rejecting and the sense of impending rejection have a visceral quality. It is the girl-child who pretends indifference to the caring parent's overtures.

Anima: stage II

The elementary positive character at the second stage of anima's development is characterized by an impulse toward joining. This impulse is energized by a nascent sexuality. There is a naturalness or even innocence to the impetus toward partnership found at this stage – a quality which gives evidence of its preconscious origins. As Psyche first receives Amor in the dark of night, embracing the anonymous and unknown lover, so the joining activity at this phase is neither fully conscious nor really personal in intentionality. It is instinctive, rather than aware; based upon feeling as opposed to choice. It is a relatedness expressing a generalized impulse which is not clearly individual in its predisposition to form connection. As such, the activity prompted by the anima here is prevenient to genuine or full relationship. It precedes and is the necessary precondition for the development of a deeper and more profound meeting that may follow in later stages of development.

The term 'ensnaring' best describes the negative aspect of the elementary character of the anima at the second stage. As is true of the negative aspect at each stage, the negative aspect here involves a distortion of the positive – in this case, 'joining' gone awry. Because the elementary impulse toward forming connection at this stage is more instinctive than fully conscious, a certain blurring of boundaries may be expected to occur. The difficulty of differentiating the 'I' from the 'not-I' is an essential dynamic throughout stage II. That which is joined appears as something of an extension of the ego. It becomes an easy 'step' for this originally neutral, primordial impulse toward relatedness to become negative. The 'other' as joined to the 'I' becomes used in the service of ego. Separation, then, can come to represent a loss of a part of the self. Hence, we see a strong element of clinging or holding fast at the negative polarity of 'joining'.

Unlike the joining activity of the positive aspect, which serves as the foundation for a more complete and fulfilling relationship, its negative counterpart parodies real relationship. It is seductive, rather than truly loving. Thus, while the 'other' may be described as 'ensnared', it is equally true to say that the anima is also 'trapped', fixed at a stage, regressed in nature, which negates further development and inhibits the anima's most essential trajectory toward deeper relatedness. Correspondingly, the observer can sense an underlying anger or even muted rage in the face of this self-imposed entrapment, an anger which infuses all its activity at this polarity, whether or not it is consciously claimed or felt.

The term 'inspiring' serves as the key descriptor for the positive, transformative character at stage II. In this mode of joining, we find an enlivening, an enhancing, an encouraging that anticipates the more mature nurturing of later stages. The difference lies in intentionality. Whereas anima at a later stage will be oriented toward the nurturing of life and creativity, here the dominant passion lies in the impulse toward intimacy. The intimacy, itself, is experienced as expansive, self-donating, enriching that which is joined. As Beatrice in her relations to Dante evoked wholly other spheres of passion, creativity, and beauty, there is something of the muse at work here.

If 'inspiration' evolves out of a nascent form of intimacy, so does 'vilifying', the negative polarity of the transformative character. Only a kind of disappointed or distorted intimacy could provoke the behaviors and expressions descriptive of this aspect of anima behavior. We must be clear here – this is not the activity of the critical or harshly punitive parent, whose attempt to control or shape the behavior of the other has, at the very least, a negative relationship to nurturing. Rather, we have here the radical distortion of an intimacy that will not complete itself. The anima is inextricably joined to the 'I', and at the same time perceives it as other. The other is received as alien, feared, and to be held apart. In its scornful and destructive mode of relating, anima proposes a pseudo sort of intimacy in place of that which cannot (will not) be had. Psyche is prepared to destroy Amor, should the midnight lamp reveal a monster in her bed, instead of a god; destruction of the other is preferred to simply ending the relationship. Like Psyche, the anima in this negative aspect is prepared to destroy again and again rather than accept the options of either 'joining' or 'separating'. The diminishment of the outer-other, it should be emphasized, is both metaphor for and projection of an alienation with regard to the inner-other, and those aspects of the self perceived as somehow foreign or threatening. Indeed, the refusal of self-intimacy conditions all such negative involvement with another.

Anima: stage III

The anima experienced in its third stage has as its unifying theme the bringing forth of life and the nurturing of that to which one has given life. One is able to foster the other, to enable the other to prosper, thrive, or flourish. Mary is the image identified by vonFranz (1964) as the symbol of this stage. It is important, however, not to take the notion of 'mother' in the narrowly biological sense or to confuse this notion of a mothering nature with the properties of the Great Mother archetype. The term 'propagator' – to increase or extend acts of nurturing – is perhaps more descriptive of the phenomenon. There is a nurturing, bountiful quality to the anima at this stage, a feeling that one is able to give unconditionally because one's reserves are limitless. This is true whether the recipient is one's own dear child, one's own dear friend, or one's own project. The operative words here are 'one's own', for the

Other is embraced as one's responsibility or as given over into one's care.

If the positive half of the elementary character is defined by a fruitfulness with regard to self and others, the negative half may be described in terms of an unfruitfulness, a withholding, or even an abandoning. Because the anima here lacks a sense of her own ability to tap the abundant resources of life, she draws back from giving life or sustenance. This drawing back occurs out of a fear of depleting her own shallow reserves. The anima at this stage and modality is neglectful of whatever is given into her care. Projects or causes may be allowed to 'die on the vine'. In fairy tales, perhaps the clearest illustration of this character is the image of the wicked stepmother.

The experiencing of creativeness evolves from the relationship an individual has with the anima in its positive, transformative character. Creativity must be differentiated from inventiveness and discovery, which are processes initiated by the animus. Creativity brings forth into existence, while invention fabricates through ingenius thinking. Creative artists and thinkers have long identified a metaphoric relationship between the creative process generally and the experience of gestation and parturition. Such metaphors serve to identify only the most transparent aspects of the phenomena embodied by the stage III anima figure in her transformative mode. Anima III is active in the artist who plunges deeply into the collective unconscious to bring forth the archetypal project. It is a primary pattern of life to which the creative individual gives birth.

The negative aspect of the transformative character of this stage is experienced in various forms of being possessed. The responsibility for one's own life is threatened and frequently taken over by this anima, and her distorted and relentless claims of ownership insist upon its own prerogatives even at the expense of the other's individuality. This negative anima reverses the creative process. Rather than relinquishing her possessive claims, she draws the individual back into the control of the archetypal forces and the unconscious. Recognition of the classic Jungian dictum that what is inside is outside (and vice versa) gives a clear understanding of the connection between creativity and madness. The anima may take the ego so deeply into the unconscious dimension that the road back has been lost. If escape from such an anima is not total, the individual moves in and out between disillusionment and depression on the one hand, or inflated exaggeration of his or her creative capacities, on the other.

Anima: stage IV

A tension comes into play in stage IV anima between integration and wholeness on the one hand, and disintegration or fragmentation on the other. The positive character of the anima assists ego to experience the feeling of togetherness as wholeness, and this experience of wholeness is visceral. One comes to it not by explanation or knowledge gained through searching out and deliberating, but through long hours of waiting filled with observing and silent contemplation. The wholeness is felt to be rather than known to be.

The positive elementary character of the anima involves the individual with the circle of life. Initially, the circle was uroboric and self-contained, unconscious and unproblematic; here it is spiritual; here it reaches toward an understanding of how life's experiences have simultaneously enlarged consciousness and enriched the 'I' by its integrative transactions with Self. The anima assists ego to experience a sense of togetherness as a kind of wholeness not through words or by direction but simply by experiencing and being. This wholeness is encountered as Self in world and World in Self.

There are two sides to the negative elementary character of anima IV, either of which may be in evidence. On the one hand, there may be an experience of disintegration, a sense that life is bereft of continuity. The sense of life as discontinuous is accompanied by a feeling of despair. On the other hand, the underlying despair may be denied, while the individual compensates through self-indulgence. This anima in her negative form abandons all ties to the Great Mother archetype and leads the individual to infant-like egocentricity and to total self-preoccupation.

The positive transformative character of anima at this stage extends to ego a wisdom that is life related, rather than word related. This wisdom has its roots in the experience of living and in a sense of wholeness with regard to life's processes. The wholeness and wisdom are as much about the relationship of ego to the unconscious as of ego to the world. In her presence, the individual knows, with a knowing that is beyond logic, that he/she is being offered the deepest and most fundamental of meaning. In the shade of an ancient tree, the dialog is direct but unhurried, often unspoken, and frequently carried by simply being with the other.

The negative transformative character of the anima at this fourth, and last, stage parades as an all knowing figure, for it attempts to cover up its sense of disintegration and emptiness. It has not traversed life's journey in the manner necessary to connect ego to the unconscious sources of wholeness. Its only interest has been a self-love that characterized the primitive emotions of the Olympian gods (goddesses), with whom it still identifies. Hence, she is an anima without substance, who can only lead the individual to meaningless and shallow dialog.

The attribute modalities of the positive and negative aspects of the elementary and transformative characters for each of the anima's four

DEVELOPMENTAL STAGES

		I	II	III	IV
Elementary character	Positive	Giving	Joining	Fructifying	Experiencing integration
	Negative	Depriving	Ensnaring	Devouring	Experiencing disintegration
Transformative character	Positive	Accepting	Inspiring	Experiencing creating	Possessing wisdom
	Negative	Rejecting	Vilifying	Experiencing madness	Showing inanity

Figure 6.1 Positive and negative modalities of the four stages of the anima's elementary and transformative characters

stages are presented in Figure 6.1. The term modality has been used here to identify the main and specific form of the relationship the ego experiences with the anima. Thus, for example, 'giving', which has been identified as the elementary positive attribute of stage I, is used here to depict the essence of the anima's relationship being experienced by the ego. The specifiers which have been employed to identify the modalities are words which have a sufficiently general connotation to portray the essential qualities of the modalities. It is recognized that the specifiers do not stand as operational concepts without a comprehensive explanation, but for such an understanding the reader is referred to the manual which was developed for the study. The purpose in presenting the material diagrammatically is to provide a ready reference to the basic modalities of the anima over its own stages of development. It is not intended to replace the explanatory discussions of the characteristics of the anima in each of its four stages.

Animus's four stages

The animus, like the anima, develops through four stages, each having an elementary and transformative character. The stages of animus development, in their positive and negative polarities, are characterized by the following words and phrases: stage one, personification of physical power – energizing and exploring vs. exhausting and inhibiting; stage two, possessing initiative and a capacity for planned action – conquering and mastering vs. evading and enslaving; stage three, bringing about by intellectual effort and words – making and inventing vs. destroying and a characteristic which might best be captured by the phrase 'foolishly contriving'; stage four, a uniting with wisdom and meaning vs. fragmenting with guile or foolishness. Separation moving toward differentiation is the masculine principle that underlies the activity of the animus at each stage of its development.

The animus manifests the masculine principle and its progenitor is the archetype of the Great Father. It is therefore a historical as well as a concurrent entity in the human psyche to be found in both men and women. The animus is experienced from a different perspective by women than it is by men because identification with the animus is by gender a different relationship. To posit this position is not to ignore the wide variance in the way that men and women have defined their identity to masculinity and, at an unconscious level, their relationship with the animus. What cannot be dismissed is the biological dimension which is a primary dynamic for both men and women as they work at defining their identity as a man or woman. Individual and gender differences are only incidentally dealt with in the following discussion on the animus. For a more comprehensive treatment of these differences, the reader is referred to the manual that was developed for this research study.

Animus: stage I

The positive aspect of the elementary character in stage I is experienced as an energizing force. The experience can be described as an upsurge of energy, a burst of power which is to be differentiated from the prudent use of energy more evident in later stages. Alternatively, energy may be perceived – i.e. invested – outside of oneself, in another individual or group of individuals. The team spirit of youthful sport activities carries this animus quality of unreflective, animated energy. This animus is a youth, eager to pit his power against a challenge, not in the spirit of conquest, but in the sheer demonstration of strength. There is a naive, unselfconscious, and also playful quality to this activity. It is qualified by neither the competitiveness nor the goal or task orientation that we shall find at a later stage. This animus is still very much a child of the patriarchal archetype, embedded in its unconscious origins; hence, the burst of power or energizing force here has a primordial and primitive quality. The animus is a Peter Pan, a youth full of energy but unlike a youthful knight, he seeks no holy grail. In a small group, a member may be observed expressing this stage of the animus verbally; 'Let's not just sit here. Let's get started and do something.' The clear implication is for action, not a specific plan with a perceived goal – just action.

In its negative aspect, the animus seems confronted with a progressive sense of inertia. The experience of enervation arises when vitality is drawn back from consciousness into the unconscious, where the energy is dissipated. The individual is viewed as listless, withdrawn, tired, de-energized. This pervasive devitalization may be described by the individual either as originating within the self or as being caused by some outside agency, either 'I feel powerless' or 'The group (or someone or something) makes me feel powerless.' Also possible is the ascription to another or others of the powerlessness to act.

The positive aspect of the transformative character can be described by the modality of exploring. The symbol of animus at this stage is that of the curious, inquisitive, probing boy – Tom Sawyer investigating his world. There is much more initiative than persistent industry here. It is a case of wanting to know without any explicit reason for wanting to know other than that one is aware of not knowing. Unlike the elementary character of 'energizing' described above, in which energy is expended without orientation to objective goal, the transformative modality of exploring presupposes something to be known and hence at least a rudimentary orientation toward an object or objects. This is the initial stage in the development of an instrumental consciousness.

The negative aspect of the transformative character has been labelled 'restraining'. This restraining activity may be imposed upon the self or upon others. The sense here is not that of being contained, as in an enclosure. Neither are we describing a lack of energy. Rather, the individual feels that he/she is being held back from going forth to explore; or, as projection, the individual feels compelled to inhibit others with regard to knowing or exploring. To give the descriptors an allegorical sense, it is as though one were told to stay in camp, rather than being allowed to explore the woods. To explore the woods might be construed as contrary to what one is supposed to or ought to do. Here consciousness is being held back by patriarchal forces – rules, structure, the superego.

Animus: stage II

The elementary character of animus at stage II is best described in terms of the polarity 'overcoming' vs. 'enslavement'.

On the positive side, the aspect is best characterized by the terms 'overcoming' or 'conquering'. When we say 'conquer' we are not implying any vindictiveness or meanness, nor is there any suggestion of intent to destroy. Instead, we have the kind of triumph which occurs from winning a competition or overcoming another or others in fair contest. The activity being described here is in the spirit of the medieval joust, where the young, untried knight challenges the best, the bravest, the most honored to the Lists. Winning itself is the goal, but it is a winning over the worthiest opponent, so that on the winner is conferred the chaplet and the honor rightfully belonging to the hero of the day. Mythologically, one might speak of 'deposing the king' (Neumann, 1954 b) – the coming to terms with authority as projection. In group literature, this corresponds to Slater's (1966) notion of the attack on the leader. The hero comes out of the arena with a sense of greater personal authority and command. That is to say, the victory initiates that process of withdrawing the authority projection, of claiming one's own inner authority, so essential to the development of consciousness.

The negative half of the elementary character at this stage is designated by the modality 'enslavement'. If the positive side of the elementary character captures a sense of victory, a triumph over another which confers its own status and authority, the negative counterpart involves a withdrawal of energy from the contest, such that the victory is not even attempted. The critical element has to do with the location of authority. Here, authority is conceded as largely and properly outside the self. Prompted by the animus, ego remains circumscribed by and dependent upon what are seemingly external givens. Tied to convention and conventional mores and submitting to restraints seen as imposed from without, the ego remains trapped in what Neumann describes as a form of 'patriarchal castration' where the ego 'remains totally dependent on the Father as the representative of collective norms...bound by traditional morality and convention' (1954b, p. 187). It may also appear in its reverse form, the permanent revolutionary, compulsively and impotently challenging authority, thereby, paradoxically, granting and remaining tied to authority's claim (1954b, p. 190).

The polarity which constitutes the transformative character of the second stage of animus development is defined in terms of the tension between 'mastering' and 'evading'.

There is a subtle, but nonetheless important, distinction between the elementary character of 'conquering' and its transformative counterpart 'mastering'. Both connote an overcoming. While the elementary character is defined by the victory, the transformative both contains the sense of victory and at the same time surpasses it in a movement that transforms the person through the activity. The focus is not so much on the outcome as it is on process and the acts of attaining. It is not primarily a case of winning over someone, but rather on mastering the obstacles encountered. Outer mastery is metaphor for mastery of the self. Hence, there is an emphasis on an inner transformation that accompanies the achievement. It is the difference between Sir Gwain challenging Launcelot as Gwynhefar's champion and the journey of Parsifal in his quest for the grail. In the latter legend, Parsifal's meeting and mastering each challenge and difficulty presented along the way corresponds to an inner achievement. The development of consciousness requires a disciplined spirit and a willingness to deal with and master the challenges ego encounters. The passion lies with the process as much as with the outcome. It is consciousness which is gradually being accomplished here. The animus, as champion, both energizes and guides in its role as psychopomp.

The negative aspect of the transformative character is experienced as avoiding the very challenges that need to be mastered if consciousness is to develop. There is a pervasive sense of flight, timidity, even cowardice here. The quest is not undertaken, or one turns back in the face of the early obstacle. Hence, transformation is not accomplished. When Psyche's lamp revealed the face of Amor, he fled, fearful of confronting his mother's wrath, fearful, too, of facing Psyche in the seering light of consciousness. Likewise, the knight Mordred refrains from the quest to which the other knights are enjoined, feigning concern for his father Arthur. The experience of 'flight' is evident, for example, when the individual, confronted with the need to relinquish his/her hold on that which can no longer serve the growth toward consciousness, hesitates, and then holds on with even greater tenacity.

Animus: stage III

The polarity of the elementary character of the third stage is between 'making', on the one hand, and 'destroying' on the other.

When the individual is in touch with the positive half of this modality, the power or energy of the spirit or word is used to bring into being, to construct, to fabricate. It is the direct and uncomplicated expression of the activity of the human spirit on material or biological or even social circumstance. The act, however, is directed wholly toward outcome, and not beyond itself. It is pristine in its utility. In the relation between person and product, the act finds its *raison d'être*.

Destroying is the negative half of animus's elementary character at this stage. This animus turns the individual to destructive acts, whether the destruction is vested upon an object or a person or upon the autonomy of an idea or thought. The negative modality, like its positive counterpart, is the expression of person upon thing.

Invent, originate, and produce are transactions between person and object which transform both the inventor and the invention, the producer and the production. When prompted by the transformative character of stage III animus, the individual expresses human energy in finding or creating connection between or among two or more objects, ideas, or notions. In this expression of person on thing, something new is brought into existence, something whose reason for existence exceeds the original relationship or utility.

The negative transformative character is expressed as inflation of one's abilities. The individual experiences a sense of being original and inventive in a world that cannot appreciate his/her brilliance. Whereas anima at a corresponding stage may also experience a form of inflation, hers is occasioned by a loss of connection to consciousness and a concomitant flooding of ego with unconscious contents; animus, by contrast, leads ego toward a spiritual hubris, a disconnection from the unconscious. That what we have here is inflation not invention becomes evident not only in the lack of workmanship, but also in the prosaic treatment of the human spirit that fails to arouse passion or relate us to either suffering or joy. The unjustified inflation is also revealed in the ego's preoccupation with the ownership of the work and with its advertised merits.

Animus: stage IV

The elementary character of the fourth stage is revealed in its attempted resolutions to the basic masculine principle of separation. On the positive side of the character, the animus struggles to unite. This uniting is different from the feminine, for the animus here is working at bringing disparate parts or elements into a union. The animus comes to see

162

DEVELOPMENTAL STAGES

		I	II	III	IV
Elementary character	Positive	Energizing	Conquering	Making (as a maker)	Uniting
	Negative	Enervating	Enslaving	Destroying	Fractionalizing
Transformative character	Positive	Exploring	Mastering	Inventing	Giving wisdom
	Negative	Restraining	Evading	Stagnating	Misleading

Figure 6.2 Positive and negative modalities of the four stages of the animus's elementary and transformative characters

connections which tie parts together whereas the anima experiences a whole and only secondarily comes to perceive the parts of the whole.

If the principle of separation remains dominant at this stage, the animus is experienced as a source of fractionalizing. The negative modality of the elementary character is being expressed when the animus works at keeping aspects of a situation discrete and opposes the ego's attempts to see patterns or connections with major life issues.

The transformative character of the animus is either the wise old man or the evil guru. Wisdom based on the masculine principle is different in kind from that founded on the feminine principle. The format is exemplified in the figures of Solomon and Merlin. They are sages, wisdom built on knowledge, experience, reflection. They explain and provide advice, and may even point the way.

The evil guru leads ego to overemphasize one aspect of life to the detriment of others, and so prevents wholeness and centroversion. It is Mephistopheles who leads Faust astray. In an attempt to develop one aspect of his life, Faust allows other elements in his character to be sacrificed. The negative element of the transformative character can also be experienced as a desperate race against time to make some meaning of one's life.

The critical modalities for each of the four stages are presented in Figure 6.2. As in the case of the anima, this chart is offered solely as a summary of the discussion on the animus's developmental stages.

An empirical study

Our work has been grounded in practice. Over many years of conducting small groups, we have come to an understanding of the explanatory power of analytical psychology. We discovered that in the theories of analytical psychology were to be found many of the answers to questions which had challenged our understanding. The explanations and insights which these theories gave provided us with new ways to see what had been only vaguely perceived and inadequately comprehended.

There is another side to our work that is complementary to practice but which has a different end in view. It is our commitment to the empirical testing of ideas. This aspect of our work has been and continues to be demanding, provocative, stimulating, and rewarding. In the final phase, our work is to be put into the marketplace for public examination. It is to this project that we now turn our attention.

The first step in carrying out this project was to describe as precisely as we could the behavioral specifications of the images that were to be empirically examined and tested. This task was undertaken, and the outcome of that work has been presented in the preceding two sections. We then faced the question: Is it possible to identify, in the flow of inter-

and intrapersonal transactions, evidence of anima/animus behavior as they were specified? This primary question was restructured to address three basic areas of our enquiry which, for methodological purposes, were set forth as conjectures.

(1) The anima/animus have stages of development which can be observed in the interactions of small groups with an acceptable level of intersubjective agreement among observers.

(2) The anima/animus take active roles in the processes of individuation as observed in the context of a small group.

(3) Anima and animus activity will be found as active images in the behaviors of both men and women.

The testing of these conjectures required the undertaking of a series of activities. Since these are generally accepted as standard procedures in the conduct of an empirical study, a brief description will suffice.

Our first task was to develop descriptions of the sixteen images of the anima and animus which would be conceptually accurate and also appropriate for the purposes of our study. These descriptions or set of specifiers had to be clearly formulated in order to clearly differentiate the specific character images of the anima and animus. The steps that were taken in the development of these specifications and a brief description of the sixteen characters have been presented in the previous section. A coding manual was the product of this work. It contains a detailed set of specifications for each of the sixteen characters as well as specific guidelines for observers (coders) to follow in recording anima and animus phenomena.

The importance of a common understanding of the sixteen characters is critical to any application that would be made of this formulation. This point has been stressed earlier and therefore does not need to be pursued further at this time. It cannot be assumed that what passes as an acceptable level of common understanding also means that this knowledge can be employed at an acceptable level of agreement among coders – thus, our concern over the level of intercoder agreement or reliability. This was our second task and the next step that had to be taken following the specification of the anima and animus characters. This task involved the development and implementation of a training schedule for coders and specific procedures to determine the abilities of the coders to observe behaviors manifesting anima and animus content. Reporting on these matters would be distractive, leading us away from the focus of our discussion. These matters were examined elsewhere (Boyd *et al.* 1989) if the reader wishes to pursue the subject. Three types of intercoder agreement were considered. When only codings for the presence of either anima or animus content were considered, the three coders reached a paired agreement at the level of 53 percent. When a finer measure of agreement was examined – pairwise agreement on the stages of development - a reliability measure of 73 percent was obtained. When the most rigorous criterion was used – agreement on the character image of the anima or animus – the coders reached a 63 percent level of pairwise agreement. In view of the number of codable categories (n=17) and the extensive time sample which was involved in the study (five hours of observation), the reliability measures were most encouraging.

These findings support our first conjecture that anima/animus stages are identifiable and can be observed with an acceptable level of intersubjective agreement among knowledgeable observers. As encouraging as these results are, it is important to bear in mind that the intercoder agreement which was obtained has been based on one set of behaviors. This fact does not minimize the results but it does remain for further empirical studies to test these procedures before we can be more assured of the universal quality of our findings.

The third task which was now before us was to corroborate or falsify the existence of the manifestations of anima/animus images in the behaviors of group members. Since there were data showing that we were able to identify such images, our task became primarily that of observing in what ways these images furthered or impeded personal transformations and constructive group dynamics. A self-study group was selected for the study. No agenda, task, or structure was given to the group when it met for the first time, other than the specific dates, times, and length of the sessions. A handout explained briefly the experiential nature of the sessions and the role of the leader (professor) whose contributions would be limited and in the form of metaphors, scenarios from literature, mythology, and familial themes. The room in which the sessions were held was equipped with three video cameras which were able to scan and record the entire group.

The group, composed of twelve members, included three nurses, three teachers, two social workers, an engineer, an educational administrator, and two persons who described themselves as graduate students. Ten participants had full-time jobs; however, all twelve members were enrolled in some form of graduate study. Their ages ranged from the late twenties to the late forties, with the majority clustered around the late thirties. The group was composed of nine women and three men.

An early and late session of the group were selected for intensive analysis. Video tapes had been made of all the sessions and these tapes were used as the data base for this study. The entire two sessions of two and one half hours were individually and independently coded by three coders. The coders met after they had completed their coding to identify where they were not in agreement and to resolve these differences or to leave them as points of disagreement.

Table 6.1 Coding of anima/animus content in two group sessions

Members	Anima Stages					Animus Stages				
	I	II	(III & IV)	Total	%	I	II	(III & IV)	Total	%
Female (N = 9)	67	39	10	116	47.5	56	57	15	128	52.5
Male (N = 3)	15	12	8	35	31.8	18	45	12	75	68.2
Total	82	51	18	151	42.6	74	102	27	203	57.4

The coding of anima and animus content from the two group sessions provided the data to test our second and third conjectures. Our second conjecture asserted that anima/animus images take active roles in the processes of individuation within the context of small groups. The third conjecture posited that both anima and animus content can be found in the behaviors of men and women. Two forms of data are presented to address these conjectures. We will first examine the coding data which provide observational evidence of anima/animus content in the behaviors of both men and women members. In the section which follows, we will present four brief case studies which illustrate how anima and animus images were manifested in the behaviors of group members and the import of these phenomena on personal transformations and group dynamics.

The coding data for the two sessions are presented in Table 6.1. We were struck by the sheer number of codings for the five hour period revealing the very active role these images play in the transactions of small groups. These results may well be a function of the type of group that was being studied; a small group whose aim was to help members become aware of the personal and group dynamics. Even taking into account this fact, the total number of codings remains impressive and may indicate that these images play a far more significant role in our interactions than would have been generally expected.

Earlier we discussed the ways these images enter into our personal transactions, namely by projection or through an upsurge of affective content. The codings provided evidence of both types.

The data show other important relationships. Contrary to that which would be predicted on the basis of the traditional formulation, men do manifest animus images in their behavior. Similarly, women manifest anima images. The presence of anima motifs in the interactions of men and of animus images in woman's group behavior appear to be more than incidental occurrences. Indeed, in the case of women, there is only a small difference between the total number of anima and animus codings. This difference is even more marked in the interaction of male group members. Men show more than twice as many animus as anima codings. This high activity of the animus may be a result of several dynamics occurring within the group. One plausible explanation would suggest that during those phases of group development when the Great Mother archetype dominates and configures group process, men in the group have to work exceptionally hard to maintain their separate identity from the Mother Figure. Whatever the source, this finding remains an interesting one in light of the classical Jungian formula on the contrasexual, which posits an anima in the psyche of men and an animus in the psyche of women exclusively.

It is of interest to note that there were far more animus than anima codings overall and that this unexpectedly high proportion of animus events occurred during those periods when the group as a system was in the Great Mother phase of its development. There are undoubtedly several levels of explanations for this finding. Two that are clearly interrelated are offered here. The group exists as a structure within a course in a university. Since the culture of a university is patriarchal and the American culture at large is also patriarchal, it would seem reasonable to assume that animus would be active in the interpersonal relations in such a setting.

There was not a similar number of men and women in the group finding which raises the question regarding the ratio of codings to gender membership. These ratios were obtained in the following manner. For example, there were 116 anima images manifested by the nine women members. The total number of anima images were divided by 9 to give a ratio of 12.8. Interestingly, the ratios are not markedly different. In the anima codings, the women were 12.8 while the men were 11.6. The differences in the anima codings were somewhat more marked as shown by a ratio of 19.2 for women as over against 25.0 for men.

The findings provided a form of predictive validity for both our methodology and the stage theory for anima/animus in general. An examination of the table shows the greatest number of anima codings in stage I, the second highest in stage II, and then the third and fourth stages were combined to make one score. The score in this combined category was lower than that in each of the first two stage categories. We would expect to see more activity in stages I and II in the initial periods of a group's life than in a later period. As reported, there was a greater number of stage I and II animus and anima images than stages III and IV images. There was one finding which did not follow the expected sequence. There was a much larger number of codings for stage II animus than stage I for the male members. There may be several forces at work which produced this result. One possible explanation may be found in the cultural context of the group. During the period in which the study was being conducted, the group was in the group phase development of the Great Mother. It is very possible that the male members were working against being 'enslaved' by what they perceived as a powerful Mother and their actions involved 'overcoming' any sense of dependency. Within a Mother culture, men may feel a strong need to establish their gender identity and engage in behaviors of 'separation'. This explanation could account for their limited activity of exploring (animus stage I) and their greater concern for 'conquering' and 'overcoming' (animus stage II).

There is much more that we could examine in this set of data but that would take us far beyond the scope of this present chapter. The purpose of this section was to present a brief discussion of an empirical study that illustrated the application of the framework set forth in this chapter. The next section presents four case studies that provide the reader with a more in-depth examination of the ways in which the anima/animus further and impede personal transformations and group dynamics.

Case studies

The following case studies were taken from a graduate course on group dynamics. The first ten weeks of the course were conducted as an experiential workshop; a setting designed to give the ten members opportunities to experience and observe the dynamics which occur in small groups. There was one session per week; each was two and one half hours in length. The role that the group leader took during these sessions is described in a later chapter.

The small group, with its complex set of relationships, transactions, and interpersonal negotiations, provides ample opportunity for projection to occur. In addition, the simple realities of group participation ensure that, in one way or another, the actor-in-group must contend with the responses others make to the perceptions or affects he/she has projected upon other group members or upon some other external circumstance. The invitation to self-reflection is all the more compelling when not just one, but two or three or more witnesses confirm or challenge an understanding, a belief, or a response. If the individual so chooses, this outer dialectic within the group may serve to initiate or further the sort of inner dialog which is the absolute prerequisite of personal transformation.

Session two had ended in intense and obvious conflict between two outspoken members, Nancy and Sandi. The perception of at least one member, Cathy, was that Nancy had 'attacked' Sandi; and Cathy had shared her perception only minutes before the end of the session. The objective observer is puzzled, then, that during the third session, a week later, it is almost a full hour into the meeting before any reference is made to the conflict. Finally, someone in the group asks Sandi how she has felt about things since the last meeting. A number of other group members follow suit, with some self-identified guilt for perhaps being less sensitive to Sandi's plight than they now see might have been helpful. These comments go on, despite Sandi's clear and repeated message that she assumes responsibility for the state of her own affect and for requesting help when necessary. Tim's and Nora's statements are typical of the group response to Sandi.

> *Tim*: I felt that we . . . that I as a member of the group let you down by not attuning myself to your concerns. . . . It would be helpful to me if you could talk about what things we could do to restore your

trust. . . . It would be helpful to our future sharing because I could see how you could be a little less willing to risk that kind of conflict.

Sandi: I don't know if there is anything you could do . . . I feel it's my responsibility to bring things up if I need to . . . but I appreciate your concern.

Nora: I don't feel that it's fair to yourself. I think that if you're under some strain, that's the time you can't ask for support.

During these interactions, Nancy, the other party to the earlier conflict, has been sitting on the edge of her chair. Nancy had made a number of comments during this phase of group transaction which an observer could interpret, with some assurance, as indicating Nancy's own level of distress. However, the group's focus is elsewhere. Finally, Nancy introjects forcefully:

Nancy: Do you know how I felt . . . I felt bad, sad, scared, hurt when you [to Cathy] said 'Why are you attacking Sandi?' And now I feel frustrated that a number of you said that Sandi was left alone. Because Sandi has this stereotypical, child-like, soft, feminine, take-care-of-me quality to her, and I don't have that, cause I've worked hard to get rid of that cause it didn't get me what it got Sandi . . . I decided to be thirty-eight in my behavior . . . I used an assertive, responsible voice . . . does this mean I have to behave like a little girl to get support?

Several members of the group respond to Nancy by indicating that they, at least, have perceived Sandi as neither little-girl cloyish nor as making a child-like plea for support. Sandi, herself, is surprised at Nancy's depicting of her feminine qualities:

Sandi: Most of my life people have been telling me that I'm too domineering, too aggressive, too unfeminine, and that they wish I'd shut up and act like a girl!

Cathy identifies the issue at stake for her, and apparently for others as well, for her comments are accompanied by acknowledging nods of several in the group.

Cathy: Sandi was speaking for the group in challenging your position [to Nancy] . . . I guess when I said that I felt that Sandi was left unsupported, it was because she was saying what I was feeling and I let her argue my position.

According to Cathy, it was not any overt, personal characteristics of Sandi which elicited the concern about supporting her, but rather the role Sandi had played for the group.

At this point in the group, Nancy has the benefit of several perspectives both on her perception of Sandi as presenting with little-girl affect and on her understanding of why group members offered support to Sandi but not to Nancy. In this context, she becomes quieter, reflecting on her own childhood in an abusive, alcoholic family, when it was literally unsafe for her to be either feminine or childlike. It is the innocent, child-Anima (Anima I) which was projected on Sandi. It is her own 'face' which Nancy sees in Sandi, a face she has not recognized in the mirror of conscious reflection. To concern ourselves with the part Sandi played in the projection would take us too far afield and into another story. Sufficient to suggest here that it is because of her own issues with femininity and assertiveness, as reported by Sandi herself, that she becomes the convenient, receptive screen for Nancy's anima projections.

As Nancy continues to interact with the group around these and other issues, it is evident that the responses of group members have left an impression which Nancy will continue to process for some time to come. Even as she shares with the group about her family experiences she enters a level of trust from which she had previously defended herself. The experience in this group has provided Nancy with an objectification of an anima issue in her life. Her encounter with Sandi has led her to confront something of herself. Other group participants offer an alternative view to Nancy's projective bias. The tasks of coming to recognize one's own projections for what they really are and of withdrawing those projections from the environment, replacing them within the Self where they belong, are ardous tasks. They are, however, the conditions *sine qua non* of expanded consciousness and of that greater wholeness which indicates movement toward the individuated person.

The relationship between individual and group is intense and always dialectical. As we have seen in the above case, the group setting affords individual members the opportunity for encountering and more consciously assimilating anima and animus elements within the total personality. It is our experience as well that as individuals confront anima or animus issues which group transactions inevitably raise, group processes are either furthered or impeded. This appears to be especially true when the anima or animus issues are engaged in their transformative character.

The literature in group dynamics, across various theoretical orientations, generally recognizes two essential group processes: that of establishing or maintaining relationships and that of advancing group tasks or goals. These two group processes appear to be advanced through the successful resolutions of individual anima and animus issues respectively. Thus, for example, in the case discussed above, as

Nancy and Sandi move toward some larger accommodation of their personal anima concerns, the quality of the resolutions will be seen to advance trust and relatedness in the group.

Similarly, as an individual engages issues related to one of anima's four stages, movement of the group toward task will be promoted or inhibited. Such a movement is observed in the following observational account. After a long pause in the group's interactions, Mary suggests 'are we skirting some issue?' and Cathy responds immediately and energetically with her concern.

> *Cathy*: That's what I'd like to talk about, and I feel pretty helpless at figuring out where we're supposed to go . . . I *am* uncomfortable with not knowing where this is going . . . I'm tired of it in fact . . . I'm curious about where this group could go.

The first stage of animus in its transformative character is specified by the polarity 'exploring vs. restraining'. On the positive side, animus prompts ego to explore simply for the sake of knowing, to try to find out for no other reason than because one is curious. There is an inquisitiveness here, but not necessarily industry. On the 'negative' pole, one feels restrained from knowing; there is a sense of being held back, experiencing a sense of limitation or constraint on one's explorations or upon one's knowing.

In this illustrative vignette, Cathy seems to be speaking as though some vague and undefined force were preventing the group from realizing something about its destiny as a collective. It is clear that for Cathy, subjectively, the capacity to 'move' the group lies outside of herself as an actor. The intensity of affect with which these remarks are delivered for group consideration alerts the observer to the possibility that Cathy's statements are more than simple commentary on group process. In a later session, we are given a glimpse of some of the dynamic issues which undergird her sense of powerlessness with regard to movement in the group.

In response to a group-level intervention made by the male, group leader/instructor, Monica, a graduate student in her late twenties, describes her relationship with male authority figures, specifically her first work supervisor and her benevolent but domineering father. Monica concludes by acknowledging that it has taken a long time for her to recognize her share of responsibility in shaping these relationships. In giving too much power away in relation to these two men, Monica notes, she ended up feeling both impotent and resentful. At this point, Cathy introjects, becoming tearful as she speaks.

> *Cathy*: I have a father like that, very loving but very autocratic. He has always treated me like a child. I want to say to him that I'm a

173

mother now, and I have my own children. I want to ask him to please change the way he relates to me . . . I've tried to bring myself to tell him. I've told my husband . . . but I haven't ever told my father.

In retrospective view, as appears to be true in regard to Cathy's inability to confront her father, when Cathy speaks of her sense of being held back from pursuing some group course or goal, it is largely Cathy who is restraining Cathy from exploring. Although Cathy does not directly confront and acknowledge the projection which is the source of her impotent restraint, her dilemma, enacted in the group, invites group members to examine the manner in which their own process has been blocked. Cathy's struggles with her animus energies provokes the kind of group self-examination which is both the goal and the requirement of self-analytic groups generally.

How are the anima and animus images played out in the lives of male members of the group? We will report on these phenomena as they were observed on two separate occasions in a group where one male member first manifested the anima image in his interactions and then, on a later occasion, an animus image became active in his behavior.

The group was deeply involved in discussing the conflict two women members had had during the last session of the group. Their differences were not fully disclosed although there appeared some readiness on their parts to begin such an exploration. The mood of the group was cautious but receptive to allowing the discussion to continue. The group was in the phase of the differentiation of the Good and Bad Mother, and had not as yet moved to the acceptance of one image over the other. Nancy and Sandi were sharing some of their feelings about the conflict but had not resolved them, nor had they clearly identified the basis of their conflict. The open conflict, although it appeared under control, was not moving toward a resolution and there was a growing sense in the group of disharmony and mistrust. It was at this point that Tim spoke up. His manner was calm, and his words were spoken slowly but with conviction.

Tim: Since I feel I let you down, as a member of the group, I want to tune myself into your concerns which somewhere along the way I missed. It would be helpful to me and to others, I think, to find out from us what things could restore that trust we were developing. It would be important to our future in our sharing. I could see where you would be a little less willing to share – express that conflict unless we had that trust. What things could restore that trust? Our willingness to risk that conflict?

As he was talking he looked directly at the two women and then as he posed his questions he scanned the entire group. Although an observer may be quite certain in his/her mind that there is clear evidence to code for the presence of an anima/animus image in a member's behavior, the procedure is to go on to see if subsequent interactions would support the coding. Following Tim's input to the group Sandi responded with noticeable warmth and tenderness in her voice. She acknowledged the point that he had made but added that it was her own responsibility to see that others understood where she was 'coming from'. In her manner she was relating to Tim's caring, nurturing, and his message of offering a more trusting and enabling way of relating. Tim nodded and appeared to accept Sandi's position. Other members quickly entered and made the point that the responsibility Sandi was trying to assume was unreasonable to ask of any member. Sandi and any other member should expect others to 'join in and work the problem through'.

These transactions provide clear evidence to support the interpretation that Tim's contributions were seen as caring and nurturing and the results that his input had for the group were to move it toward a culture that would further more helpful relationships within the group. Whether such a culture did develop or not is not at issue here. The task before us is the interpretation of Tim's behavior. What we observe is that Tim's behavior showed the upsurge of anima content and it was responded to as anima content.

In a later session, the group was dealing with the separation of the Great Parents. The specific topic was the sense one had of one's family and the way it handled conflict. They spoke about the different roles that fathers and mothers take in family conflicts. Tim said that what they were discussing recalled the feeling he got in faculty meetings with fellow teachers. It was like a family that had conflicts but were not aired because father (the principal) interceded before any conflict could be clearly framed. Mary said that is so like many families. When father and mother begin to have a disagreement which could turn into a serious conflict the children are sent out of the room. Ann, in her usual direct manner, brought the discussion back to the group itself, 'What do we do when it looks like a conflict is going to develop?'

Tim: We have already done it. We clumsily offer wrong things. Then we realize it. We ignore it. We act as if there is no conflict.

Sandi talked about the conflict she and Barbara had in an earlier session and how their conflict had left the group out.

Tim: I think there was a failure on our part to notice that you were in conflict. Lacking support, however, I think it would not have been helpful for any one of us to jump in and try to help because that would have appeared as rescuing one of you and that would not have been helpful. That is clearly my perception as I reflect back on it. So I think

175

we should not intervene unless the person can't take it anymore. After all, when it comes down to it, we want to help each to face and not to run away from the problem.

There is a sense that this 'wisdom' is coming deep from within Tim. There is a quiet conviction in his voice and manner. It falls on the group as a statement that is profound and sagacious. Here the animus is addressing the group; an animus which shares its wisdom and attempts to move the group forward in its development.

Cathy then spoke about the caring aspect of their behavior when the group would become involved in the personal differences which arise in the group. Tim agreed but emphasized the point he had made earlier that helping does not mean stopping conflicts. His statement was supported by many nodding heads of those members who were in agreement. There was a sense that he had become an older brother who had much good advice to give to his brothers and sisters.

A concluding statement

The chapter has examined the images of the anima and animus as developmental elements of the human psyche. Our many years of working with small groups have been the empirical basis for our views which have so deeply affected our practice and the notions which have been pursued in our research. Building on the foundations given by Jung and the works of several investigators, in particular, the writing of Erich Neumann, we were able to formulate methodologies that allowed us to examine empirically the roles the anima and animus took in the behaviors of individuals within the context and dynamics of the small group. Our studies have shown that the anima and animus are active images which may impede or help in furthering personal trans-formations and which affect the dynamics in a small group in small but also in significant ways.

Up to this point we have presented several methodologies that have been developed in our laboratory to study both the small group and individual members from the perspective of analytical psychology. The group and the individuals constitute an indivisible whole. Yet it is often necessary to hold one apart in order to examine the other. What we have attempted to do is to move back and forth between our view of the individual as he/she struggles toward a personal transformation and our view of the group as it develops through its transitions and its phases to a richer collective consciousness.

In the next chapter we will focus primarily on one individual member. It will become apparent that our understanding of this person's personal meanings and his/her behaviors reflecting those meanings can only be realized to the extent that we perceive the contexts in which those meanings are developed and expressed. This view reflects again the Gestalt point of view presented in the Matrix Model. Mary is an individual but she is a person who lives in social contexts.

References

Bion, W. F. (1963). *Experiences in groups*. New York: Basic Books.

Boyd, R. D. (1989). The developmental stages of the anima and animus in the small group. Part one. *Group Analysis, 22*, 135–47.

Boyd, R., Kondrat, M. E., and Rannells, J. S. (1984). *Manual for coding anima and animus images*. Laboratory of Group Dynamics, University of Wisconsin-Madison.

Boyd, R. D., Kondrat, M. E., and Rannels, J. S. (1989). The developmental stages of the anima and animus in the small group. Part two. *Group Analysis, 22*, 149–59.

Erikson, E. H. (1950). *Childhood and society*. New York: W. W. Norton.

Harding, E. (1965). *The 'I' and the 'Not-I' : A study in the development of consciousness*. Princeton, NJ: Princeton University Press.

Hillman, J. (1973). Anima I, *Spring* (The Analytical Psychology Club, New York).

Hillman, J. (1974). Anima II, *Spring* (The Analytical Psychology Club, New York).

Jung, C. (1966a). The relations between the ego and the unconscious, Part 1. *Collected Works of C. G. Jung*, Vol. 7. Princeton, NJ: Princeton University Press.

Jung, C. (1966b). The effect of the unconscious upon conscious, Part 2. *Collected Works of C. G. Jung*, Vol. 7. Princeton, NJ: Princeton University Press.

Jung, C. (1967). Comment on 'The secret of the golden flower'. In *Collected Works of C. G. Jung*, Vol. 13. Princeton, NJ: Princeton University Press.

Jung, C. (1968a). Concerning the archetypes, with special reference to the anima concept, Part 1. In *Collected Works of C. G. Jung*, Vol. 9. Princeton, NJ: Princeton University Press.

Jung, C. (1968b). The syzygy: anima and animus, Part 2. In *Collected Works of C. G. Jung*. Vol. 9. Princeton, NJ: Princeton University Press.

Jung, C. (1982). *Aspects of the feminine*. Princeton, NJ: Princeton University Press.

Neumann, E. (1954a). On the moon and matriarchal consciousness, *Spring* (The Analytical Psychology Club, New York).

Neumann, E. (1954b). *The origins and history of consciousness*. London: Routledge & Kegan Paul.

Neumann, E. (1955). *The great mother*. London: Routledge & Kegan Paul.

Neumann, E. (1956). *Amor and psyche*. Princeton, NJ: Princeton University Press.

Neumann, E. (1959). Psychological stages of feminine development, *Spring* (The Analytical Psychology Club, New York).

Samuels, A. (1985). *Jung and the post-Jungians.* London: Routledge & Kegan Paul.

Slater, P. (1966). *Microcosm: Structural psychological and religious evolution in groups.* New York: John Wiley and Sons, Inc.

Ulanov, A. (1971). *The feminine in Jungian psychology and in Christian theology.* Evanston, IL: Northwestern University Press.

vonFranz, M. L. (1964). Chapter 3 in Carl G. Jung (ed.), *Man and his symbols.* New York: Doubleday.

Whitmont, E. C. (1982). *Return of the Goddess.* New York: Crossroad.

Chapter seven

Mary
A case study of personal transformation in
a small group

Robert D. Boyd

In Chapter Five we discussed a methodology for identifying archetypal
themes as they are manifest in the ongoing life of a small interacting
group. In this chapter we will show how these group-wide themes relate
to and facilitate personal transformations by presenting a case study of
a woman who encountered a psychic dilemma as a member of a small
group in which archetypal themes related to and facilitated her struggles
toward a personal transformation. The small group observed in this
study was a self-analytic group – a group that provides its members with
opportunities to examine their own behaviors, interpersonal transactions, and group dynamics. Before turning to the case study a brief
discussion of the conceptual framework is presented in order to make
explicit from what viewpoint the data were being interpreted.

Personal transformation and the psychic dilemma

The concept of transformation is used here as it has been formulated
within analytical psychology. Transformation refers to individual
change in the deepest sense of the word, a form of rebirth (Jung, 1969),
or the 'discovery of a new life-form which goes hand in hand with the
successful conduct of life as a whole' (Jacobi, 1965). Jung (1969)
identified eight forms of transformation, of which our work is concerned
only with the form he described as 'enlargement of personality'. This
form of transformation is characterized by movement from an attitude
of ego-centeredness to one of ego-transcendence. This change is
brought about, either suddenly or gradually, when there are insightful
linkages and/or revealing dialogs between aspects of an individual's
inner life and vital components of the individual's life-space. When
meaningful linkages are made, the outcome is an expanded consciousness and a movement toward greater integration of personality.

A personal transformation is frequently initiated by a psychic
dilemma which exists at or just below the level of consciousness. It can
be described as a semi-conscious discord – an unresolved conflict that

179

the individual is generally able to acknowledge with prodding or encouragement. The psychic dilemma is in this major respect different from a complex, as it is more readily accessible to consciousness while the latter, existing as it does in deeper layers of the unconscious, is more difficult to make conscious. A person experiencing a psychic dilemma is confronted with two opposing choices. A complex, on the other hand, has a clear and unmistakable goal. In addition, the conflicting choices presented in a psychic dilemma have the effect of draining off energy. Frequently, individuals encountering a psychic dilemma complain of feeling drained of energy. That condition is contrasted to the powerful upsurge of energy, whether constructive or destructive, in the manifestation of a complex. In the grip of a psychic dilemma one feels rooted while a complex takes hold and is experienced as a powerful and moving force.

We are proposing that, for many individuals, personal transformations start, not with the realization of a complex, but the identification of the choices set out in the psychic dilemma. The individual's first task is to clearly recognize the choices and the meaning they hold in his/her life. Then with a firm understanding of the nature of the choices, the individual can begin to examine the deeper structures underlying the choices and to that extent begin to bring into consciousness those aspects of the complex or complexes that are expressed in the choices.

The social system of the group (which we will refer to hereafter as the group) and other members play major roles in helping an individual member to identify and work on his/her psychic dilemma. There are three basic functions that the group can provide in helping a member. First, the group as an entity, may come to be experienced symbolically as a central figure in the individual's yet unrevealed complex, but the symbol, holding a fascination for the individual, is seldom realized as manifest content of the complex. Our research indicates that the member will initially relate the symbol to his/her personal unconscious and begin to talk about the symbol in terms of past personal experiences. For example, the designated leader offers interpretations of the group's behavior – the dynamics of the group – in terms of a familial scenario in which the mother is the central figure. A member picks up the symbol of the mother and shares with the group certain relationships she has had with her mother that speak to conflicts still existing between them. With sufficient time, a good deal of work, and the support of the group, the symbol may begin to have transcendent value for the individual, suggesting involvement of the collective unconscious. In this example the symbolic function of the group serves to identify a particular psychic dilemma for an individual member. Furthermore, the group provides the social milieu in which the individual can develop further insights into the dilemma, thus contributing to the potential for personal transformation.

The second function which the group serves in crystallizing psychic dilemmas for individual members was alluded to in the previous paragraph. Identification of and working on psychic dilemmas requires a supportive structure, a setting in which an individual feels sufficiently safe and secure to engage in this difficult work. The research literature within the field of small groups provides substantial evidence for the value of supportive groups in facilitating the personal development of group members (reference on nurturance, Luft, 1984; Schein and Bennis, 1965; Smith, 1980; and others). This is often a difficult function for groups to perform well. There is perhaps only a 'fine line' between a nurturant and supportive group structure and one that is constraining and potentially smothering of its members. Therefore, a significant task of the groups is to come to grips with this polarity in such a way that individuals are able to work toward expressions of their true selves while in community with others. The small group which was the focus of the case study reported in this chapter was able to develop such a supportive structure for its members.

Finally, the third function a group serves in an individual's psychic dilemma is to provide a context for a variety of events from which group members can vicariously learn. Transactions within the life of a group are a rich source of learning for its members. Individuals struggling with psychic dilemmas are frequently able to observe other members struggling with similar problems. For example, an individual may have a psychic dilemma that on the one hand poses the task of independence from a figure of a powerful father and, on the other hand, a wish to have his love and protection which may be forfeited if the course of independence is pursued. This dilemma may be played out in the individual's relationships to the designated group leader and in the member's concerns with the distribution of authority and power in the group. Such an individual will often confront and criticize the designated leadership, often openly challenging the leader's position in the group. This confronting and challenging does not occur, however, without considerable uncertainty, ambivalence, and holding back on the part of the member challenging the leader. Other members will often relate to this individual's dilemma by asking questions, advising, empathizing, and even exhorting. Another individual, with a similar dilemma, will carefully watch and observe this particular unfolding of events in the group and, in the process, clarify and deepen his/her understanding of his/her own dilemma.

Individual members of the group, through their relationships with each other, also play significant roles in helping each other discern and work through their psychic dilemmas. One aspect of these relationships

Robert D. Boyd

is intentionally and mutually acknowledged. For example, one member may question another to help the person identify the choices that are present in his or her life. In the course of this dialog, the individual's psychic dilemma may be more clearly revealed. But, perhaps even more significant are the unconscious dimensions of these relationships, particularly the way in which they become conduits for projections. Members who exhibit certain characteristics may become the object of projections by other members. They are what Jung (1969) referred to as 'hooks' upon which projections are placed. Such projections, expressed through the dynamics of group interaction, can be constructive moves toward personal integration, provided that the individual grasps the meaning of projection in his or her life. Left unexamined, however, the problem expressed through the projection will remain or may even deepen. In the description of the case study to follow, it will be evident that projections among group members played an important part in the unfolding and working through of the psychic dilemma illustrated in the behavior of the individual who was the focus of the study.

In the next section, we provide a brief narrative of the periods of group life relevant to a psychic dilemma of one individual member, whom we shall call Mary. This description is intended to provide the reader with a sense of the particular relationship that existed between Mary and the group, and how that relationship contributed to Mary's identification and work on a particular psychic dilemma of immense importance to her.

Mary

Mary's story took place in a particular context and from a personal historical perspective. Thus, to tell her story it is necessary to briefly describe the group of which she was a member and to report upon those aspects of her life that were involved in her psychic dilemma.

The group

The small group, of which Mary was a member, is generally referred to in the literature as a self-analytic group (Gibbard et al. 1974). The purpose of such groups is to provide its members with opportunities to observe and examine their own behaviors as well as interpersonal transactions within the context of a group setting. From these experiences, members are expected to derive insights, develop deeper understandings of group behavior, and expand their consciousness. The group observed in this study was set up as the experiential component of a graduate course on the dynamics of instructional groups. The experiential session extended over the first 10 weeks of the semester, with weekly sessions of 150 minutes in length. No explicit curriculum or agenda was assigned to these meetings. Other than specifying the meeting time and place, the designated leader (the professor) gave no further structure to the sessions. This group was composed of eight women and two men. The professor, who assumed the role of a nondirective leader, made few interventions. Those that were provided were in the form of metaphors, familial scenarios, and references to myths or incidents in literature. The members had been told that the interventions would be statements of the leader's observations and were not given as directive, judgements, or forms of censure. In addition, the members were informed that interpretations were directed at the group as a whole and not to any one individual. A more detailed description of this type of group and the forms of interventions used are described in Chapter 8 of this volume.

Within the life of a self-analytic group, several members will identify and begin to work on particular psychic dilemmas. The individual that we chose to focus on in this study reflected our particular research interest in the matriarchal elements of group life. Mary's dilemma, as it unfolded in the group, proved to be an especially dramatic illustration of the complex relationship that exists between an individual and the group as the individual attempts to work through a psychic dilemma. It is for these reasons that we chose to focus this case study on Mary and her relationship with the group.

Biographical data

Mary was a woman in her late thirties who had recently started her own business. Divorced for several years, she was a single parent with one teenaged daughter. Although she was apparently doing well in her business, Mary decided that further study would be helpful to her and, therefore, began working part-time toward a degree in education. She was an attractive woman whose general bearing gave the impression of a self-assured and business-like person, with obvious feminine qualities. Her mother, of whom more will be provided later in the case description, was the dominant force in Mary's nuclear family. Her father was alcoholic. She had one brother who left home at an early age. Mary's accounts of her early childhood gave a picture of an unhappy and troubled family life.

It is our intention in the following material to illustrate how certain group conditions served to identify and activate a psychic dilemma for Mary that related to this troubled family life and deep-seated conflicts with her mother. In focusing our case study on this particular issue, we are aware that much of what transpired will be left out of the analysis we present. The involvement of any one individual in the life of a time-limited group is obviously complex and multi-faceted. No single analysis can do justice to this complexity. For this reason, we do not purport to represent the totality of Mary's participation in this group. Our goal is rather modest – to describe and understand the significant events in the group, and Mary's role in those events, that lead to her discernment of and decision to work on a particular psychic dilemma in her life.

The emergence of the psychic dilemma

It is our position that Mary's behavior in the group was influenced to a large extent by a psychic dilemma that emerged early in the life of the group and persisted throughout the life of the group. In addition, certain events that occurred in the group can be better understood if one is aware of the saliency of Mary's dilemma for the group. Stated in analytical terms Mary's dilemma involved the opposing dynamics of the animus and feminine elements of her personality. This dilemma was activated and given shape both by the content of the group's discussion and the matriarchal motifs which characterized its symbolic life. Furthermore, a mutually facilitative relationship existed between Mary and the group, in that Mary's need to give voice to her dilemma was activated by the matriarchal symbolism of the group. In turn, the group's need to work through issues regarding trust, relatedness, and caring – qualities associated with the matriarchal motif – found expression in Mary's dilemma. In this section, we will illustrate the process by which Mary's dilemma emerged, as well as its specific nature.

The first session of the group began with the leader giving a general description of his role in the group, the purposes for videotaping the sessions, and additional matters related to the scheduling of the group sessions. The leader then spent several minutes answering questions of a clarification nature for the group members. Following this period, members then introduced themselves. The atmosphere during this time was polite and friendly but somewhat tense and observably constrained. Because no structure or agenda was set by the leader, the group tried repeatedly to decide what it would undertake as work. Members frequently turned to the leader for guidance and direction. Unless directly requested to answer, he remained silent. His response to direct requests was to state that the answer to their questions and concerns rested with the group. The first session ended with no agenda having been adopted. Several members were obviously frustrated with the way things had gone, but Mary did not appear to be one of these individuals. She seemed generally relaxed and pleased about what had taken place during the session.

Other than setting the stage for what might follow, the group's first session provided little indication of the eventual role that Mary was to

play in the group or the particular psychic dilemma with which she came
to reveal and to struggle with in the group sessions. In many respects,
the session was fairly typical of the kind that usually characterize the
first meeting of a self-analytic group. It was in the second session that
we began to see indications of the relationship that Mary was to form
with the group, and how this relationship served to identify her dilemma. The second session began with some members raising questions
and concerns about administrative matters, such as arranging times for
viewing the videotapes. Following the expression of these concerns a
period of silence ensued. Mary then made a direct overture to Mark, one
of the two male members of the group.

> I thought about you quite a bit this past week, Mark.
> (*Mark*: You did – well!) The talk we had on the steps on the way out
> after the last meeting. What I would label courage when you asked
> Dr B___ [leader] about what was going to happen; give me some
> details. What I perceived to be your frustration with that. I can relate
> to that from other experiences I have had in groups. I wonder if you
> thought about it this week?

Mark responded to Mary by describing his reactions to the first session
of the group. He indicated that he had shared this experience with his
wife, who was apparently more familiar than he with these types of
groups. She advised him not to expect much structure and to relax and
learn from the experience. Mark's description of his reactions conveyed
an underlying sense of caution, a sense which characterized the group as
well at this time. His answer was delivered in a controlled, analytic, and
rational manner. Following Mark's response to Mary, two women
proposed that the group needed to get down to some plan of work. It
soon became apparent that what they were proposing was to use a plan
of work as a means of developing structure in the group. These
individuals apparently felt a lack of structure in the way the group was
operating and found this troubling. This feeling appeared to be shared
by the group as a whole, as demonstrated by a quiet consensus to the
concerns the two women had expressed. Barbara may have been
speaking for the group when she stated: 'It is interesting to see that when
there isn't any structure provided, we seek to impose structure.'
   At this point and with obvious emotion, Mary joined the discussion:

> I got a little tight feeling in my stomach when you talked about
> structure. We need structure because we have been raised that way in
> an authoritarian system. We must help people to trust each other so
> they can be more free from structures. Building trust is very
> important – critical for this type of learning.

She went on to describe that what she now finds exciting in working with groups is to see them 'going by themselves'.

In stating her position the way she did, Mary clearly set herself in opposition to the group. There were indications that the members heard and understood what she said. Some members talked about openness in groups and how structure sometimes hinders openness, but the tone of these comments was analytical and rational. There was little evidence of emotional support or acceptance for Mary or her position. To Mary, however, there was something ominous in the group's insistence on creating a structure. This concern is clearly articulated when, after a short silence in the group, Mary said: 'Do you know what I would feel safe in doing, is if someone said, "Here is an idea", and ten of you said "great". I would feel free to say "I am not going to do that."'

With this response, Mary was attempting to differentiate herself from the group. In insisting on a form of structure, the group was eliciting fears in Mary that the group would not allow her to express her own individuality. The group is coming to represent for her a form of con- strictive containment, quite possibly, at one level of perception, reminding her of her unhappy experiences with her own mother, and, on another level, of the terrible aspect of the Great Mother.

These fears were apparently reinforced with the group's response to her statement. The group appeared stunned and several members voiced strong reactions to her. To whom in the group did she feel responsible? Did she not see her behavior as affecting the group? One member commented that if everyone did it would break up the group. Joyce asked Mary: 'Would you continue to separate yourself even if the group wanted you to join?' Mary responded by saying that it is important to be truly yourself.

With this brief but provocative interaction, Mary had called the question: How does the group and the individual coexist? One has the sense that she was really testing and challenging the group. Her question was much more than a group process concern. At one level she was beginning to examine her personal dilemma. It was for her an issue of her independence, a reflection of a primary conflict she shared with her mother. When any agency attempted to challenge her independence it took on the symbolic dimensions of her struggle for independence from a domineering and unloving mother. At another level she appeared to be attempting to determine if the group as mother is a good mother or a bad mother. Evidence for this statement can be found in the subsequent group discussion. Led by Joyce, the members began to talk about commitment and belonging. During this discussion, Joyce said, 'In community work, it is essential that members be committed, otherwise you cannot trust them.' The implications of this statement for Mary's relationship with the group were obvious. Sandie found this comment to be so potentially inflammatory that she felt it was necessary to point out that she didn't believe that Mary 'would take her marbles and go home if you are not going to play her game'. Although Sandie appeared to be siding with Mary in saying that it wasn't necessary for Mary to do everything the group wanted, the issue appeared to remain unresolved.

Further evidence that this interchange symbolically represented the relationship of Mary to the group as mother is found in the group's response to the leader's intervention at this time, 'You have to get to know mother before you can come to understand father.' Surprisingly, Margaret quickly interpreted mother to mean relationships. 'Is the relationship's mother and father the task?' Although Mark attempted to shift the discussion to a rational analysis by proposing a working definition of what constitutes an instructional group, Mary brought the focus of the discussion back to mother, as if she had not even heard Mark's comments. The parallel between the group as mother and her relationship with her own mother was now clearly explicit in her consciousness. 'Do you know what I know about my mother? She wants what she wants and it has to be her way or else. It is still a big deal in our relationships.'

The similarity between Mary's last comment and the one she made earlier regarding the group is striking. Through her brief interaction with the group, at a time when it was just beginning to struggle with the realization of its potentially powerful and destructive capacities, Mary had identified a critical psychic dilemma in her life – her troubling and unsettled relationship with her own mother. Furthermore, this dilemma emerged in the context of the group when it was fully receptive to such an issue, as evidenced by the focus of its subsequent discussion. The group continued to talk about the qualities of mother and contrasted these with the qualities of fathers. Several individuals pointed out how these different qualities were being manifested in the group. During the remainder of the session, Mary continued to examine her relationship with her mother, reestablishing the personal history component as if she had to rework it until it was clearly in focus and undeniable.

> I learned much in a supportive group. Ties in with all the work I have done with my mother and myself. Since I have been 35 I can define myself as getting free. She had much power over me and I had to learn to fight against it – just to be free.

As some members spoke about how their mothers were caring and helpful, especially during adolescence, Mary said, 'All my mother wanted was to be approved of by the system. I started out that way but I found it got in my way.' The group appeared to have discerned Mary's struggles and some members followed with questions encouraging her to talk further about how she now saw things. Various group members spoke about mothers as having both good and bad qualities. Cathy said that she thought most women worry about taking on the bad qualities of their mothers. Mary agreed and said it was difficult not to do so because mothers played such an important role in their lives. She went on, 'I looked like my mother when I argued. My husband made quite a point of that. I hated the way she attacked people and I hate that in myself when I do it.' Later, when members were speaking about how this group had moved away from being superficial and was now dealing with honest content, Mary spoke quietly and in a reflective voice: 'I had, no, I still have a fantasy of a mother I wanted to have. I think it influences the way I relate to my own daughter.'

The degree of sharing that Mary was doing at this time was clearly a statement of the degree of trust, support, acceptance, and caring that was present in the group at this time. The group had to come from a position of direct confrontation with Mary to a position in which she seemed to be focusing for the group on its concerns regarding the group's symbolic role as mother. The session ended with the group members coming to recognize that a set of ground rules had been generally accepted as defining the group. Members could 'open up' if they wished to but there was no expectation that they had to do so. Sharing was a way of helping everyone to come to a deeper understanding of themselves and of each other. The group existed as a means of increasing relatedness. Relatedness, in turn, was an expression of caring and help. Although these affirmations appeared to represent this stage of the group's development, subsequent sessions proved their tentative nature. This is to be expected, for development in such groups is characterized, within phases, by a process of differentiation and cohesion (Beck, 1974), a process that is perceived by both participants and observers as a forward and backward movement.

These first two sessions of the group's life proved to be crucial in assisting Mary to discern a particular psychic dilemma and to identify some of its critical characteristics. That the conduit for the emergence of this dilemma was Mary's relationship with the group is obvious. Furthermore, the evidence strongly suggests that this relationship was mutually facilitative – as Mary's dilemma became more clearly focused in her eyes, so too the group's crisis regarding its matriarchal nature was brought into sharper relief.

Movement toward transformation

For the next four sessions, the relationship between Mary and the group did not appear to change in any substantive way. This period was punctuated by occasional and somewhat tense interchanges between Mary and the group. In particular, Mary's relationship with Joyce seemed to be strained and tense. For the most part, however, Mary's participation was not as confrontational and assertive as it had been in the second session. She often paused and appeared to be reflecting upon the situation at hand, in contrast to her earlier, more spontaneous and forceful manner. Reviewing the group's behavior over these four sessions, it appeared to be aimed, in a symbolic sense, at further clarifying the polar sides of the matriarchal theme and at flirting with patriarchal issues. Relatively little time was spent on the latter, while the mythological motifs reflecting matriarchal issues generally dominated group interaction (Dirkx, 1987). The group's progress in this area mirrored the gradual unfolding of the matriarchal element of Mary's psychic dilemma.

The seventh session of the group provides evidence of a considerable shift in the relationship between Mary and the group. After a light and somewhat superficial beginning, Ruth began to discuss her family.

> We have a relationship with each member of my family [a family of nine children] but we also have a relationship to the total family. I may get in a fight with one of my brothers but still the whole family is still together – we are a whole.

Ruth was apparently attempting to address the lingering conflict that continued to characterize Mary's relationship with Joyce. Following her statement, Mary said, 'We can learn from this.'

As this session proceeded, there was a feeling of intense involvement in the group. Heavy silences occurred frequently, indicating a fairly high level of anxiety and tension, a tension that was not being addressed. During this time, there were some shared examples of trust and conflict in family relationships. For a brief period, Tim, one of the male members, and Mary talked with each other as the group watched. Tim, a member who also had difficulties in developing a positive relationship with his mother, talked about the existence of the 'dark side of our personalities'. He asked Mary if she had struggled with this issue. Mary responded by identifying the struggles she had had in developing a sense of trust in others, but, especially, in herself. She works hard, she said, at telling herself that she is basically a good person. Tim concurred, saying 'I am finding that I am getting to feel it before I can intellectualize about it.' Nodding her head, Mary agreed.

The conversation between Mary and Tim dwindled uncomfortably to a close. A reflective silence followed, with members staring down at their arm-desks or at the floor in the center of the circle. Then, as if from nowhere, Mary drew in her breath, turned to Joyce and said in a quiet voice: 'I wish you would get angry. I know you are really mad about the metaphors B___ throws into the group.' A heated exchange then took place between these two women, as the group stood by, both troubled and fascinated by this latest development. Joyce accused Mary of wanting to take control and of seeking power. In turn, Mary referred to Joyce's behavior in the group as terribly controlled and emotionally restrictive. In watching this interchange, one had the sense that these two members were making public the view each held of the other. A few members attempted to intervene, as if to assuage the growing tension between these two women and in the group. Sandie attempted to explain the conflict on the basis of the difference in the family backgrounds of Mary and Joyce. She made specific reference to material each woman had shared in the group about their family relationships. Barbara, however, was more direct, commenting that she thought it was an issue of power between Joyce and Mary. With considerable emotion, Mary responded: 'The terms of win and lose have been tossed around. I don't see why it has to be a win or lose situation.' Joyce responded immediately in her characteristically calm but deliberate manner, 'Because you want it your way.'

Following Joyce's comment, a long silence ensued. Then, another member proposed that the group look at the role of authority. Appearing to want a reprieve from the intense emotionality of the last 30 minutes, the group pursued a series of rational discourses on authority and leadership in groups for the remainder of the session. The tension seemed to subside and some levity and lightness surfaced in the discussion. Little reference was made to the difficult encounter between Joyce and Mary. Toward the end of the session the leader made the following intervention: 'Mother is sitting at the kitchen table and all the family has gathered in the kitchen. Everyone is having a good time. Then someone says, "Where is father?" Someone answers, "He's up in the study."' The intervention was treated with humor and appeared to be dismissed by the group. A few comments were made about father and their involvement in family life, as the session came to a close.

Before we move to a description of the next session, it may be helpful to reflect for a moment on the meaning of the events of this session to Mary's psychic dilemma and to the evolution of her relationship with the group. As was indicated in Ruth's opening statement, a conflict had developed earlier between Mary and Joyce. In one sense, the persistence and potential destructiveness of this conflict represented to the group the terrible side of the group as mother. This conflict stood as a barrier and a threat to the group's efforts to establish a nurturing, supportive, and caring environment. Evidence for this statement is found in the group's response to Ruth's statement, a period of relatively high levels of tension and anxiety. The group was up against something big and all the members seemed to be tacitly aware of it. The dialog between Tim and Mary that occurred during this time can be seen as a further attempt by Mary and the group to clarify and focus energy on this struggle. The content of their conversation clearly reflected an attempt to define polarities within the issue of relatedness. They spoke of this problem in terms of a struggle to establish trust in relationships with others and to come to terms with the 'dark side' of ourselves.

In this episode, Mary was beginning to give voice to the polarities that characterize her particular dilemma, the opposing elements of the animus and the feminine elements within her personality. Her aggressive, sometimes opinionated positions showed the animus element of her dilemma. Her caring and expressions of relatedness revealed the feminine component that was active in her dilemma. Within the context of the group environment she appeared to be clarifying and focusing these polarities. At the same time, her work was also furthering the developmental issues for the group as a whole, moving the issue of relatedness front and center stage. This issue and the group's need to resolve it were made explicit in the heated interaction that occurs in this session between Mary and Joyce. The intensity of the emotions involved in this encounter suggest that each was involved in projective identifications. Something about Joyce's manner really irritated Mary. That 'something' apparently involved the controlled and relatively emotionless way in which Joyce interacted with her and others in the group. It is possible that the depth of Mary's reaction arose from a deep-seated fear that she herself was overly controlled and controlling, like her mother before her.

Thus, we have evidence that Mary's group behavior was being heavily influenced by the presence of her dilemma. The group's own need to resolve questions concerning relatedness and nurturance served to facilitate continued expression of Mary's dilemma and the need for her to further clarify its elements. Mary gives us indications that she was willing to engage in this struggle. While she did not explicitly state her dilemma and her desire to work it through she provided verbal indications of a growing commitment to engage. One can infer from her behavior in the group that, at a symbolic level, Mary was indeed beginning to work through the dilemma. But she had yet to establish and open dialog between the poles of her dilemma, a fact which was also played out symbolically in her interactions with group members.

Further evidence for Mary's hesitancy in taking the 'next step' with her dilemma can be found in Mary's responses to the leader's interventions. Up to the seventh session, most of the leader's interpretations of the group process made reference in one form or another to mother and, in more primitive terms, to the feminine archetype. These interpretations were presented as metaphors, familial scenarios, or references to mythological figures. While some members found the interpretation interesting, frustrating, or even 'weird', Mary, up to session seven, did not make a direct reference to the metaphors. It is interesting, however, that, given the particular nature of her psychic dilemma, she chose not to pick up and specifically address the content of these interventions. This particular observation will be explored further in the following section.

When the group reconvened for its eight session, discussion returned to the topic of the father. Barbara informed the group that she would like to talk about her father. She then proceeded to describe in considerable detail her relationship with her father before he died prematurely from a hereditary disease. She recounted his early life and his relationship with a cruel and uncaring father, from whom he ran away at an early age and made a life on his own. Barbara spoke of his kindness, his firmness, and his strength of character. With tears she talked about their family and how his love was expressed toward his children and his wife. Her account of her father was quite emotional and it had a substantial impact on the group.

As Barbara ended her moving account, the group lapsed into silence. Mary was the first to speak. She spoke in a quiet voice which conveyed empathy and caring: 'That was a beautiful story. I really admire the way you handled it. You certainly have had sufficient pain in your life.'

The group continued to discuss Barbara's story. Mary recalled she had earlier stated that Barbara had not had enough suffering in her life. She told Barbara that she wanted to take that back. And again, somewhat later in the discussion, Mary said:

> I was interested to hear how your father had been abused as a young person, but he did not relate to his children in that way. Some parents who were abused as children do relate that way and so abuse their children. You wonder why there is a difference.

The group continued on the topic of personal fathers for a while and, during this discussion, Mary revealed that her father was an alcoholic. Although he was a kind person, he could not be depended upon. He was weak and could not face up to things. She added: 'I suppose in some ways that was why my mother was the way she was. But my brother and I believed that she was the way she was before Dad became an alcoholic.'

The intensity of Mary's psychic dilemma was revealed in her many comments. Mary's observations of her own family elicited similar observations from other group members, and moved the focus of discussion away from fathers and more onto the relationships between parents. Sandie spoke of how her father was also an alcoholic and that so much of what Mary had described about her parents was also true for Sandie's parents. Sandie and Mary then talked about how the parental roles that are typically expected in our culture were reversed for their parents in many ways. In the process, both women described their relationships to their mothers that reflected disappointment, very little affection, and even hostility. Yet they seemed unable to let go of or to terminate the relationship, revealing an area of 'unfinished business' for both of them. One had the sense that each had helped the other acknowledge this situation, even though neither woman had explicitly voiced this realization.

For a period of time, the group discussed topics without pursuing any in great depth. Then, the conversation moved to a consideration of what children learn from their parents. Mary turned to Barbara as she remarked: 'I see you as an ambitious person. Do you believe this has anything to do with your ancestry? You are a person with energy.' Barbara responded by saying that she had been told this before, adding that she saw Mary as an ambitious and a hard worker. Mary seemed to accept this picture of herself, saying in a joking manner, 'Perhaps this is how single parents generally are like – especially women in this culture.'

Group interaction within this session was quite different from the preceding one. In contrast to session seven, which was marked by relatively high levels of tension, anxiety, and a heated interaction between Joyce and Mary, group behavior in session eight was reflective, introspective, and caring. The content of the conversations, however, revealed an intense desire on the part of the group to further clarify and get through the potentially negative aspects of the group. In particular, Mary and Sandie seemed to be speaking for the group as they described their unhappy and troubling relationships with their own mothers. This content had the effect, on a symbolic level, of bringing into bold relief the dual nature of the group viewed symbolically as the bad and terrible Mother.

In this session, Mary continued to explore and deepen her understanding of her dilemma. Still, in listening to her talk about her relationship with her mother, one had the feeling that Mary was hesitant to move from the past into the present, to claim and own this relationship for herself in the here-and-now. She speaks of it almost as a historical phenomenon, something that was quite painful, but a relationship that she has put behind her. To the observer, however, this is clearly not the case. The troubling aspects of Mary's relationship with her mother continued to be manifest in Mary's transactions with the group. So invested was the group in Mary's dilemma that one has the sense it was waiting for her to take the next step, of realizing that she has yet to accept what has been and move on to what she can be as mother to her daughter – the symbol of the good mother.

The ninth session provided very little new insights on Mary. She shared as did several other members her feelings and perceptions on issues of authority and supportiveness. There was a sense, in observing Mary, that she was doing more internal reflection than she was revealing in what she was sharing with the group. The tenth session was quite another story. The issue of control came up early in the meeting. Mary related the topic of control to her daughter saying that she did not want relationships in which control was an issue between them. As the group continued to deal with this topic it became clear that the issue of love was there but had not been spoken to. The leader, intervening, presented the analogy of the choice Christ had to make between the crown and the cross. Certain members made immediate application of the analogy's message to the group. Tim went on to state that growth involves a symbolic death: 'You have to give up a part of who you are and go on to a new you. I suppose we would call it a transformation.' Mary agreed with Tim and went on to point out that love plays a critical role in such transformations. She went on to discuss the conflict that occurs between power and love. 'One must risk to give love and to move away from using power. I am not too good at that yet, but I find that I can stay with that longer now.' The group then went on to talk about wholeness. During this discussion Mary spoke of the spiritual side to relationships. On two occasions she stated that, 'My body speaks to me – it is my growing consciousness.' At no time during this session did Mary take the discussion back to her mother. In observing her, it was as if, at this point in time, she had moved the critical issues beyond the confines of her relationships with her mother to a larger terrain. The issues she was struggling with were certainly part of the conflicts with her mother but they were far beyond this restricted field. Mary appeared much more relaxed during this session and it appeared that it was not necessary for her to 'win' her point. She exhibited those qualities which describe the feminine archetype – relating, caring, patience, and supportiveness.

Interpretations and discussion

Mary's behavior clearly showed that she had agendas which she wanted to work on. Two questions arise about these agendas. First, do these agendas express a psychic dilemma? Second, is the description correct that she 'wants to work on' or is it simply a matter of rehashing personal concerns? Although the questions raise different issues, they are nevertheless, interrelated.

We turn first to Mary's demonstrated show of affect which occurred shortly after the second session had begun – the third hour of the group. The members were reestablishing their ties to the social system in its initial phase of expressing relatedness, the initial phase of the Great Mother theme. Whether this was a factor which may have contributed to Mary's behavior remains for now an open question. After the close of the previous session a male member had privately shared with Mary his frustrations about the lack of structure being provided by the leader. It was to this member that Mary now turned. She showed concern and caring when she asked him how he was feeling this week as a member of the group. Her reaching out to him showed empathy and a concern for his well-being. The members were most attentive to this interchange between Mary and Mark. More than one explanation can be offered to explain their attentiveness. Mary's expression of caring was a symbolic manifestation of the Good Mother. At this point in the life of the group-as-a-whole this dynamic had a high valence. The members were also obviously affected by the quality of Mary's concern. Her behavior revealed not only the work that the social system was engaged in but also an aspect of Mary's personality.

Both explanations for this episode appear to have validity in light of other observations reported below. The significance of these initial observations is that they point to critical behaviors that alert us to the possible existence of a psychic dilemma. The affect level of Mary's behavior in her expression of showing caring was higher than would normally be the case at this point in the group which prompted the question: Is caring a critical concern for Mary? If it is a concern and thus conceivably one side of a dilemma, then there is a counter part to be identified as the other side of the dilemma. Evidence for the other side of the dilemma, counter to caring, was found shortly after the above event. Following the interaction between Mary and Mark, the group again took up the topic of structure. The discussion, unlike the previous discussions on structure and agenda, was more relaxed. There was evidence, as shown by the willingness of the group members to hear each other's wishes, that the social system had qualities of the Good Mother. Different topics for the group's agenda were proposed; however, at this phase of the social system's development the group was not ready to become a task group. It was working to determine its symbolic nature in terms of the qualities of the Great Mother. The social system was still in the phase of differentiating the Good and Bad Mother. It was at this point Mary spoke up. She stated that if she was not interested in the topic that the group decided upon she would not take part. As reported earlier the group was stunned and certain members were confused if not angered by her statement. Her behavior appeared to be a threat to the growing solidarity of the group. This act revealed the other dimension of her psychic dilemma – her right to personal independence.

The members had been working at developing a supportive climate in the group and further group cohesiveness. Mary's statement appeared as a rejection of these developments. In view of the caring behavior shown earlier, her present position, at best, seemed inconsistent. How was it possible for her to show such concern over another member who felt out of it and then to take the position of appearing to separate herself from the group? This was the position taken by those members who confronted her with the obligations of her membership in the group. But to take this interpretation would completely miss the thrust of her concern. Although Mary had not expressed a link between her relationship with her mother and the symbolic relationship with the group as mother, it is very likely this occurred to her consciously or unconsciously. Her mother had been a domineering and demanding person. It is not difficult for us to understand how the emphasis on solidarity could readily evoke images of these negative relationships Mary had experience of with her mother. Caring can be truly acts of helping but it can be a facade behind which one can use and dominate another. Those members who insisted on Mary giving up the position she had taken were obviously not aware that they were raising images of the Bad Mother not only for Mary but also within the group. There was a sense in the group that it was experiencing the Bad Mother who is possessive and who denies the child room to explore and to transgress.

In these behaviors there were indications of a dilemma Mary had been struggling with for some time. She wanted to relate to others in a caring and supportive manner but she was fearful of having her independence denied by the group. In this we can see unresolved difficulties with her mother. As long as Mary controls the giving of caring and support there is no problem. When other powerful agents, in this case the group, seek cohesiveness then she had difficulties differentiating whether the intent of the relatedness is positive or negative. When some members spoke about her behavior as an act of rejecting her membership in the group, they failed to see that Mary was trying to determine whether she could be independent within the boundaries of the group. In this way she was testing herself and the social system of the group. Although the context was different the dilemma Mary encountered in the group was the same basic dilemma she had experienced with her mother.

There is another aspect of Mary's dilemma which was first noted in this episode. She defended herself in a forceful manner when Joyce questioned her about her commitment to the group. She answered that she was not going to go along just because she was a member. When questioned further whether she wanted to be asked by the group, she replied brusquely that that was not the issue. What drew our attention to these exchanges was the aggressiveness of Mary's behavior. Her reaction was far more assertive than would be generally expected in this type of situation. For example, her case could have been reasonably argued on its merits; that any member had the right to object to being forced to accept an agenda just because the majority wanted it. Approached in this manner, the pros and cons would be examined. This was not what occurred. Mary's position was to stand her ground.

Setting aside our observations on the group for the moment, there are two further observations that should be noted about Mary's behavior in this event. As reported above, Mary's behavior was more assertive than the situation called for; however, it was not unusual for Mary to behave in this manner. She confronted different women members in the early sessions of the group. We later learned from Mary that her mother was a very forceful woman and Mary had to adopt the same mode of behavior in order to stand up to her mother. The confrontations Mary had with Joyce, Barbara and Sandie then could be seen, in part, as projections. In all three cases it was apparent that the three women were unprepared for Mary's aggressive behavior and appeared mystified by Mary's behavior toward them. Another member asked why Mary had 'attacked' one of the women. Mary initially denied that she was attacking but later she acknowledged that 'sometimes she came on heavier than she intended'. It was after these exchanges that Mary shared her experiences with her mother.

We may now add another aspect to Mary's psychic dilemma. Women who were assertive and would stand their ground presented Mary with behaviors that may have evoked relationships she had had with her mother. The threat to her independence must at all cost be countered and being strong and assertive were her modes of responding. The force of her assertiveness and her frequent behavioral pattern of using logic in place of understanding would indicate the presence of the animus element. Counter to this was her behavior of caring and her wish to be accepted within the group. There are several interactions that provide evidence to support these statements. For example, on two specific occasions Mary shared with the group that she was aware that her mother's aggressive manner frequently prevented a loving relationship to develop between them and on occasions she behaved like her mother. Mary wanted to be accepted in the group and Sandie recognized this when she said Mary did not want to take 'her marbles and go home'. Mary had a growing awareness of her dilemma – to be strong and assertive on the one hand and receptive and accommodating on the other. The animus and feminine elements were opposing dynamics in her personality. Mary was becoming increasing conscious of this polarity – her psychic dilemma – and the need to develop a working resolution to it if she were to move toward self-actualization.

There is an interplay between the individual personal struggles of members and the developmental phases of the social system. Mary's struggles contributed to this dynamic. Her personal history with her mother illustrated qualities that defined the Good and Bad Great Mother. As the members worked with Mary and her symbols of mother, they dealt with the images of the Good and Bad Mother and through this differentiation phase the social system evolved primarily as the Good Mother.

Robert D. Boyd

One of the major contributions the small group makes to the working through of a psychic dilemma is bringing to consciousness the archetypal elements that underlie the dilemma. For example, when a social system of a small group is manifest as a Great Mother, individual members can then relate their personal histories to the wider and more fundamental dynamics of primordial patterns in their daily lives. Mothers are expected generically to perform certain functions and to manifest certain attitudes. This knowledge exists in the unconscious of every child. This knowledge becomes lost to the developing ego and the relationship with the mother is viewed solely in terms of personal history. The ego fails to see the links between the personal mother and the Great Mother and thus the anguish and celebrations that are experienced are viewed from a limited and often a distracted perspective. The social system of the small group progresses through the archetypal themes and in doing so provides opportunities for individual members to reexamine these primordial patterns in their lives. Thus experiences in small groups have the potential to bring the ego back into relationship with the self-experiences of discernment and dialog.

Mary gave no indications in the early sessions that she was aware of the psychic dilemma in her personality other than in terms of her personal history. Mary did become an active participant often after some reference to the symbol of the Great Mother. This behavior does not warrant the conclusion that she was conscious of any links between the dilemma she began to see centered around her mother and the symbol of the Great Mother manifest in the social system of the group. In the early sessions Mary appeared to focus solely on the personal history of her dilemma. As the sessions progressed there was some evidence that she was coming to sense the existence of something else as a part of her dilemma in addition to her personal history. Our observations document two fundamental steps on the way toward a personal transformation. First, it is necessary to make public, primarily for ourselves, the historical dimensions of our dilemma. In making public such personal content it is difficult if not impossible to deny it or to hide it away again. It is reasonable to assume that since Mary repeatedly brought the content of her dilemma into the group then this must have been precisely what she wanted to do. Second, having made the dilemma public the task then becomes one of confronting it as a difficulty to be worked through. There is much evidence that Mary had taken this task on. The third step toward a personal transformation brings the individual to that point where the primordial elements are recognized as playing critical roles in the psychic dilemma. As noted above it took several sessions before this awareness could be observed in Mary's behavior. Notwithstanding, Mary was making meaningful progress toward a personal transformation.

Mary had shared with the members certain aspects of her dilemma in the early sessions of the group. They appeared as fragmented pieces of a larger picture – a picture that was filled in more completely as the sessions progressed. The dilemma may have been held at a poorly defined state because of the mother complex in Mary's personality. The autonomous nature of this complex may have prevented Mary's conscious attempts to understand and move toward personality integration. The openness of the group, the risk-taking and self-exposure that were accepted and supported in the group, may have been the conditions that provided the space and time for Mary to define the missing aspects of her dilemma and, if there were a mother complex, to free herself from it sufficiently to focus on the counter aspects of her dilemma. We do not know if this was the case; however, this interpretation is consistent with our observations. As our observations of Mary continued it was evident that she progressively demarcated the aspects of her psychic dilemma. She appeared to become increasingly aware of the counter choices that defined her dilemma. The mother complex did appear to have played a role in her struggles, but Mary's observable weighing of her choices centered the drama of her expanding consciousness on her psychic dilemma rather than on any complex.

Jung pointed out (*Golden flower*, p. 92) that 'problems of life in a certain sense are insolvable' and that if, in any sense, they appear to be resolved, it is only that they have been 'outgrown'. Our observations of Mary revealed that she was, in most cases, going over terrain she had gone over before. She, herself, spoke to this very fact. In observing her dealing with these relational conflicts, there was a sense that she was beginning to accept them as an inescapable passage in her life but also that they were losing their relevancy to her present life. She spoke about them always in the past tense. She was coming to acknowledge that things may not be as we would have wished and that these last encounters projected into the group were fixing this realization. Two patterns had been played out in Mary's behavior. On the one side the supposedly logical and assertive pattern – the animus element – and on the other side the caring, relating and accepting pattern – the feminine element. In the last two sessions these two patterns were moving toward an integration within her personality.

There were several occasions where Mary demonstrated an increasing integration of personality through her expanding consciousness. One such occasion was when Tim, in a later session, made the comment that he saw Mary having worked at developing independence from her mother. Mary immediately agreed with this observation. Here we can see that the group provided Mary with the setting to put her subjective perspectives out into a public domain to be looked at as forms of objective content. In taking these steps Mary was able to develop the necessary distance that enabled her to de-energize the psychic images that had held her. She was making real progress in outgrowing the problems she had brought to the group to work on.

There was further evidence that Mary's behavior showed her working toward a personal transformation. Mary had long been aware of the difficult relationships she had had with her mother. Her statements in the group provided sufficient evidence of this fact. What developed over the course of the group sessions was expanding consciousness of the polarities that constituted her dilemma. They were increasingly differentiated and these differentiations were taking place in a public domain. She disapproved the way her mother held on to what she wanted and her aggressive manner in getting what she was after. Yet Mary was aware that she behaved in a similar manner. Her husband, she reported, pointed out to her that her assertiveness and argumentativeness were very much like the way her mother behaved. She stated in the group that this is not how she wanted to be. Mary exhibited this pattern of behavior in her interactions with Joyce who pointed this fact out to her. In her initial interactions with Joyce, Mary was persistent and aggressive in ways that prevented a constructive exchange between the two women. In a later session a similar incident appeared to be developing, but Mary was now aware of what she was doing for she became more receptive of Joyce's position. In addition Mary tried to reconcile their differences as contrasted to her earlier behavior where she stood steadfast for her own position. This change was more than just the opportunity to practice another more acceptable behavior pattern for it gave evidence that upon the basis of her expanded consciousness Mary had made a choice and in doing so was moving toward the resolution of her dilemma.

In the last two sessions Mary began to see that the personal historical dimensions of her dilemma could not define all the dynamics which were operating in her dilemma. There were other forces more universal than the particular dynamics which she had come to see in her personal dilemma. The conflicts clustered around her relationships with her mother were not unique but reflected primary patterns in human relationships. These patterns were more than cultural configurations; they were patterns embedded deep within the human psyche. Her involvement in the discussion on love and power clearly documented Mary's expanding consciousness and her awareness of these deeper psychic patterns. This step is necessary in realizing a personal transformation as only a superficial resolution of a psychic dilemma can be had in the examination of personal history conflicts. Evidence would indicate that Mary has made significant movement toward a more fundamental discernment of the forces in her life and thus toward a personal transformation.

Some concluding observations

There was ample evidence that Mary projected aspects of her dilemma into the social system of the group, as well as onto certain members of the group. It was necessary for her to get this material out in order that she might deal with it but for it to remain as projections would do nothing in moving toward a resolution of her dilemma. The aim is to have these projected aspects of her dilemma made conscious and to have her own them as part of her personality. From that point the possibilities would then exist for her to develop ways by means of which she could outgrow the dilemma she was experiencing.

The twenty-five hours did not provide sufficient time for significant changes to occur. The realization of a personal transformation can rarely be expected in such a time frame. The case study did document movement toward an expanding consciousness of the critical components of her personal dilemma and that formed the beginning basis for a personal transformation.

It would be instructive to consider which components of her psyche may have been playing central roles in her personal dilemma. It is to be understood that any interpretation must remain speculative at this point because of the nature of our evidence. Earlier the observation was made that the animus may have been actively involved in Mary's interactions with her mother. The animus may have been the source of the aggression that Mary displayed in the group when situations conveyed symbolic content which reflected personal history with her mother. When, for example, the social system was working at developing cohesiveness, Mary insisted upon her rights as an individual member. In this situation Mary may have perceived cohesiveness as a manifestation of a controlling mother – The Terrible Mother. The affect that was evident in her behavior would lend support to our interpretation.

Although Mary was making noticeable strides in becoming increasingly conscious of the various aspects of her dilemma, she was only beginning to go beyond her personal history in understanding the conflicts she had encountered. Becoming aware of this content of the dilemma is essential but not sufficient. It is necessary to discern the deeper and universal images or pattern that are manifest in the content of personal history, that is to say the presence of archetypal elements. Jung (1969) observed that his clients frequently attributed to their personal mothers much that really belonged to the Great Mother. Initially Mary was never a part of the discussions that involved the Great Mother. It appeared as if she were holding back although she was attentive to the discussions. The integration of personal history and archetypal elements must be made if there is to be a transformation. This development was only beginning to take place as the group terminated. Her clarification and ownership of the dilemma demonstrated important growth on her part and were significant steps toward a personal transformation. Her attentiveness to the discussions on the Great Mother may be an indication that there was a growing awareness to this dimension of her personal dilemma. Her involvement in the discussions on love and power as universal forces in human affairs gave further evidence that she was becoming increasingly conscious of archetypal content.

References

Beck, A. P. (1974). Phases in the development of structure in therapy and encounter groups. In D. Wexler and L. North (eds), *Innovations in client-centered therapy*. New York: John Wiley & Sons.

Dirkx, J. M. (1987). *The self-analytic group and the Great Mother: An analysis of matriarchal consciousness in an adult learning group*. Unpublished doctoral dissertation, University of Wisconsin-Madison.

Gibbard, G. S., Hartman, J. J., and Mann, R. D. (eds) (1974). *Analysis of groups*. San Francisco: Jossey Bass.

Jacobi, J. (1965). *The psychology of C. G. Jung*. New Haven, Ct: Yale University Press.

Jung, C. G. (1962). *The secret of the golden flower*. New York: Harcourt Brace Jovanovich Publishers.

Jung, C. G. (1969). The archetypes and the collective unconscious, 2nd edition, *Collected Works of C. G. Jung*, Volume 9, Part 1. Princeton, NJ: Princeton University Press.

Luft, J. (1984). *Group processes: An introduction*, 3rd edn. Mountain View, CA: Mayfield.

Schein, E. H. and Bennis, W. G. (1965). *Personal and organizational change through group methods*. New York: John Wiley & Sons.

Smith, P. B. (ed.) (1980). *Small groups and personal change*. New York: Methuen.

Chapter eight

Facilitating personal transformations in small groups

Robert D. Boyd

The starting point

This chapter reports on the ways personal transformations may be facilitated within the setting of a small group. Small groups include a wide variety of associations which are convened for many different reasons. Although their purposes may be quite different, certain types of these small groups can be a setting in which personal transformations can be promoted and fostered. There are specific conditions that must be present, however, and critical among these are the structural and functional nature of the small group, the approach the leader uses in relating to the small group, and the commitment of the members to the goal of experiencing personal transformations on their journeys toward individuation. Before considering each of these conditional components in greater detail, the meaning of personal transformation will be clarified.

Transformation has been used to designate a number of psychological changes within the personality of an individual. Here personal transformation is conceptualized within the framework of analytical psychology and in particular as was set forth by Carl Jung (1969). A personal transformation is a fundamental change in an individual's personality involving conjointly a resolution to a personal dilemma and the expansion of consciousness resulting in a more fully realized personality integration.

The first condition identified above was concerned with the structural and functional nature of the small group. There are specific types of small groups which, generally, are structurally and functionally potential settings for encountering and dealing with personal dilemmas which in being resolved lead to personal transformations. Among these are support, counseling, therapy, interpersonal relation groups and certain types of educational groups. Since there are many meanings given to these types of groups, it will be more instructive and to the point to identify the distinctive features or specific properties the small group must possess if the proposals which follow are to be adopted to facilitate personal transformations. These requirements fall into two classes – first, the characteristics the group must possess, and second, the general orientation the leader must provide to the members of the group.

Every member must have a reasonable hold on reality – severely disturbed individuals must be excluded from the group. This stipulation does rule out certain types of therapy groups. Those who work with interpersonal training groups and instructors in educational settings must also be aware of severely disturbed individuals who may be in their classes. These persons should not be included as members of the group. On the other hand it must be recognized that certain neurotic patterns herald the onset of a possible personal transformation. A pre-session interview with members will generally reveal those who should be advised against joining the group. It has been my experience that those persons I failed to identify in the pre-session interview dropped out of the group on their own volition. Others I have been able to help to move out of the group to individual therapy or to couple individual therapy with their continuation as members of the group.

There should be no more than twelve members and no fewer than eight. The membership cannot be increased once the group has begun and all members must agree to stay with the group, which means attending all sessions. There should be no fewer than ten sessions and no fewer than twenty-four contact hours. Sixteen to twenty sessions are preferable and recommended with a proportional increase in contact hours. These specifications have been spoken to here because educational, counseling, and interpersonal study groups are often arranged for much shorter time periods. Personal transformations take time to work through. The meeting room should allow for privacy, and the room and furnishings should provide for a modest degree of comfort and a congenial ambience.

The leader is responsible for providing an orientation which makes explicit the general structures and purposes of the group. I propose that the leader provide a written description of the group's purposes, administrative arrangements, a general description of the members' responsibilities, and the roles the leader will take during the group sessions. The objective of such a statement is two-fold: first, to offer a minimum but functional structure; second, to provide an orientation for an open and enquiring community to come into existence within the group. The manner and specific content of such a statement will vary from one type of group to another.

It is clear from what has been proposed here that the leader has the initial responsibility of informing the participants of the nature and purpose of their small group. There is a real possibility that what I have proposed here could be misunderstood unless I explain the leader's initial orientation interventions more fully. The statement, whether written or spoken, is given to make explicit, in simple and direct language, the reasons why the group has been convened and the broad categories of interactions that are acceptable and likely in the group. Although this orientation appears to be and may be experienced as patriarchal, the tone of this introduction must convey the expectation of openness and experimentation. The leader through the statement must acknowledge his/her contract with the members involving the purposes of the group and his/her specific and unique commitments to the group and to the members. The statement must acknowledge the concerns of the members. It may serve, for some members, to reaffirm their understandings on what they have committed themselves to in joining the group. For other members, the statement may help to define the boundaries, giving to some members the structure they require and to other members the permission they are seeking in order to test and experiment.

It is naive to assume that orientations of this sort get the group immediately on track whatever its purposes may be. But that is not my reason for proposing this form of orientation. It is my position that a leader has the responsibility to make explicit his/her orientation to the roles and duties of the leader. It is also my position that a leader has the responsibility to make explicit his/her perceptions of the group's broad purposes and the ways she/he will attempt to relate to them. Such actions are a critical component of the open community which I am advocating. If explorations and experimentations are to be undertaken then there must be a relationship of trust between the leader and the group otherwise he/she will be able to do little to facilitate personal transformations.

There is another aspect to the notions of an open community which needs to be conveyed in the orientation statement the leader makes. It announces that in so far as his/her relationships to the group are a concern, there is no 'game-playing' involved.

With all of this, we can observe some members who appear totally lost in their attempts to understand what is taking place in the group. 'I've never been in a group like this and I feel completely lost – I don't know what's going on.' Other members are suspicious and act as if the leader is cleverly manipulating them. 'I'm not certain that I understand what you said. You will make your interventions only when you think they may help us?' There are still other members who, on later occasions in the life of the group, will admit that they had failed to hear when the leader described his/her role in the group. An orientation statement does not eliminate the fears and anxieties but it does put on record the ways the leader will relate to the group. Although the members may not initially understand, believe, or trust and may even fail to hear what has been said, their extending experiences with the leader come to confirm his/her words. It is important to have these words in place so that a basis of building trust can be made.

The emphasis that has been given to the initial orientation and the leader's role in the conduct of the orientation would appear to place the leader in the key position within the approach that is being described in this chapter. Although the leader has critical roles to take in the life of the group, he/she is not the only contributing and significant agent in facilitating personal transformations. The group and of course individuals contribute to their own and other members' personal transformations. The discussion of the ways to facilitate personal transformations is organized around the leader, the individual members, and the group. The group is examined first because it is the context within which the transformations occur and it is one of the three dynamic entities acting to block or to facilitate the members' personal transformations.

Before considering the ways a group may block or facilitate personal transformations, there is the matter of naming what we are about. I have been reluctant here to describe the ways to facilitate personal transformations in the small group as a method. My reason arises from the concern I have that labelling an approach 'a method' reduces it to a set of techniques or at least to the level of a technology. An approach is at one and the same time a conceptual framework and a flexible, highly adaptive, and uniquely sensitive set of empirical precepts. It is for these reasons I have avoided the use of the term *method* and have employed *approach* as my reference term.

The group as a social system

To understand the role played by a group in facilitating personal transformations it is necessary to have a conceptual framework of a small group to examine how it operates and affects the behaviors of its members. The Matrix Model (see Chapter one of this volume) has been used here. It describes the small group as composed of three interacting and autonomous structural systems – the social, personality, and cultural systems. When we speak of the group affecting personal transformations we are referring to the social system. The social system comes into existence at the time when the small group is formed. Its unique character is developed over the course of the small group's life. As a dynamic structure it influences and is influenced as it expresses its own existence. It asserts itself on other structures within the small group and expresses its own developing nature in the life of the group. It is proactive and reactive from the initial formation of the group to that moment when the group terminates.

There are three ways in which the social system impacts on the members that may prove helpful or impeding to the facilitating of personal transformations. One impact arises from the powerful feelings and images the members perceive manifested in the social system. A second way the social system may contribute to a personal transformation is when an individual identifies his/her personal dilemma being raised within the transactions of the social system. The third way involves the supportive structure the social system can provide for an individual which enables the member to take on the task of his/her personal transformation. Each of these three ways will be considered in turn.

The members experience the social system as a source stimulating images and powerful feelings. These images and feelings are related directly to the social system. For example members speak of the group as being 'controlling'. 'I sometimes feel that the group has some kind of power over us as members and I find this frightening.' The reference to group is obviously to the entity or structural agent I have identified as the social system. The feelings and images which the members experience and describe are primitive in the sense that they express primary relationships and emotions. Research (Boyd *et al.*, 1989; Dirkx, 1987; Slater, 1966) has shown these feelings and images arise in relationships with archetypal elements. For example, feelings of being smothered or, on the other hand, having a sense that the group cares about its members are experienced as personal emotions. They are emotions which invade and take hold of the member's being-in-the-group. These emotions, or what Jung (1972) has spoken of as feeling-toned, have their counterpart in numinous images. The smothering and caring are manifestations of the Great Mother – the image of primary archetype (Boyd, 1984, 1987; Dirkx, 1987). In the early sessions of a small group the members confront the principles of femininity and masculinity (archetypal elements; Neumann, 1959) as content and agenda of the social system (Boyd *et al.*, 1989). That is not to say that the members describe or even consciously perceive the social system as if it were the archetype of the Great Mother or that they are aware of their struggles to define their relationships in terms of the principles of masculinity and femininity. That there is some level of awareness of these dynamics, however, is evident from verbal transactions and the members' reactions to the leader's references to archetypal images and mythologems. Members speak of the group (social system) in such terms as a caring, supportive, comforting, accepting group, or they describe it as restricting, unfriendly, fault finding, and cold. The leader's metaphor of the group as Mother, arouses many reactions from most if not all members. Some members open themselves to the images, and their expanding relationships to the group experiences are evident in their body language and their sharing of personal insights. Other members retract and only later do we sometimes learn about painful relationships they have had with their personal mothers. For some of these persons the Great Mother is so much a part of their own mother that it is extremely difficult to separate the one from the other.

It will prove instructive to stay with the discussion of the Great Mother to demonstrate the impact images as manifested by the social system have on furthering or hindering the realization of personal transformations. The archetypal images which are manifested by the social system as a dynamic entity are clearly evident to any observer knowledgeable of analytical psychology. For the members who generally do not have this knowledge, it is often necessary to describe the social system in familial terms (mothers, fathers). With some groups, depending on the members' knowledge of mythology, deity figures can be used to characterize the social system. Familial references or deities are both bridges to the archetypal figures which reveal the inner world of the collective unconscious. The social system, by manifesting itself in the forms of archetypal elements, provides the member with the opportunities to have a dialog with his/her collective unconscious.

In my work with small groups I generally introduce metaphors which have a mother as the central figure, for the reasons given above, when the members have described their group, over a period of time, in such terms as caring, supportive, withholding, giving, attentive. The members had been informed in my orientation statement that my interventions would be focused on the dynamics of the social system. With the introduction of the image of mother in my metaphor (I observe the social system as the Great Mother), the members are being invited to use this symbolization of their transactions to further their expansion of consciousness. My interventions are intended to serve as stimuli for the members to explore and then relate their immediate and conscious experiences with the social system, moving from the outer world of their existence to the active interfacing of their outer and inner worlds, thus developing a more integrative mode of being-in-the-world. They are being invited to go beyond the immediate situation of their feelings of caring, withholding, etc., to the world of the primordial patterns which play such a significant role in structuring their projections which define their world.

Some members relate the image of mother or some goddess immediately and claim its validity for the social system as a dynamic entity. Others reject the notion of the group as mother or as Aphrodite, which I may have used in a metaphor, referring to the symbol as a conceptual fabrication or sheer nonsense. These initial rejections are generally abandoned by most if not all members as the sessions progress. There is the possibility that such acceptance, when it does occur, may be tentative and even a position adopted as a public posture because of some perceived form of pressure. There may be some individuals who desire to 'please the leader' and accordingly say they accept what they truly do not experience. In both cases we would look for superficial accepting behaviors, contradicting behaviors, slips, and other such indicators that would reveal some difficulty in the member's acceptance of the symbolization. When such evidence is not found, it would appear reasonable to conclude that the members have come to experience the group symbolically.

We have spoken briefly above on how personal transformations are facilitated when the social system is experienced as an archetypal image or element. This is a major impact that a social system of a small group may have on facilitating personal transformations and therefore a more extensive examination of this phenomenon is called for at this time. The encounter with archetypal elements provides opportunities for members to become aware of the ways primordial patterns affect interpersonal relations and influence as well as direct behaviors. In acknowledging these experiences the individual furthers his/her expanding consciousness. The expanding consciousness is frequently described by members as disturbing, awesome, and frightening. The ego can no longer be seen as the central and only determining entity in one's personality. The familiar must be given up and the premiss of the conscious and the controlling ego must be abandoned. The initiate is about to learn that the disciplining of the ego must be complemented by sympathetic relationships that foster open and facilitating dialogs between the ego and the collective unconscious. Personal dilemmas involving basic personality crises are now resituated into a larger context than one's personal history. The social system is a milieu in which individuals can experiment working on placing their personal dilemmas in the larger context involving both the conscious and the collective unconscious. This resituating of the personal dilemmas is facilitated by the social system as it manifests primordial patterns during its course of development.

It is commonly accepted that personal dilemmas appear to have their origin in personal histories but it has not always been accepted or more generally, it has not been recognized that there are archetypal components to personal dilemmas. Elsewhere (Boyd, 1987) I have presented a case study of a woman in which the interplay of these two components was illustrated. Her relationships with her mother, who was alcoholic, were not only tragic and odious, but were a source of nagging apprehension that she, herself, had not been at all times a 'good mother' to her daughter. She had been one of the members who initially rejected the notion that the group could be experienced as the Great Mother, although later she appeared to perceive the symbol of the Great Mother. There was a slow step-wise progression in her coming to openly acknowledge the group as the Great Mother which occurred over several sessions, during which she first spoke of her relationships with her own mother and then, incident by incident, she began to relate qualities she saw in her mother to properties she saw being manifested in the group. She recognized that there had been both good and bad times in the group. Along with other members she shared her perceptions that the group had often been caring and supportive but on other occasions it had been also smothering and even punitive. At some point as the sessions progressed, she came to an enveloping awareness that the experiencing of mother and mothering were more universal and primary than can be attached to a personal history. This awareness reflected a knowing which is primordial in nature transcending millennia of generations. 'It is as if I knew this all along. As if it were part of me and I only had to let it out to know it.' In this expanding consciousness of the mother archetype, she moved toward calmer relationships with her mother, in her own self, and toward a more accepting and balanced perception of herself as a mother. This personal transformation in progress was a function of Sara's acceptance of and then her encounter with the symbol of the Great Mother as manifested in the social system.

In the course of a group's life the social system expresses many different primordial patterns. The Great Mother, as critical as this archetypal figure is in the life of a group, is only one of many primordial elements that are encountered. Other chapters in this volume have documented the presence of the Great Father, anima and animus, and the shadow among others. As any one of these primordial patterns becomes an active symbol of the social system, members may take such opportunities to work through dilemmas within their personalities which involve any one of these archetypal elements.

The social system may interact with members in another way to facilitate the members in identifying personal dilemmas and initiating personal transformations. To understand how the social system can contribute it is necessary to return to a reexamination of the Matrix Model which was discussed in Chapter one of this volume. The social system goes through developmental phases which are delineated by specific and different crises that are encountered as it works at defining its identity and expanding its collective consciousness. In establishing its identity the social system defines itself in terms of a trusting or a mistrusting entity, followed by issues of autonomy, initiative, and on through a sequence of eight phases. In the expansion of its collective consciousness the social system develops from the stage of a mere collective (the Uroboric stage) to the next stage where the social system is experienced as caring and supportive on the one hand and the indifferent and rejecting on the other (Great Mother). From these the social system moves on to encounter the separation of problems of relatedness and problems of productivity (the Separation of the Great Parents). The issue of defining acceptable productivity is the next phase

(The Great Father). Finally, the phase of discovering and pursuing the unique goals of the social system is undertaken (the Hero Journey). The social system's identity development and the expansion of its collective consciousness provide opportunities for individual members to re-examine their resolutions to these crises in their own psychic development.

Resolving the crises of trust versus mistrust is the first crisis encountered by the nascent social system. Evidence is everywhere to be found in the initial sessions of a group bearing on this crisis. 'I am aware that sharing one's feeling is becoming an expectation of this group but I'm not sure yet that I can trust this group.' Such exchanges illustrate the relationship between the social system's task of developing its identity in working through a resolution to being a trusting or a mistrusting entity, and the individual's struggle with his/her own resolution of trust versus mistrust – a crisis long ago encountered in his/her identity development. Here the situation is demanding that this previously resolved crisis be reexamined. The individual is thrust horizontally back to an early stage of development. Where dilemmas exist in these epigenetic crises (Erikson, 1950, 1959), the possibilities are presented to the individual for a reworking of the troubled crisis and here the social system may facilitate personal transformations.

The developmental phases in the social system's collective consciousness present similar opportunities for personal transformations. As stated above, the social system begins its existence in the Uroboric phase – the Great Round as Neumann (1954) describes it. It is common to observe in this initial phase of the social system the verbalization of members, in various stages of agitation, insisting upon their individuality. They fear a loss of control over their lives, that somehow the group will strip them of their individuality and that they will become one in a mass – an undistinguishable entity. The apparent irrational quality of this fear must have an explanation other than in the terms in which these members are expressing it. A closer inspection reveals the fear is often linked to revealing content which initially appears threatening in the development of consciousness. As the social system symbolizes the state of unconscious in its Uroboric phase fears are awakened in the memories of these individuals that they may be drawn back into the darkness of the unconscious. This is an unreasonable explanation only for those individuals who have a strong enough ego to resist the possibility of such a reversal. It has been my observations that those members who have been frightened by the social system's Uroboric phase are those who during the course of the group's existence reveal an ego which is unstable and lacks the strength to maintain itself against invading forces. Such persons are fearful that they will be swallowed up and forces beyond their control will possess them. This is how they generally describe their feelings because the basis of their fears is still unconscious; they can only express their fears as a pressure to conform made by the group. It is interesting to observe other members who are astonished and not uncommonly bewildered by the way and nature of these imputations that have been lodged against the group. For still other members the sense of primitive oneness that the Uroboric phase imparts can serve to awaken conditions of estrangement existing between the ego and the Self. Statements of the following sort often are the beginning of the discernment of this estrangement and the beginning of work leading toward a transformation: 'I feel some kind of peace in this group when I stop worrying about myself. It is as if I am letting the waves roll over me without fighting to always keep my head above water.'

The movement of the social system through the phases of consciousness development provides members with the opportunities to revisit and to restructure earlier stages of their own struggles in the development of consciousness. When the members are open to and willing to experience the struggles of the social system in its phase movement in consciousness development, then they too can gain a greater expansion of their own consciousness. Within such relationships the social system may serve to facilitate personal transformations.

A social system can provide supportive structures which facilitate an individual in realizing his/her personal transformation. The willingness of members to share, to reveal their feelings, to experiment is evidence that a supportive culture exists in the group. The impact that a supportive culture can make on facilitating personal transformations can be illustrated in the following case where Joan gives evidence of the exploration which is necessary in the initial movement toward a personal transformation. 'I would like to try something', she began.

> I have been taken with the idea of shadow, you know, what we have been calling our hidden personalities. Could we look at how these affect the group? I would be willing to begin. I would be willing to share those personal qualities in myself that I have been seeing in others but have been unwilling to see in myself.

She paused at this point and looked around at the other members. Several members were nodding agreement and Sara appeared to be speaking for the group when she said, 'That's pretty gutsy but I'm with you.' The sense of support in the group was being experienced. Joan went on, 'I am proposing this because we could learn a lot about what is happening in this group; I know I certainly could. I think if we all worked at it we could see how these things affect the group.' The support that can exist in the social system is critical for such events as this one to occur in small groups. We have known for a long time, from the study of group dynamics, the positive impact that a supportive climate can make to the personal growth of the members and conversely the disastrous affects of a nonconforming social system.

In addition to these contributions the social system makes to facilitating personal transformations, there are other benefits the social system provides for the individual in his/her expansion of consciousness. These contributions have to do more with the context the group provides than with the impact the social system has on the members. That is to say, a social system is a context as well as a dynamic entity and it is the context of the social system which can also serve as an arena for an individual to work on his/her personal transformation. Certain phenomena occur in the context of a social system, such as projections, which, if examined and understood, may lead to personal transformations. It is often the case that many group projections, which operate extensively in interpersonal relationships, are made without being examined or even experienced. The possibility exists, however, that projections, as they occur in the context of the social system, could be perceived and examined. In a small group where there is an agreement to facilitate personal transformations, projections are legitimate content to be analyzed and understood. To focus on projections is critical because they are frequently centrally involved in personal dilemmas and their part in these dilemmas must be explicitly discerned if a personal transformation is to be realized.

There are three steps involved in dealing with projections. Obviously, the first step is the awareness of the projection and taking one's ownership of it. This step does not occur easily for most people. I will discuss ways in which this encounter may be more readily undertaken in the section which follows describing the leader's interventions. Once the individual has accepted ownership of the projection, the next step is the self-disclosure of the nature of the projection. For example, Hal first came to realize that he was projecting a teasing and denying anima onto Ann and now he is beginning to see the figure of this anima as a part of his previously unconscious personality. He has been both fascinated and unsettled by women on whom he could place this projection. Again, the self-disclosing of the nature of the projection is a difficult task and it is not one that is achieved, generally, on the initial attempts. Knowledge of the nature of the projection leads to the third step to be taken. The individual must develop a conscious working relationship with the processes that lie at the core of the projection. In developing this relationship which is carried on in the form of internal dialogs, the autonomous unconscious nature of the projection is largely removed and in the light of the individual's consciousness it becomes another force that must be reckoned with when it becomes active. These tasks are worked at in the context of the social system and when a supportive climate exists there is a greater likelihood that more projections will be examined.

There is yet another way the social system may facilitate personal transformations. Like a scenario of a play, the dynamics of a social system come to have focal actors. Critical issues arise in the life of a group and on some occasions the group turns to a specific member while on other occasions a member takes the initiative in focusing the group on the issue. In either situation the member serves as a focal point around whom the group coalesces (Dirkx, 1987; Myers, 1986; Redl, 1942). Beside the value such events may have for the life of the group, it may also have value for individual members. The behaviors of the focal person (see Chapter three) provide opportunities for members to learn vicariously by observing the dynamics occurring between the group and the focal person. They may see themselves in similar roles and reflect on their possible reactions were they to be in the focal person's situation. In addition the focal person may help them to more clearly perceive issues that could have gone unnoticed. Such opportunities do not exist in dyadic situations, as is the case in individual therapy practice. Such opportunities do exist in small groups and are a valuable source for personal growth.

In summary the social system has been shown to contribute in five ways to facilitate an individual's personal transformation. It can serve as a symbol representing for the members archetypal elements and principles. As such it can bring to consciousness the archetypal components of an individual's personal dilemma. A second form of contribution the social system can make is demonstrating a corresponding development between its phase movement within the identity and reality-adaptive tasks and those stages of development an individual encounters in his/her personal life course. As the social system moves through a particular phase individuals as members of the group are compelled to revisit earlier stages of their own development. This revisiting of previous life stages provides individuals with opportunities to reexamine resolutions of earlier stages and to rework them if they so desire. A third contribution is the supportive structures and climate the social system can provide for experimentation, explorations, and disclosures which are basic to the realization of personal transformations. A fourth contribution is made as the dynamics of the social system provide a context for projections. The awareness of a projection is frequently the first major step in an individual member's personal transformation. Finally, the transactions taking place in the context of the social system reveal insights into the dynamics of personal dilemmas and it is through expanding consciousness that experiences take on meaning and may lead to personal transformations.

The individual member

Our discussion now turns first to consider how other members of a small group may facilitate an individual member's personal transformation and then what steps he/she must take to further his/her own personal transformation.

Individual members may not always be aware that they are making a contribution to a fellow member's personal transformation. Early in the life of the social system, members may be unaware that they are objects of a projection. The existence of a projection can be the first step in revealing and working on a personal dilemma which could lead to a transformation. This may be illustrated in David's case, who, becoming conscious of his projections of a father figure onto an older member, is taking the first steps in coming to grips with primordial patterns of dependence and authority. In addition, members serve as sources of vicarious learnings which give insights to personal dilemma. Mary witnesses the coquettish whims of Diane and she is disturbed to see herself having acted in this manner. John becomes more able to share his feelings on his sense of being rejected by others following a discussion in which David revealed his basic feelings on the issue. The argument between members which resulted in a more open environment in the group helped Nancy to reconsider her perceptions about personal confrontations. Watching the interactions among members provides a rich source of insights about the games people play in their interpersonal relationships (Berne, 1963). Members through these many ways can serve in starting the expansion of consciousness that may lead to personal transformations.

The realization of a personal transformation demands that the individual take the responsibility for his/her own growth. The awareness of the dynamics occurring in the social system and the vicarious learnings gleaned from the observations of other group members is not sufficient to bring about a personal transformation but is only the first step in that direction. It is not sufficient only to acknowledge this responsibility; it must be fully accepted. The existence of personal responsibility for one's own growth initially opens the individual to consider what is and what possibly could be. When this has taken place the individual has moved from the phase of mere acknowledgement to the receptive phase. The individual, in being receptive, is taking the necessary step in recognizing and taking ownership of that which has been hidden. The unknown in its many aspects comes to be known. Peter's rejection of the need for emotional cohesiveness and his distrust of those proposing the expression of personal feelings comes to be experienced slowly as his own personal crisis of intimacy and isolation. Such explorations are carried forward cautiously and in a limited manner. There is also both forward and backward movement, where individuals advance to and then fall back from knowledge about themselves. In some cases what has been gained appears to have been lost. In most cases this apparent loss of knowledge about an aspect of personality is only temporary. It often happens that such retreats appear to be necessary in order that advances may be consolidated. Like many significant insights, a particular awareness may take a period of time of living with it before it is fully accepted. Being receptive, that is being open to look at one's psychosocial difficulties and to recognize them as personal dilemmas, is not by itself to resolve them. To reach some form of a working relationship with a personal dilemma, an individual must move beyond receptivity and recognition. In developing some form of resolution to a personal dilemma, the individual must come to know the nature of his/her dilemma and this is experienced through the expansion of consciousness.

This expansion of consciousness involves more than simply the personal ego. It is commonly assumed in our western culture that the ego is the sole agent in the expansion of consciousness. Although the ego is the center of consciousness, the development of consciousness comes about in triadic transactions dynamically determined by the psychic components of Self, the outer world, and the ego. Not all of the psychic components of the Self would be involved. In one set of transactions it may be the shadow that plays a major role, while in another situation it may be the anima – similarly with the outer world. Specific aspects of the environment would be critical in one situation and another group of environmental factors would be critical in another setting. All three components are always involved in any transaction which involves a personal transformation. The conscious relating of the transaction among these three is here described as a 'dialog'. Such dialogs result in the expansion of consciousness. Among the potential results of the expansion of consciousness can be the revealing of a personal dilemma – a core personality malintegration.

Since the concept *personal dilemma* has a specific meaning here, a brief discussion of the concept is called for at this point. A personal dilemma is an unresolved set of critical choices bearing on an individual's life course. There are three components common to all personal dilemmas, specifically: (1) archetypal elements; (2) personal history; (3) current existential conditions. If we use cultural histories and mythologies of cultural groups as the basis of our evidential argument, then it is reasonable to assume that there is a common body of archetypal elements shared by all humankind. The configuration of these archetypal elements, however, varies among individuals. In one individual certain elements are more prominent than they are for another individual, thus this difference, in part, accounts for the differences in

216

personality. The phrase 'in part' is a critical proviso in that personality is also a function of one's personal history which weaves the warp and woof of the unique pattern of personality. It follows that if personal history is an active and primary constituent of personality, then it must be an active component of an individual's personal dilemmas. We speak of dilemmas because our lives evolve many dilemmas and there is no period when our lives contain only one dilemma. There are times when a particular dilemma dominates our lives and other dilemmas drop from our immediate attention. What then moves a particular dilemma to center stage? Something in the individual's environment focuses the person's attention on the dilemma. This awareness is experienced initially in most cases as disequilibrium – something yet unnamed but disturbing is experienced. Seldom does the individual immediately recognize the nature of the feeling-toned she/he is experiencing as a personal dilemma in the terms in which it has been defined here. The existential condition has aroused the individual to the dilemma and it remains only for the individual to take the responsibility to develop a workable resolution to the dilemma. The working through involves coming to understand how archetypal elements and personal history structure the dilemma and how they are played out through the dilemma. These are the difficult and demanding tasks involved in realizing a personal transformation.

As noted above, several dilemmas exist at any given time, but fortunately, not all of them are energized at one point in time. They are like quiescent volcanoes ready to erupt under specific conditions. More specifically, a dilemma remains in a relatively inactive state until existential conditions excite it or the existential conditions are favorable to the expression of personal history problems or/and archetypal elements. The case of Karen illustrates the interaction among these three components of a personal dilemma. Karen voiced her disturbance at the way the leader was conducting the group. She criticized what she saw as a labile, non-directive form of leadership. 'Either join the group as a member or act as a group leader.' In the sessions which followed this attack on the leader, Karen came to recognize her own ambivalence toward issues involving power and control. Her growing awareness was evident in the exploration of her personal history which she began to share with the group. Her explorations were resulting in an expanded consciousness. Her father was an overcontrolling but caring person who appeared to dominate aspects of her life on the one hand, yet on the other hand gave lovingly of himself as a gentle and benevolent patriarch. This relationship illustrates a common quality of dilemmas – namely, as distressing and frequently painful as dilemmas are, they generally contain some form of gratification. Karen apparently wanted to keep the particular father–daughter relationship alive because it must have given her some form of gratification. Her experiences in the group were raising to consciousness the choice that was the dilemma; the choice to reject or to hold onto this relationship was now becoming painfully clear. One aspect of her dilemma had not as yet become evident. Were she to gain an insight into the archetypal component of her dilemma she would gain a transpersonal view of a universally human developmental epic. Toward the end of the group's life the myth of Electra was introduced by the leader. During one of the later sessions, Karen related her feelings about the leader and other persons in authority roles. She shared her growing awareness that there were basic questions of control and autonomy that were underlying her relationships with her father and persons in authority generally. Here she was beginning to incorporate the archetypal elements in an understanding of her dilemma.

In summary other members can play a significant role in facilitating personal transformation. In addition to direct and explicit help that other individuals can give, they serve as objects of projections and players in vicarious learnings. Nothing can be made of the extended help or of the potential learnings unless the individual him/herself takes the responsibility for his/her own growth. A major task in expanding one's personal consciousness is accepting the responsibility to understand one's personal dilemmas. A personal dilemma has as its basic components both archetypal elements and personal history. Dilemmas remain in a relatively inactive state until existential conditions excite them or the existential conditions are favorable to the expression of personal history problems or/and archetypal elements. There is an expansion of consciousness when an individual takes ownership of the dilemma and undertakes to resolve the dilemma. Movement toward a personal transformation is evident in these actions.

The group leader

To this point, we have examined the ways in which the social system and the members of a small group can facilitate personal transformations. We will now consider the roles a leader can take in helping individual members of a small group expand their consciousness and realize personal transformations. The roles and the general structures of the approach proposed here for the leader can be used with different types of small groups. It is recognized that designated purposes of groups vary; however, leaders can make use of the approach to be set out in this section provided that a principal end-in-view of the group is to facilitate personal consciousness. This section describes the ways the leader is to carry out his/her commitments to the members and the group. In addition to a discussion on the conceptual structure of the approach, I report on its practice as I have conceived it.

A principal aim that continuously guides the leader's interventions is to raise the members' personal consciousness. I propose that these interventions be primarily in the form of metaphors. I describe my interventions as metaphors because I use images or pictures or story sketches as a way of putting into bold relief what I discern to be the critical aspects of the group's current life. What follows is an explanation of the reasons for using metaphors and the ways they are presented in the leader's interventions. It needs to be pointed out at this time that there are occasions when I speak directly to an issue, examine an event, or ask a question but such interventions are made rarely. The conditions which prompt these types of interventions are described in a later part of this section.

The discussions and explanations which follow are organized to address specific questions. These questions focus on key aspects of the approach which is being proposed in this chapter.

Why the metaphor?

It is first necessary to ask a prior question. Why do I make interventions into the life of the group? My interventions are given as a way to encourage the members to bring to consciousness the unconscious content which they are encountering but which, for some reasons, they are not raising to consciousness. Although the general nature of the struggles in such encounters can be discerned, the nature of that struggle is yet to be made explicit in the consciousness of the member. Metaphors as general sketches of such encounters have the quality of revealing the essential nature of encounters with the content and elements of the unconscious while at the same time giving individuals the latitude to relate the import of the metaphors' messages to the members' common and unique struggles. Members can also deny the metaphors on the grounds of not understanding them and thereby reject the invitation to examine their struggles. To relate to the messages of the metaphor initially requires the courage to encounter the unconscious and then the will to engage in a dialog with unconscious content and elements which requires reflection and active imagination.

Active imagination plays a crucial role in understanding metaphors. Barbara Hannah describes active imagination in the following terms:

> a form of meditation which man has used, at least from the dawn of history, if not earlier, as a way of learning to know his God or gods. In other words, it is a method of exploring the unknown, whether we think of the unknown as an outside god – as an immeasurable infinity – or whether we know that we meet it by contemplating our unknown selves in an entirely inner experience.
>
> (1981, pp. 3–4)

Robert D. Boyd

My interventions, structured as metaphors, are attempts to enlist the members' active imagination. The development of consciousness is largely the result of the dialogs between the ego, as the center of consciousness, and the other components of the Self which reside in the unconscious. Metaphors are employed to encourage such dialogs when movement toward the contemplation of the inner realms is already evident in the group.

I have come to use metaphors for several reasons. One of their most obvious virtues is that they can be used to describe in very general terms a critical aspect of the group's dynamics. They convey the primary features of that dynamic which could not be adequately presented in literal or conceptual terms unless the observations were recounted to the group in some detail. To do so would very likely diffuse attention and the focus on the critical dynamic could be lost conceptually and emotionally. In brief, metaphors have the potential of revealing the essence of a given dynamic within the life of a group.

Metaphors, because they do not specifically describe an event, behavior, or a transaction, do not put any member's behavior in the limelight to be examined. The situation the metaphor addresses is described in a way that does not direct the members' attention inescapably to a transaction involving particular individuals. It focuses on the dynamics of the group-as-a-whole. Thus, a member who does not want to look at the difficulty may claim ignorance of the metaphor's message on the basis that he/she is not accustomed to thinking in metaphors or is unable to see how this vague input has anything to do with what the group is working on. In this manner the member has a legitimate excuse not to deal with the context of the metaphor. This behavior is observed when the content is too threatening to the member for him/her to consider. Unlike methods which use an encounter approach – one which directly confronts the member – I am proposing here an approach that does not so invade a person's or a group's life space such that there is no choice but to confront what is perceived to be an attack. We will examine later the issues that arise in directly confronting a member or a group; however, at this time it is obvious that there are moral and ethical issues as well as psychological considerations that such an approach raises. But these questions aside, there is the strong possibility that a confrontative approach provokes mechanisms of defense and unless this can be shown to lead to personal insights, we may have created stronger barriers to the development of personal transformations.

Metaphors, in their very construction, are vague allusions. Since they do not specifically and literally point to this or that, they have the potential to be adapted within some given limits, of course, to private and personal interpretations. Thus the general configurations of metaphors provide the individual and the group with the opportunity to apply their unique interpretative variations on the theme presented in the metaphor. Examples of specific situations may serve to illustrate these points. When the social system is in the phase of the Great Mother and it is uncertain whether the Good or Bad Mother will come to characterize the social system, the myth of Aphrodite may be cited in part. In a familial scene the mother could be described as listening to a daughter's difficulties but not saying anything or offering any advice. For some members, the mother is not judgemental and therefore seen in a favorable light. For others she is not helpful and is viewed negatively.

Metaphors are presented as descriptions of the group and are always addressed to the group-as-a-whole. There are very specific reasons for doing this. One purpose is to keep the notion of the group as an entity before the members. The members must come to see that the social and cultural systems of the group affect what happens in the group and that they influence every member's behavior, decisions, and feelings. The phase development of the social and cultural systems has a profound effect on member's behaviors. Most members start from the assumption, however, that a group is a collection of individuals and the only dynamics are interpersonal. This perception is challenged when the metaphors are continually referenced to the social or cultural systems. Another outcome in focusing on the social and cultural system is that it may remove for some members the sense of being put on the spot. When the group is the focus of the metaphor, individual members may be provided with some space in which to consider their own developmental concerns without feeling directly challenged or threatened.

Earlier the Matrix Model was identified as the conceptual framework for the approach which is being set forth in this chapter. In that framework there are three primary tasks that individual members, the social and cultural systems encounter and work on. All these tasks are being worked at in some fashion and to different degrees at any given time although generally task one is receiving more attention than the other two. Metaphors, in most cases, give a sufficient latitude whereby members may read into them an insight as to what they see the difficulties are with handling a given task. A metaphor is offered about a father who never spends his time with the family but yet hands down expectations. Some members interpret the metaphor to mean that they are letting an outside agent define their group (identity task). Other members suggest that there is too much dependency in the group (emotionality task). Still others might propose that the members are not dealing with the symbols of authority in their lives (reality-adaptive task). There may be aspects of all three elements in the group. What follows is that one of these problems comes to be seen as most central. When the group focuses on one of the three tasks, they, as well as the leader, would then become aware of what the primary task is and then begin to explore the direction the work should take. There are two points that need to be made explicit at this time otherwise the reader may assume I am ascribing a level of sophistication to members which is seldom the case. First, they may recognize the general nature of the task but not its conceptual status. Second, there may be a general sense of the group's malaise but what should be done about it is frequently not clear to the members initially.

Although the metaphors speak to the critical issues the social system is encountering, the message of the metaphor has a counter-part in the personality and cultural systems. In the example above the father may symbolize the social system's encounter with issues of power and autonomy. The same metaphor may serve in bringing to consciousness a member's personal dilemma involving his/her own struggles with taking autonomy. The cultural system may also be involved in the group's encounter with autonomy. The struggles of both the social system and the personality systems to constructively deal with issues of autonomy may reflect the dynamics of the current *Zeitgeist* – the cultural system of the group structured upon the patriarchal character of the larger society. Metaphors, when they get hold of the essence of what is occurring in a small group, reveal insights into the workings of all three systems because all three systems constitute the dynamics of a small group.

Of what subject matter are metaphors composed?

Metaphors are composed of one of four types of subject matter. One form of subject matter may be structured as familial scenarios. For example, when members are in a pattern of approaching and then flighting from dealing with their relationships to the social system revealed in the symbols of the Great Mother, the leader may make an intervention in the form of a familial scenario.

> I am getting a picture of a family; brothers and sisters sitting around on the back terrace of their home on a summer afternoon. They are behaving as any group of young adults just waiting for somebody or something to get them started doing something. Then one sibling asks in a casual, off-handed manner, 'Has anyone seen Mother this afternoon?'

The subject matter of metaphors may be structured from mythology. Myths are a powerful medium because they speak to primitive and universal dilemmas. The interplay among the three systems of a small group is portrayed in symbolic and dramatic form in myths. The myth of Prometheus, for example, may be briefly outlined at the time when the members are struggling with the issue of dependence/independence but appear to be unable to raise the problem to a conscious level. Psyche's difficulty with Aphrodite may be shared with the group to help the members formulate their resolve to accept the tasks the Mother group has placed before them.

A third source of content for the metaphor is drawn from literature. In confronting the leader, in order that the group can deal with authority symbolized by the leader, there may be a sense of conspiracy in the group. This can arise when all members are not explicitly committed to confronting the leader as a symbol of controlling authority. As a symbol (and sometimes as an actual condition) he/she stands in the way of the group achieving autonomy. If the sense of conspiracy is not dealt with, it will block any meaningful movement toward handling the issue of autonomy involving the leader. On such occasions I have made reference to the conspiracy against Caesar as dramatized by Shakespeare. There are a large number of such episodes in literature which capture the essence of the various problems a group encounters.

Biblical literature provides a wealth of material for metaphors. It goes without saying that the religious faiths of the membership must be taken into account. When a group, in its attempt to escape a gripping sense of directionlessness, turns to the practice of laying down explicit norms, I have made the following kind of intervention:

> You may recall the story of the prodigal son. After lovingly taking his prodigal son back into their home the father had to explain his actions to the other sons who were angered by their brother who had not obeyed their father's wishes or accepted his duties.

On other occasions when many members feel they are gaining little knowledge and understandings from their struggles, I have recounted the story of the loaves and fishes shared by the multitude. The account of Christ's encounter with Satan on the mount when told as a metaphor places the confrontation of love and power before the members. The wandering of the Jews in the desert portrays for the group its own sense of wandering.

What are the content topics of the metaphors?

The content topics of the leader's interventions are determined by what she/he perceives to be facilitating input. It would seem therefore that the subject matter of these interventions would be almost an infinite range of topics. I have found, however, that the content topics of my interventions can be classified into one of seven categories. I am not proposing that these seven categories are exhaustive but I have found that these categories do reflect the common problem topics which small groups encounter.

223

Major life dilemmas of members are manifested in the life of the group. Personal dilemmas become evident in three contexts: interpersonal transactions; as the social system moves through its developmental phases; as the cultural system struggles toward its unique configuration within the group context. For example, in any one of these three dynamic contexts, members may be observed confronting such dilemmas as independence–dependence, cooperation–competition, trust–mistrust, matriarchal and patriarchal relationships.

Projections are another content area which is commonly observed. There are two forms of projection which can be observed. There are projections which are structured from repressed material, the classic example being of the father complex being played out with the leader. There is also the other form of projection (vonFranz, 1980) by means of which we construct our descriptive meanings which structure the world in which we have our being. Both forms of projection are content areas the leader must be aware of and take into consideration in his/her attempts to facilitate personal and group transformations. In the case of either form of projection, the individual member is dealing with his/her environment on the basis of unconscious elements. When there is some evidence that such projections are or are becoming barriers to group development or to personal growth (seldom are they ever separate) the leader has the responsibility to consider making an intervention.

The interplay between personal history and archetypal elements forms another category of content. A woman who had a domineering father must relate the experiences based upon that type of relationship to the archetypal Great Father involving such elements as power, autonomy, and linear logic. I have found in my studies that many women have severe struggles relating their personal histories with their own mothers to their relationship with the archetypal Great Mother.

Seldom if ever do we find a member of a small group aware of and practicing active imagination. In recent years there has been an increasing number of persons who are becoming aware of such practices. The leader must help members to explore the experience of dialoging within themselves which, I here describe, as personal dialogs. This is a form of active imagination which has the potential of bringing conscious and unconscious elements and content into an encounter with each other. Members speak of feeling something in their gut. They speak of knowing before they have been aware of consciously reflecting upon it. Learning about personal dialogs is a content area a leader can address through his/her interventions.

Most members, as I have noted earlier, view the dynamics of small groups solely as interpersonal transactions. They must be helped to perceive the existence of the social and cultural systems as dynamic entities within the small group. Thus coming to understand this conceptualization of the small group becomes a content area for the leader's interventions. Members must come to recognize that the three systems affect each other. Their increasing knowledge of these interrelationships is critical if they are to understand the dynamics of their small group. For example, when members do not have this knowledge, they find it difficult to understand the changing appropriateness of various behaviors at different times during the ongoing life of a small group.

Another content area is the relationship between the developing cultural system of the small group and the larger society within which the group exists. Most members attempt to structure the small group's cultural system solely on the basis of the cultural structures of the larger society. Members must come to recognize the existence of the unique cultural system that is being developed within the small group. This involves not only an understanding of the relationships between the two cultural systems but also the commitment to evolve a workable cultural system within the life of the small group.

I have stated in several places within this chapter that the interventions do not speak directly to the behaviors of individual members. Although metaphors focus on the social and cultural systems, it is expected that individuals will gain insights and understandings from the metaphors about their own behaviors. It is the case, however, that personal transformations can only come about if an individual takes ownership of his/her personal dilemma. That is to say, members must relate themselves to the dynamics of the social and cultural systems and when they do, personal dilemmas should make themselves evident where unresolved conflicts exist. There are specific stages to taking ownership of one's dilemma. First, the individual must come to recognize the possibility that there is evidence of a personal dilemma. Then the individual must become receptive to the idea of a commitment to examine and deal with the dilemma. Finally, the individual must struggle to resolve the dilemma. By identifying an issue or a crisis that exists in the social or cultural system, the ground has been prepared for members whose dilemmas also involve those concerns, to begin to work on their individual dilemmas in the social or/and cultural context within which their dilemmas are contextually defined. For example, the social system appears to be unable or unwilling to accept the responsibility for its own inertia. There are references to a leader that will not lead. It will not accept ownership for the state of affairs it now finds itself in. I have described such a condition by referring to the play *Waiting for Godot*. I have also used a familial scenario in which the children are sitting together wondering what they can do to help Mother who is fighting a serious illness. Personal responsibility for one's own and the group's growth is clearly a content topic in a small group.

Robert D. Boyd

What are the occasions when an intervention may be helpful?

There are four types of occasions in the life of a small group when I have made an intervention. One such occasion is when I observe the group to be mired down. For example, the social system appears to be fixated on an issue and is going nowhere with it. There is much talk about building trust in the group but there is no evidence that trust is being furthered in any observable way. The same ground is covered over and over again; it is variations on the same theme.

Another occasion when an intervention may facilitate the forward movement of the social system is at times when flight becomes a pervasive emotionality. For example, there are several occasions which follow in sequence when the members' flight from openly recognizing the social system can be both supportive and rejecting. The members appear to be threatened or frightened by the possibility that the group can be destructive in different ways. They often desperately cling to the illusion that their group has only the welfare of its members at heart. Their unconscious dread of the Bad Mother creates a fictitious Good Mother. In cases where there is flight on such critical issues, I have found that these occasions frequently require a number of interventions.

Interventions are frequently helpful on occasions when members appear to be unable to make connections that would shed light on the difficulties they are encountering. The social system has become symbolized primarily as the Good Mother yet the members, expecting the issue of their autonomy to have been taken care of, find it is before them again in even a more pressing manner. I have used the familial metaphor where the mother advises the adolescent son or daughter that it is up to him/her to ask dad for the use of the car for she is not going to run interference. Such interventions may strike the reader as lacking sophistication and therefore somewhat offensive to adults. My experience does not support this position. The fundamental nature of the social system's crisis and of specific members' personal dilemmas requires the elementary quality of such messages.

There are occasions when the group has reached a particular development but has not explicitly recognized it and, were it to do so, it would facilitate further development. If it appears the group is not going to identify for itself where it is now at, the leader could offer an intervention which may facilitate the group in coming to perceive the connections. A caution should be noted here. There is a tendency for most leaders to enter too soon and thus deny the group the opportunity to develop its own realization.

226

What considerations should be taken into account in making interventions?

How interventions are made and what considerations must be taken into account are two key features of the approach being set forth here. There are some fourteen advisory statements which speak to the practice of this approach. They are the product of my experiences and study and thus cannot be viewed as an exhaustive statement. They are, so far as they go, critical considerations in furthering the expansion of consciousness and facilitating personal transformations.

It is difficult, understandably, for a leader to be part of a small group and not be actively engaged in directing the group. The approach I have been advocating in this chapter will not work unless the leader comes to understand and thoroughly appreciates the necessity to relax. It is important, indeed essential, that the leader not force him/herself to do something simply because he/she feels that is the leader's role. This taking charge of things by the leader is not only a cultural norm and a wishful expectation of many members but often the stimulus from an overactive ego. The ego is frequently guilty of seeking recognition at the expense of more worthy goals and so the leader searches for a 'brilliant' remark that must be given to the group for its salvation. Surrendering to such human impulses can be most disruptive to the work of the group.

It is difficult for many if not most leaders to remain quiet when the group appears to be making little progress. I recognize this difficulty in myself by a tension I experience after long stretches of time during which I have not made an intervention. When I feel myself becoming tense, I immediately try to identify possible conditions for it. The tension I feel may be a reaction to my own inability to define what I am sensing to be a difficulty the group is experiencing but not handling successfully. There are steps I can take to deal with this condition which I discuss later. Even though the group may be struggling with an unresolved problem the tension may be centered more within me than in the situation I am observing. The question arises: Am I searching for some way to take a more active part in the group's transactions? The possibility may exist that my role of observing at this time may not be meeting some personal need I have. If I, as leader, enter the group without carefully examining my own motives I may be building my own agenda into my interventions. This possibility exists because I may be projecting myself into what I believe I am observing taking place in the group. The responsibility of the leader is to be aware of his/her tension, to recognize its probable sources and to relate these to the symbolic content with which the group is actively involved.

The personality, social, and cultural systems work at three primary tasks: the development of identity; the establishing of emotional patterns of relating; the expansion of consciousness. Although all of these tasks are ongoing in the life of a small group, one is generally focal. The leader needs to be aware of which task is focal in order that his/her intervention addresses the prominent dynamic of the group. An intervention which redirects the attention of the group to the symbolic content of a task which is not currently focal may prove disruptive to the group. There are occasions when the leader needs to help the group to become aware of content that is not directly involved in the focal task. For example, the group may be working to establish its autonomy, when the leader observes a member who gives the appearance of withdrawing from the group. This behavior has gone unnoticed by the group in its eagerness to establish autonomy. Since it is very likely this member's withdrawal may present serious difficulties to the social system in the immediate future, the leader decides to draw the members' attention to what is happening. Any number of metaphors could be employed to convey the leader's observation.

The symbolic language and content of the group is of central concern in the proposed approach. The symbolic content is carried by the manifest subject matter of the group's discussions. It is necessary to listen carefully therefore to the group's discussions to identify and comprehend the symbolic content in order to perceive what primary task is now focal and how it is being handled by the group. The leader has to work at listening to the symbolic content as it is so easy to become involved in the ongoing business of the group conveyed in its manifest language. Bion (1959) was one of the first to speak to this problem.

In stating that the leader must focus his/her attention on the symbolic language and content of a group, it should not be understood thereby that the leader should disregard the manifest content. There is an interplay between the manifest and symbolic content of a group's work. To understand what is occurring in the group requires an understanding of how the two forms of content interconnect and carry forward the concerns being expressed in the group. Although it is necessary for the leader to be aware of the manifest content, it is the symbolic content that unmistakingly expresses the primary task concerns of the group. The manifest content is much easier to follow and often, because it is direct and seemingly of more immediate concern, has a seductive quality that draws an observer's attention away from the symbolic content. The symbolic content is recognized by a theme that runs through the discussion. Often the presence of these themes can be identified by either strong affects or at the other pole a sense that affect is being repressed. Themes are often embedded in periods of inertia. During such periods when the group appears to be going nowhere the leader may find it difficult to identify themes. But the leader can be certain that a theme or conflicting themes are present. Trivia can occur in such periods. When it fascinates the members, or when it continues to return, the leader has strong evidence that the trivia, as symbolic content, is expressing some central concern for the group. This work is occurring at the unconscious level of the group's life and thus the leader's role becomes one of helping the group to expand its awareness of the unconscious content.

Understanding the nature of the content expressed in symbolic language is a difficult undertaking. This means that the leader may not know what is taking place at all times in the life of a small group. I believe it is unreasonable to expect she/he should. When I am uncertain as to what is happening I take my notebook and start writing every word which is accented or is given weight in verbal utterances. This may go on until I have filled a page before I begin to perceive a pattern. I have noted that when I am faced with this problem one of the following three conditions is present. The group is not focused on an agenda either because it is in the process of moving from one concern to another or it is having difficulty in perceiving what its task is. The problem may lay with the leader. There are times when personal problems unconsciously distract the leader's attention. Focusing on the group by note taking redirects one's attention. Fatigue may be part of this phenomenon. Above I spoke of the issue that there are occasions when the leader becomes intent on bringing his/her own agenda into the group. This preoccupation with one's own agenda distracts the leader's ability to see what is going on. The practice of noting what is going on is so highly structured that it seldom fails to bring the leader back into touch with the dynamics of the group. Forcing one's attention on the discussion by writing down the critical words and phrases (expressions weighted with affect) is a successful procedure for overcoming the lack of concentration whatever the cause.

It is always necessary to test the validity of a metaphor. Its validity can only be tested after the fact; however, there are some considerations which should be taken into account before the leader shares the metaphor. Does the metaphor feel right? This test is problematic in that we humans have a large capacity to mislead ourselves; however, our intuition can provide insights in the absence of point-to evidence. Often the sense of what feels to be correct alerts us to evidence. Here again we must be cautious for the same reason that was identified above. With the metaphor fully formed by the leader and ready to be shared with the group, the leader can ask him/herself: How would I react to this metaphor were I a member? This directs the leader to look for further evidence. Waiting for a period of time to see if further transactions support the use of the metaphor is an advisable practice. There is a caution in spending too much time in protesting the validity of a metaphor. It can happen that the dynamics may change radically and what could have been of help now is no longer relevant. Inaction on the part of the leader can result in missing an occasion where help could have been given.

Determining the validity of a metaphor after it has been shared will provide many insights to the leader. A metaphor may be described as having validity when it portrays essential(s) quality(ies) of the group's current life. But the validity of a metaphor is tested by what occurs subsequently in the group. The group may respond in a variety of ways ranging from ignoring, rejecting and flighting to accepting, explaining, and integrating. These reactions in themselves are not the critical evidence but whether, is there evidence of one of the following types of events occurring in the group? First the group increases the type of behavior portrayed in the metaphor. One should be careful, however in assuming this to be always the case. A case in point is that a group in the phase of dependency will often take up whatever the leader offers. An experienced leader is aware of this possibility and will take this into account. If the increase of behavior leads to a more meaningful examination of the group's difficulty then it is reasonable to assume some level of validity to the metaphor. In other words, a measure of validity for the metaphor is affirmed when the group uses the message of the metaphor to expand the consciousness of its members. A third form of evidence for the validity may be found in the emotional reactions that follow the leader's intervention. There are two types of emotional reactions which may be observed. The group's response can be an emotional reaction against the content and/or the message of the metaphor. If there is a sense that the reaction is defensive then in all probability the metaphor has reached a critical problem. The other reaction may be an emotional response as a result of a powerful insight – darkness yielding to light. The desire to seek validity must always be tempered by doubt. Seeking to falsify the validity of a metaphor is frequently more instructive than finding corroborating evidence. The difficulty with this advice is that tests of falsification can be much more readily applied in *post hoc* examinations than they can be applied in situations demanding ongoing analysis.

Metaphors are not to be explained. If metaphors do not make sense readily then one of four possibilities exist:

(a) The metaphor is premature – the leader presented the material before there was sufficient knowledge and experience in the group to have it make any meaning.

(b) The metaphor is too late – the leader presented it after the group had already dealt with the topic and had moved on to another problem. The metaphor makes no sense in terms of what the group is now dealing with.

(c) The metaphor is incorrect – the leader presented an interpretation or an observation that does not describe the dynamics of the group accurately. Therefore it properly should be ignored.

(d) The metaphor is accurate but for reasons or causes operating in the group it cannot be accepted or understood.

My reasons for not explaining a metaphor are found in my earlier discussion which presented my reasons for using metaphors. It was pointed out in that discussion that metaphors are structured in symbolic language which is the language or the medium the unconscious employs to structure and communicate its content. Metaphors which are in the same language medium that is used by the unconscious speak directly to the content elements of the unconscious. Thus to explain my metaphors would be to undo what I am setting out to encourage and foster. Specifically, I am trying to help the group members to relax their egos sufficiently that they might hear messages from their unconscious and eventually engage in intrapersonal dialogs. Metaphors are viewed as bridges, where, for most members, no bridges exist.

There is another reason which has to do with dynamics of group interactions. There is always the issue of dependency on the leader that may be present and must be taken into consideration. Being informed by the leader allows the person to keep the content as information – keep it at a distance – and thus avoiding the anguish of it becoming personal knowledge.

There are occasions when I discuss a metaphor with the group. These occasions are few in number because I am committed to facilitating the expansion of consciousness and not instructive leadership. The discussion explores aspects of the metaphor which were not included when it was initially presented.

I never make any comments on an individual's behavior. Sometimes after I have contributed a metaphor a member may believe it was directed at him/her and will share this perception with the group. I then state, as I have in the orientation statement, that my interventions are my observations on the group and never on any member. I acknowledge that it may seem that my interventions follow a particular statement of a member; then I go on to point out that a member may be a spokesperson for an issue the group is confronting. I have several reasons for focusing on the group and not on individuals. It is less threatening to the membership and yet all the content that needs satisfaction can be spoken to by focusing on the group. It continually alerts the members to the social and cultural systems. It promotes the idea of a learning community – mutual enquiry – while at the same time it promotes the qualities of supportiveness, cooperation, and risk-taking. In addition, by focusing on the group, individuals are given time and space within which to consider and work at their own development. This last point is a critical aspect of this approach.

I frequently make use of dialogs in my metaphors. For example, I have brothers and sisters discuss the health of their mother when the phase of the Great Mother is focal. I have them discuss their ambivalent feelings toward their father in comparison to how they feel toward their mother. Such a familial scenario would occur during the phase of the separation of the Parents. I recount a scenario in which children are afraid to go into dark places in the basement of their home – the exploration of the unconscious. These metaphors share not only my perceptions of the place where I observe the group to be at, but in their own way they demonstrate the function of dialog between the conscious and the unconscious. I do not make this point explicit as the metaphors are always presented without explanations.

Patience and waiting are hallmarks of this approach. When a group is failing to deal with an issue, problem, or task, I wait for a period of time to see if the members will begin to deal with it. A group must be given time to struggle with the task before it. I have waited an hour and often longer before I enter with a metaphor. I have been unable to discover a universal precept which would direct a leader when to intervene. There is much that is gained through experience and also much to be attributed to intuition.

If the group continues to avoid the task that is before it after my intervention or flights from it completely, I then present another metaphor which carries the message of its avoidance or flight.

The second intervention may be viewed as a type of 'follow-up'. If the group does not appear to be helped by these interventions, I do not intervene further at this time. My decision not to intervene is based upon my view of education. If my follow-up intervention is not helpful to the group, then there are reasons for this response which I must then try to discover. Rather than being disturbed at the group's inability to move, I need to recognize there must be reasons and I have a responsibility to try to find out what these reasons may be. The following are some of the possible reasons. The members may need more time to integrate the messages of my interventions or what may be more fundamental, the conflict they are sorting out for themselves. As illogical as it may appear they may need to flight, to deny, or reject before they can consider and accept. They may need to own the messages as their own and also come to them not through my metaphors but through their own reflections. As leaders we need to avoid any attempt to preempt situations by our impatience with what we may consider intransigent and unresponsive individuals. Individuals need the room to experience and thus to fail as well as to succeed.

Projections and transference are often directed at the leader. I suggest that the leader faces the member when he/she is engaged in either of these behaviors. By facing the speaker, the leader is indicating he/she is hearing the message, but in turn the leader makes no reply. The leader neither rejects nor accepts the behavior verbally. The leader is aware of what the speaker is conveying in his/her behavior. When the leader does not appear to be upset, disturbed, or even moved by the member's behavior the member frequently becomes more emotional and the feelings toward the leader are heightened. The leader responding in this manner does not diffuse the issue or the emotionality but lets the transaction serve as the content for the group's and also the individual's learning. I do deal directly with the projection or transference when either of two conditions exist. If the affect of the projection or transference is so strong that there is a possibility that the individual or group may lose control of the situation, then I actively intervene. The second condition involves the repetitive nature of the projection or transference. When the group does not recognize what is occurring and therefore fails to modify the situation, I will address the projection or transference by means of a metaphor. Above all I want the member to clearly realize he/she is not being rejected.

Epilogue

My purpose in writing this chapter was to share the approach I have used with small groups to facilitate personal transformations. I have done so by describing it in some detail. Except for short sorties here and there, I have not addressed conceptual or philosophical issues involved in my approach. My focus has been confined to a narrower range of concerns, what is often referred to as the practice of small group theory. My discussion of the approach has emphasized the practice with only a nod once in a while to theory which is generally the case in such presentations. For myself, I would find it difficult to end this chapter having only given a nod to conceptual and philosophical issues. There are several I would wish to examine but I have chosen only two to speak to at this time. These are so central and critical to the approach set out in this chapter that I am compelled to speak to them even if only briefly. A more thorough treatment of other issues must be left for future publications.

Rousseau's admonition, as stirring and provocative as it may still read, now strikes many people in the western world as no longer a description of the state of affairs regarding individual freedom. It would be pointed out that we need only look about us, for the evidence is everywhere. There is no bondage; if individuals do not choose to exercise their freedom, that is another matter. There are others who disagree.

They point out that there are segments of our population within our society which do not have political power and certainly not the access to economic resources. These people, they assert, are in bondage. And so the debate is joined, but the issues are seldom resolved through constructive actions.

What has this discussion to do with small groups? Perhaps if this book had been an examination of negotiating, political or action groups the connection would be clearer; however, the book was not specifically about these groups. But the book has been about human bondage. When socialization does not encourage the processes of examination, criticism, and rejection of social traditions, expectations, premisses, and roles then we are right to speak of bondage. Political and economic premisses have been part of our socialization and they have become reified. They have their counterpart in the reifications of social and psychological suppositions.

These reifications are not the source of our bondage, they are the chains that manifest the bondage. The source lies much deeper than social, political, and economic structures and forces. The bondage is of our own doing and it is structured upon our own individual unexamined life. We submit to external bondage; it is sought and surrendered to as our way of being in the world.

The small group can be a setting to begin and to further those unexamined parts of our lives which hold us in bondage. But this cannot be done unless we accept our personal responsibility to shoulder that task. Where once we turned to God, we now expect the state, or some technique, or a great individual to rescue us – to deliver us from our own freedom. The individual, in facing him/herself in the small group – the individual who will accept the responsibility of his/her own growth – will encounter the unexamined self. This is the task of every person who accepts the journey toward individuation.

References

Berne, E. (1963). *The structure and dynamics of organizations and groups.* New York: Lippincott.

Bion, W. R. (1959). *Experiences in groups and other papers.* New York: Basic Books.

Boyd, R. D. (1984). The self, ego and the archetypes: The study of the small group from the perspective of analytical psychology. In *Proceedings of the Adult Education Research Conference*, Lincoln, Nebr: University of Nebraska.

Boyd, R. D. (1987). A women's group encounters the Great Mother (unpublished manuscript).

Boyd, R. D. and Myers, J. G. (1988). Transformative education, *International Journal of Lifelong Education*, 7 (4), 261–84.

Boyd, R. D., Kondrat, M. E. and Rannells, J. S. (1989). The developmental stages of the anima and animus in small groups: Part 1 and 2, *Group Analysis*, 22 (2), 135–59.

Dirkx, J. M. (1987). *The self-analytic group and the Great Mother: A study of matriarchal consciousness in adult education*. Unpublished doctoral dissertation. University of Wisconsin-Madison.

Erikson, E. H. (1950). *Childhood and society*. New York: W. W. Norton.

Erikson, E. H. (1959). Identity and the life cycle: Selected papers, *Psychological Issues*, Vol. 1 (1), New York: International University Press.

Hannah, B. (1981). *Encounter with the soul: Active imagination as developed by C. G. Jung*. Cambridge, MA: Sego Press.

Jung, C. G. (1969). The archetypes and the collective unconscious. *Collected Works of C. G. Jung*. Volume 9, Part 1. Princeton, NJ: Princeton University Press.

Jung, C. G. (1972). The psychology of dementia praecox. 2. The feeling-toned complex and its general effects on the psyche. *Collected Works of C. G. Jung*, Volume 3. Princeton, NJ: Princeton University Press.

Myers, J. G. (1986). *Grief work as a critical condition for small group phase development*. Unpublished doctoral dissertation, University of Wisconsin-Madison.

Neumann, E. (1954). *The origins and history of consciousness*. Princeton, NJ: Princeton University Press.

Neumann, E. (1959). *The great mother: An analysis of the archetype*. Princeton, NJ: Princeton University Press.

Redl, F. (1942). Group emotions and leadership, *Psychiatry*, 5, 573–96.

Slater, P. E. (1966). *Microcosm: Structural, psychological and religious evolution in groups*. New York: John Wiley & Sons.

vonFranz, M. L. (1980). *Projection and re-collection in Jungian psychology: Reflections of the soul*. London: Open Press.

Index

active imagination: and metaphors 219–20, 224

adaptive point of view: group tasks 25; of groups 18, 22; symbolism of groups 25

amplification: conceptualizing anima/animus 145

anima 5–7, 138; animus stages 158–64; case material 170–7; conceptualizing 139–48; with group as facilitator 210, 213; identifying stages of 148–51; with member as facilitator 216; research on 164–70; stages 151–8

animus 138; anima stages 151–8; and case material 170–7, 184, 191, 197, 199, 201; conceptualizing 139–48; with group as facilitator 210; identifying stages of 148–51; research on 164–70; stages 158–64

Aphrodite 208; and metaphors 223

aptitudes: conceptualizing 144

archetypal component: with group as facilitator 209, 214; with member as facilitator 218

archetypal content 3; in group tasks 37

archetypal elements 2; and group as facilitator 207–10, 214; and member as facilitator 216–18; and metaphors 224

archetypal figures: and anima/ animus 138; conceptualizing anima/animus 139–40; and group

as facilitator 207, 208

archetypal images *see* archetypal figures

archetypal influence 50–1, 54

archetypal paradox 65, 79–81; and focal person 86, 92–4; and influential member 74, 77

archetypal phases *see* archetypal stages

archetypal stages: coding archetypal themes 60; rationale for social grieving 98; themes 48, 50

archetypal symbol: in adaptive view of groups 20; and research on individuation 132

archetypal themes 48–51, 54; case study 179; coding 56–7, 59–62; methodology for 45, 47; rationale for social grieving 97; research on individuation 136; small groups in analytical psychology 41; within case material 198

Argyris, C. 24, 39

attachment 101

authority: psychic dilemma 181; within case material 190, 193

authority figures 173

authority structure 55 *see also* structure

Bad Mother: case material on anima/animus 174; group tasks 36–7; within case material 186, 195–6

Bales, R.F. 18, 23, 27, 39, 67, 94

236